Culture and Customs of Cuba

William Luis

Culture and Customs of Latin America
and the Caribbean
Peter Standish, Series Editor

GREENWOOD PRESS
Westport, Connecticut • London

Library of Congress Cataloging-in-Publication Data

Luis, William.
    Culture and customs of Cuba / William Luis
       p.   cm.—(Culture and customs of Latin America and the Caribbean, ISSN 1521–8856)
    Includes bibliographical references (p. –) and index.
    ISBN 0–313–30433–5 (alk. paper)
    1. Cuba—Civilization—20th century.   2. Cuba—Social life and customs—20th century.   3. Arts, Modern—20th century—Cuba.   4. Arts, Cuban.   5. Popular culture—Cuba.   I. Title.
    II. Series.
    F1787.L945   2001
    972.9106—dc21   00–035324

British Library Cataloguing in Publication Data is available.

Library of Congress Catalog Card Number: 00–035324
ISBN: 0–313–30433–5
ISSN: 1521–8856

First published in 2001

Greenwood Press, 88 Post Road West, Westport, CT 06881
An imprint of Greenwood Publishing Group, Inc.
www.greenwood.com

Printed in the United States of America

The paper used in this book complies with the
Permanent Paper Standard issued by the National
Information Standards Organization (Z39.48–1984).

10 9 8 7 6 5 4 3 2

Unless otherwise noted, all photographs appear by courtesy of William Luis.

To my mother's family in and outside Cuba:
Alexander, Haydee, Justo, Elizabeth, Phillip, Rubén,
Zenaida, Juanita, Consuelo, Fernando, Lázara, and Pilar.
Petra, Domingo, Aralia, Domingo, Evelia, Ventura,
and Eva in memoriam.

Contents

A photo essay follows p. 98

Series Foreword

"CULTURE" is a problematic word. In everyday language we tend to use it in at least two senses. On the one hand, we speak of cultured people and places full of culture, uses that imply a knowledge or presence of certain forms of behavior or of artistic expression that are socially prestigious. In this sense large cities and prosperous people tend to be seen as the most cultured. On the other hand, there is an interpretation of "culture" that is broader and more anthropological; culture in this broader sense refers to whatever traditions, beliefs, customs, and creative activities characterize a given community—in short, it refers to what makes that community different from others. In this second sense, everyone has culture; indeed, it is impossible to be without culture.

The problems associated with the idea of culture have been exacerbated in recent years by two trends: less respectful use of language and a greater blurring of cultural differences. Nowadays, "culture" often means little more than behavior, attitude, or atmosphere. We hear about the culture of the boardroom, of the football team, of the marketplace; there are books with titles like *The Culture of War* by Richard Gabriel (Greenwood, 1990) or *The Culture of Narcissism* by Christopher Lasch (1979). In fact, as Christopher Clausen points out in an article published in the *American Scholar* (Summer 1996), we have gotten ourselves into trouble by using the term so sloppily.

People who study culture generally assume that culture (in the anthropological sense) is learned, not genetically determined. Another general assumption made in these days of multiculturalism has been that cultural differences should be respected rather than put under pressure to change.

But these assumptions, too, have sometimes proved to be problematic. For instance, multiculturalism is a fine ideal, but in practice it is not always easy to reconcile with the beliefs of the very people who advocate it: for example, is female circumcision an issue of human rights or just a different cultural practice?

The blurring of cultural differences is a process that began with the steamship, increased with radio, and is now racing ahead with the Internet. We are becoming globally homogenized. Since the English-speaking world (and the United States in particular) is the dominant force behind this process of homogenization, it behooves us to make efforts to understand the sensibilities of members of other cultures.

This series of books, a contribution toward that greater understanding, deals with the neighbors of the United States, with people who have just as much right to call themselves Americans. What are the historical, institutional, religious, and artistic features that make up the modern culture of such peoples as the Haitians, the Chileans, the Jamaicans, and the Guatemalans? How are their habits and assumptions different from our own? What can we learn from them? As we familiarize ourselves with the ways of other countries, we come to see our own from a new perspective.

Each volume in the series focuses on a single country. With slight variations to accommodate national differences, each begins by outlining the historical, political, ethnic, geographical, and linguistic context, as well as the religious and social customs, and then proceeds to a discussion of a variety of artistic activities, including the press, the media, the cinema, music, literature, and the visual and performing arts. The authors are all intimately acquainted with the countries concerned: some were born or brought up in them, and each has a professional commitment to enhancing the understanding of the culture in question.

We are inclined to suppose that our ways of thinking and behaving are normal. And so they are . . . for us. We all need to realize that ours is only one culture among many, and that it is hard to establish by any rational criteria that ours as a whole is any better (or worse) than any other. As individual members of our immediate community, we know that we must learn to respect our differences from one another. Respect for differences between cultures is no less vital. This is particularly true of the United States, a nation of immigrants, but one that sometimes seems to be bent on destroying variety at home, and, worse still, on having others follow suit. By learning about other people's cultures, we come to understand and respect them; we earn their respect for us; and, not least, we see ourselves in a new light.

Peter Standish
East Carolina University

Introduction

CUBA, the largest island in the Caribbean Sea and only ninety miles from the United States, has had a significant impact on world history, politics, and culture. Events such as the Spanish American War of 1898, the Cuban revolution of 1959, the Cuban missile crisis in October 1962, and the recent custody battle between the Cuban father and grandmothers and relatives in Miami over Elián González, the boy whose mother drowned while trying to leave Cuba, have received international attention. In the area of culture, Cuba has produced some of the most renowned writers, artists, musicians, and athletes of the twentieth century.

Cuba's government considers culture to be a weapon of the revolution, which serves to support the political establishment. If bourgeois culture helps to sustain the capitalist system, then a politicized culture was created to promote Cuba's revolution. However, this has not been an easy task, and it has been achieved with varying results. Certainly at the outset of the revolution, general enthusiasm favored Fidel Castro's political goals. Facilities that had been reserved for the privileged few were made available to all. The number of writers and artists increased, as did the publishing houses, which began to print record numbers of books. Books were made affordable, and education and culture began to flourish. As the revolution began to define itself as communist, government supporters promoted a more dogmatic type of culture. Some writers and artists were forced to curtail their freedom of expression, and others looked for ways to vent their creative activities. Understandably, these events were tied to the economic and political backdrop unfolding on the island. Many of the original goals of the revolution, for which the

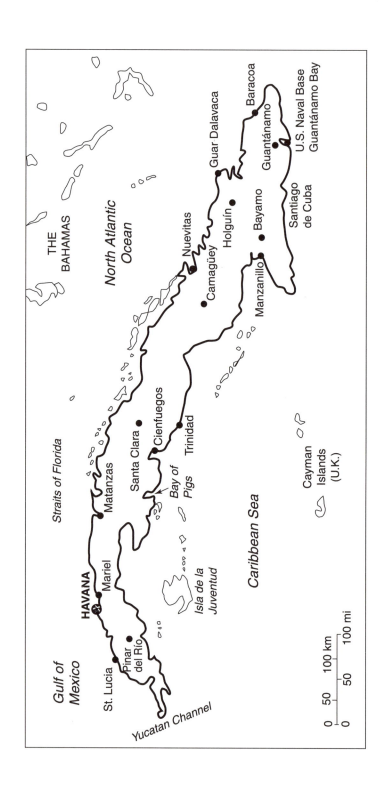

average Cuban has sacrificed, have been placed on hold, perhaps permanently. With the collapse of the Soviet camp and the beginning of the Special Period in Cuba, Castro has moved in the direction of a market economy, and the country has returned to being the type of nation many Cubans had once rejected. (The Special Period refers to a temporary stage in which Cubans had to sacrifice more and socialist reforms were suspended. It was caused by the collapse of the Soviet camp and it has forced the Cuban government to make social and economic reforms.) The dollar has returned to a position of preeminence as the unofficial currency on the island. While this means that those holding dollars are now members of a privileged class, Cubans are beginning to express themselves more freely, and culture on the island continues to evolve. One often hears among high-level officials, "You can play with the chain but not with the monkey," meaning that there is leeway as long as Castro is left unscathed.

Cuban history, society, and culture can be divided into four periods: the colonial, the nineteenth century, the republic, and the revolutionary. Although an argument can be made for a periodization of culture in Cuba, these four stages can also be viewed as interrelated. This is certainly the case if one views the colony's nineteenth-century fight for independence from Spain and the nation's struggle in the twentieth century for sovereignty from the United States. The interrelatedness is also evident in the social, economic, and political position that blacks have endured since the nineteenth century. Emancipation, the republic, and revolution marked distinct historical stages, but the position of blacks has changed very little; they continue to be at the bottom of the socioeconomic ladder.

This book provides an understanding of the culture and customs of Cuba in the twentieth century, which for Cuba means from the country's inception as an independent republic to the present. Nevertheless, it is not possible to understand Cuban society without considering aspects of the nineteenth century. Although Cuban independence was late in coming, the emergence of a national culture took place in the same period in which its sister republics had already shed Spanish colonialism. With this in mind, this study begins in the nineteenth century.

Equally significant, Cuban culture developed on the island and also abroad, particularly after Castro assumed power in January 1959 and hundreds of thousands of Cubans abandoned the island in four migratory waves, mainly to the United States. However, Cuban culture has always existed outside the island's geographic boundaries. In the early part of the nineteenth century, writers like José María Heredia, Félix Varela, Cirilo Villaverde, and José Martí joined many of their Cuban and Puerto Rican counterparts living in New York, Philadelphia, Tampa, and other U.S. cities. They formed part of an exile community in which Cuban culture was maintained and reinforced. They formed political and cultural organizations, gathered funds, and continued to conspire against the Spanish government. But these and other intellectuals also contributed to the unfolding of events in their adopted country.

Cuban history and culture have responded to events taking place on the island. However, because of its proximity to the United States, Cuba has also been influenced by events taking place there. The reciprocal is also true: Cuba has had a significant effect on U.S. history and culture.

The contact between the two countries in the nineteenth century allowed Cuba to be the recipient of the technology offered, for example, by the steam engine, used for the mechanization of the sugar industry. The Louisiana mulatto (of mixed black and white blood) Norbert Rillieux and the engineer Charles Derosne created a vacuum boiler that combined the grinding and evaporating process in the same steam engine that became a necessity for any successful sugar mill. In the twentieth century, radio and television were in place on the island before they became available in other Latin American countries. Cuban businessmen had close contact with their North American counterparts, who viewed the island as an accessible market for their products.

In the area of culture, Cuban music has influenced music in the United States. U.S. businessmen traveling to the island in the early part of the century became enamored with Cuban music in general and in particular the son, a sound created by the island's unique mixture of Spanish and African cultures. Cuban singers were among the first to be recorded by the newly established RCA Victor and Columbia record companies. George Gershwin went to Cuba and composed his "Obertura cubana." And Cuban singers traveled to the United States, where Moisés Simón made Don Aspiazu's "El manicero" (The Peanut Vendor) an instant success. There were the famous musical and dance styles of the rumba, the mambo, the cha-cha-chá, and Cuba's influence on the salsa. The Buena Vista Social Club, a group of musicians popular before the revolution and recently rediscovered by Ry Cooder, continues a long tradition of cultural sharing between the two countries. (Their record *Buena Vista Social Club* won a Grammy in 1998.) The popular sit-com *I Love Lucy*, featuring Desi Arnaz and Lucille Ball, became a symbolic marriage between Cuban and U.S. cultures in the 1950s, but with the actors' divorce, also the tension between the two countries.

In the contemporary period, the sons and daughters of Cuban exiles are contributing to the expansion of culture in both Cuba and the United States.

Pop singer Gloria Estefan has blended the music of her parents' island culture and that of their adopted country. In literature, Cuban-American or Latino writers like Cristina García and Oscar Hijuelos are redefining the boundaries of U.S. and Latin American literatures. Because of the many contributions of Latinos to North American culture, Cuban-American culture is also recognized in this book.

The Cuban family continues to be divided—in some cases members of the same family are forced to live in separate geographic locations. Both the U.S. and Cuban governments must recognize that the strategies of their current foreign policies have not worked. They must abandon their fixed positions and engage in meaningful dialogue and negotiation. We are currently in a period in which the United States negotiates with the Chinese, the Israelis with the Palestinians, and the Irish Protestants with their Catholic counterparts. Is it not time for the United States and Cuba to do the same? My hope is that this book will bring a greater understanding of the interrelations of the two countries and how they affect one other.

ACKNOWLEDGMENTS

As always, I thank Roberto González Echevarría and Antonio Benítez Rojo who unknowingly continue to influence my work. In my estimation, their writings set the standard for our profession. I also acknowledge my student David García, who is a source of inspiration and strength. Ricardo Pau-Llosa read the section on art and made valuable comments, Narciso Hidalgo helped with the music section, and Vanderbilt University provided me with a sabbatical that allowed me to complete the manuscript. Peter Standish and Wendi Schnaufer of Greenwood Press were patient and supportive, and Rebecca Ardwin and Beverly Miller helped with the manuscript.

Equally important, I recognize my family in Cuba and the United States. Although my Cuban mother and Chinese father migrated from Cuba to the United States before Castro gained control of the government, I also have been affected by the politics dividing Cuban families on the island and in the United States. I thank my children, Tammie, Stephanie, Gabriel, and Diego, for their understanding of my professional obligations and my wife, Linda, whose invaluable support cannot be measured in words.

Chronology

1812   The Aponte conspiracy. The black Aponte was accused of conspiring to create a black republic in Cuba.

1844   The ladder conspiracy, in which blacks were accused of conspiring to overthrow the colonial government. Blacks were tied to a ladder, whipped, and coerced into confessing.

1847   The first ships with Chinese indentured servants arrive in Cuba.

1865   The last slave journey across the Atlantic.

1868   The Ten Years' War, fought by those seeking independence from the Spanish colonial government, begins.

1878   The island is divided into six provinces.

1879   The Guerra Chiquita (the "little war"), another war between Spain and its colonies, begins and lasts until 1880.

1886   Slaves are emancipated.

1895   The Second War of Independence begins. José Martí, Cuba's national hero, is killed fighting for his country's independence from Spain.

1898   The U.S. battleship *Maine* explodes in Havana harbor, and the United States declares war on Spain.

1901   The Cuban Constitution is completed, and the Platt Amendment is included in it, giving the United States a legal right to intervene in the internal affairs of the newly created republic.

1902   The Republic of Cuba is born. General Tomás Estrada Palma is Cuba's first president.

1912   In the race war, La Guerrita del 12, thousands of blacks lose their lives.

1933   The dictatorship of General Gerardo Machado comes to an end.

1934   The Platt Amendment is abrogated from Cuba's constitution. Women receive the right to vote.

1940	Fulgencio Batista is elected president of the republic by a coalition that includes communists. He writes and institutes the liberal Constitution of 1940. He leaves office in 1944.
1952	Batista ousts President Carlos Prío and takes over the government.
1953	Fidel Castro and 134 rebels attack the Moncada barracks (Batista's army barracks) in Santiago de Cuba. He and other survivors are captured and sent to prison.
1956	Abroad the *Granma*, Castro and eighty-one rebels leave Mexico and land in Playa de los Colorados, near Belic, in Oriente. They make their way to the Sierra Maestra and wage a guerrilla war against the Batista dictatorship.
1959	Batista flees the island, and the rebel troops enter Havana. The first wave of Cuban exiles flees the island. In January Manuel Urrutia becomes the president of Cuba; in July the position is filled by Osvaldo Dorticós.
1960	The United States establishes an economic embargo against trade with Cuba. The French ship *La Coubre* explodes in Havana harbor. Castro accuses the U.S. government of sabotage.
1961	The United States and Cuba break relations. Castro declares that the Cuban revolution is socialistic. Cuban exiles invade the island and land at the Bay of Pigs. Castro convincingly defeats the exile invaders. Campaign for Literacy eradicates illiteracy in the island.
1962	The United States demands that the Soviet Union remove its intermediate-range ballistic missiles from the island, producing a superpower confrontation and a possible third world war.
1965	A second wave of exiles abandons the island and seeks asylum in the United States.
1970	Failure of the ten-million-ton sugar harvest that produced a record 8.5 million tons. This begins a period of increased repression of writers and artists.

1971   The poet Heberto Padilla is arrested, producing a split among Western intellectuals between those who support and those who criticize the revolution. The Congress on Education and Culture establishes important cultural policies.

1975   The First Congress of the Communist Party of Cuba is celebrated in Havana.

1976   The Communist party ratifies the new Cuban Constitution. The six provinces are divided into fourteen provinces and the municipality of Isla de Pinos.

1977   U.S. President Jimmy Carter allows travel to Cuba. The Antonio Maceo Brigade, made up of children of exiles, visits the island.

1978   Cuban-Americans are allowed to travel to Cuba.

1980   Cubans escaping the Castro government seek refuge in the Peruvian embassy. Cubans are allowed to leave the island through the port of Mariel; 120,000 arrive in the United States. Established Cuban writers, some who held high official jobs in the government, seek exile abroad. The Second Congress of the Cuban Communist Party announces a five-year plan to increase efficiency on the island.

1986   The Cuban Communist party hold its Third Congress to increase economic and social efficiency.

1987   Cardinal John O'Connor meets with Fidel Castro.

1991   The Special Period, caused by the fall of the Soviet bloc countries, begins. The government embraces tourism as a way of obtaining hard currency.

1998   Pope John Paul II visits the island. He calls for the lifting of the U.S. blockade, but also demands the release of political prisoners in Cuban jails.

1999–2000   Elián González's mother drowns while escaping from Cuba. His family in Miami wants him in the United States, and his father, grandparents, Castro, and the Cuban people demand his return. Elián's situation is emblematic of the separation of the Cuban people. It is political and renews tension between the two countries. After failed attempts by the Miami relatives to keep him in the United States, U.S. courts order Elián's return with his father to Cuba. The decision represents a major public relations victory for Fidel Castro.

1

Context

CUBA'S geographic location and size have helped to define its unique history and culture. Christopher Columbus visited Cuba, the largest of the Caribbean islands, on his first voyage to the New World in 1492. Although the island did not contain the large deposits of gold later found on the Spanish mainland, the Spaniards were not disappointed. They soon realized that the island's geographic position was as valuable as any precious metal. Cuba is situated at the crossroads of three important water passages: the straits of Florida, the Yucatan channel, and the windward passage. Whoever governs the island also controls the adjacent waterways. The first governor of the island, Diego Velázquez, founded the capital city of Havana. By 1519 this port city had become a strategic center for exploring the continent and returning to the mother country. In the contemporary period, the island's proximity to the United States has forced it to play an unwanted role in U.S. foreign policy, influencing many decisions made by the U.S. government. (For example, Kennedy's Alliance for Progress was a reaction to Castro's influence in Latin America, the presence of Soviet missiles in Cuba helped to define U.S.-Soviet relations, and the Elián González affair is helping to clarify U.S. immigration policy.)

Spaniards, Africans, and Chinese make up the island's population and culture. To obtain economic wealth and improve their social position, Spaniards enslaved the native inhabitants of the island. Hard work beyond physical limitations and exposure to previously unknown diseases practically eliminated Cuba's native Tainos and Ciboneys. West Coast Africans soon replaced the Amerindian population. They first accompanied the Spanish conquerors as servants. Others arrived later in large numbers as slaves to work alongside Amerindians in the mines and agriculture.

In the nineteenth century, the Chinese contributed to the development of Cuban culture. The coolies, as they were known, first traveled from southern China to Cuba in 1847 as indentured servants. They arrived under a five-year contract, with the option of returning home at the conclusion of that period. Although conditions on the island were less than ideal, those on the Chinese mainland were even worse, so many of these immigrants chose to make Cuba their new home. Chinese Cubans, fewer in number than Spaniards and Africans, made a small but significant contribution to the island's culture. They also represented a way of diffusing the racial tension between whites and blacks; during the first half of the nineteenth century blacks outnumbered whites, and Chinese immigration was a means of changing this ratio.

Cuba's size and climatic advantage allowed the island to be a leader in agriculture. Indeed, in the nineteenth century, Cuban sugar became the most important crop in the world. (Haiti had held this role previously, but after the Haitian Revolution, Cuba filled the sugar vacuum.) However, the rise in demand for the product also led to increased trafficking of Africans to replenish slaves working on the sugar plantations, at all stages of production. By the middle of the nineteenth century, Cuba's black population surpassed that of whites and augmented the racial tension on the island. The need to accelerate the sugar process and meet consumer demand led to greater punishment of slaves. The strategy failed and incited slaves to rebel. A fear of rebellious blacks has persisted throughout Cuban history and has become a part of the Cuban psyche.

TOWARD INDEPENDENCE

Cuba was Spain's last colony. Except for a brief period of British control in 1762, the island remained a Spanish possession until 1898. Most other countries in Spanish America obtained their independence from the colonial center in the early part of the nineteenth century, but Cuba continued to be a Spanish colony until the end of the century, and it did not become an independent nation until the beginning of the twentieth. Cubans nevertheless had initiated their struggle for independence much earlier, thus coinciding with Spanish American national liberation movements against the mother country. The road to Cuban independence can be traced to the Aponte conspiracy of 1812, in which blacks, with the help of whites, attempted to liberate slaves and establish an independent republic. The colonial authorities suppressed the uprising, accusing and sentencing to death the black Aponte and his followers for conspiring to create another black republic, similar to the one founded on the nearby island of Saint Domingo in 1804.

The "Soles y Rayos de Bolívar" (Bolívar's suns and rays) conspiracy attempted to overthrow the colonial government in 1823. José Francisco de Lemus headed the organization with the help of Colombian agents living in Havana and the United States and supporters of the Spanish Constitution of 1812 and other liberal Spaniards. Taking advantage of turmoil in Europe and at home, which included a French invasion of Spain and a Spanish attack on the constitutionalists, the newly appointment and savvy Captain General Francisco Dionisio Vives moved against the insurrectionists, which included Lemus, José Antonio Miralla, Diego Tanco, Juan J. Hernández, José María Heredia, and Miguel Teurbe-Tolón. There were 602 accused conspirators, some of whom were professionals, mayors, judges, military officials, and laborers. The organizers of the conspiracy also appealed to blacks and slaves. However, the appeal backfired and instead created a black fear among whites.

The fight for Cuban independence can be traced more appropriately to the Ten Years' War (1868–1878), when white planter Carlos Manuel de Céspedes emancipated his slaves and rose against the Spanish authorities. Dissatisfied with the Pacto de Sanjón (Sanjón Pact), which concluded the war, Cuban black patriots, like General Quintín Banderas, continued the armed struggle in the short-lived Guerra Chiquita (the "Little War," 1879–1880). The struggle for Cuban independence also continued abroad. Many Cuban exiles who lived in U.S. cities like New York had become an integral part of armed resistance.

Cuba finally obtained its independence after the Spanish American War, which for Cubans began in 1895 and ended with U.S. participation in 1898. The Republic of Cuba was established three years later, in 1902, with the proclamation of the constitution and the insertion of the Platt Amendment, which ensured U.S. intervention in the internal affairs of the newly created nation.

Although Cuba's independence was late in coming, Cuban culture, like that of its sister nations, was forged in the first part of the nineteenth century. It emerged when sugar, coffee, and tobacco growers competed for the same agricultural land and struggled with questions related to race, slavery, freedom, and independence.

Fernando Ortiz's (1881–1969) *Contrapunteo cubano del tabaco y el azúcar* (Cuban Counterpoint: Tobacco and Sugar, 1940) is a book that captures many issues confronting the developing culture. In this groundbreaking work, Ortiz studied two Cuban plants, tobacco and sugar, and showed how they helped shape Cuban national identity. Relying on the Spanish medie-valist Juan Ruiz's dialogue, "Pelea que ovo don Carnal con Doña Quaresma" (Fight Between Don Carnival and Dona Lent), in his *Libro de buen amor* (Book of Good Love), Ortiz uncovered a similar relationship in Cuba be-tween tobacco and sugar. Ortiz viewed tobacco and sugar as representing two extremes. One crop is native, the other foreign; one natural, the other artificial; one black, the other white; one takes the male article, the other female; one depends on free workers, the other on slaves; one demands skilled labor, the other unskilled; one thrives on central control, the other on small parcels; one desires shade, the other sun; one is delicate, the other robust; one appeals to the five senses, the other only to taste. Cultivating these crops led to the formation of a social and political position that influenced the development of culture. Sugar producers favored Spain's dominion over the colony. They supported slavery and the slave trade, necessary to harvest, produce, and market sugar. Unlike sugar, tobacco was grown in small parcels, required skilled labor, and the workers were independent thinkers. Cigar makers were among the best-paid craftsmen; they supported the abolition of slavery and Cuba's independence from Spain.

During the first half of the nineteenth century, a period in which Cuban culture developed, Cuba's agriculture did not depend exclusively on sugar or tobacco; the island's economy also included coffee. In the early part of the nineteenth century, coffee and sugar competed for the same fields, and coffee even outperformed sugar. In the first quarter of the nineteenth century, sugar mills grew at a rapid pace, but the figures for coffee were even more aston-ishing. During the same period, tobacco production did not increase. It was a controlled industry until 1817, when a royal decree authorized its sale for export, providing jobs for many whites and free blacks. By the end of Captain General Dionisio Vives's government (1823–1832), tobacco, sugar, and cof-fee were flourishing.

Like tobacco and sugar, coffee and sugar are also opposites, and Ortiz's counterpoint applies here too. For example, one takes the male article and the other female; one is dark, the other white; one requires high elevations, the other does not; one grows in the shade, the other in the sun; one is bitter, the other sweet. Unlike tobacco, both coffee and sugar are foreign crops and may best represent the foreign influences that set into motion the development of island culture.

Ortiz's idea of counterpoint between sugar and tobacco has made an enor-mous contribution to understanding Cuba's economy and culture. Never-theless, the idea of a counterpoint between the two crops in literature can be traced to the nineteenth century. Cirilo Villaverde (1812–1894) had already developed it in his *Cecilia Valdés* (1882), Cuba's most important novel. The novel's Gamboa and Ilincheta families represent sugar and coffee interests, respectively, and are described within their historical context. Members of the wealthy Gamboa family were absentee landlords and a component of the sugar aristocracy. They supported sugar, slavery, and central control of the island, and they routinely punished their slaves. In contrast, the Ilincheta family grew coffee; they lived on the plantation and were benevolent toward their slaves. Isabel Ilincheta, who ran her father's plantation, can be understood as a precursor to the feminist movement. The marriage between Isabel and Leonardo Gamboa, in spite of Isabel's liberal thinking, implied the dominance of sugar over coffee.

The coffee plantation represented a different aspect of Cuban culture. It was the center of liberal ideas. French coffee growers, who escaped the rebellion in Saint Domingo in 1791, like their sugar counterparts, sought refuge in Cuba and continued their interests in agriculture in their adopted island. Coffee growers brought knowledge of French culture with them, which embraced promoting the arts and supporting the liberal ideas of the French Revolution: equality, liberty, and fraternity. During the narrative time of Villaverde's novel, which coincided with the Vives government, the two most important crops, sugar and coffee, represented two types of slavery, the ruthless and the benevolent, with which the country struggled. This was also a period in which sugar was becoming more important than coffee. As a crop that promoted its own set of values, sugar spread at a disproportionate and alarming rate, and Captain General Dionisio Vives and the sugar aristocracy continued to run the colony with a firm hand. Tobacco and the values it represented did not become viable until the middle of the nineteenth century.

By the time Ortiz completed his work, tobacco had gained in importance and consequently played a significant role in the formation of a society that supported independence and freedom. Tobacco workers supported national independence in the nineteenth and twentieth centuries in the Caribbean and the United States. Many Cuban intellectuals and cigar makers lived in U.S. cities such as Tampa, Ibor City, Key West, and New York. They favored armed resistance against the Spanish colonial authorities in the nineteenth century and opposed U.S. interventionism in the twentieth.

Tobacco ultimately surpassed coffee in economic importance, a trend evident when Villaverde completed his novel in New York in 1882 and certainly when Ortiz wrote his work some eighty years later. But Ortiz and Villaverde addressed two different debates during distinct moments in Cuban history. Villaverde captures the one at the beginning of the nineteenth century, and Ortiz describes the other unfolding in the twentieth.

By constructing one of his theses around tobacco, Ortiz was arguing for independence and freedom, a political and nationalist discourse in history that gained momentum in the twentieth century, especially during the period in which he wrote. This position was first manifested against the Spanish colonial government during the Ten Years' War and the Spanish American War. In the twentieth century, it opposed the U.S. control of Cuba's economy and government, represented by the highly controversial Platt Amendment, incorporated into Cuba's constitution. The amendment provided for U.S. intervention in Cuba's internal affairs. Although it was abrogated in 1934, the U.S. presence continued to be felt in all aspects of Cuban life well after Ortiz published his work. For Ortiz, his research on tobacco was a way of narrating the nation's need for political and economic independence, this time against U.S. interests. Ortiz reacted to events while researching and writing his book; he uncovered the crop's genealogy and read the past as a manifestation of the present. Tobacco, for Ortiz, became a crop that symbolized Cuba's sovereignty and the island's contribution to the world's economy.

If we read the history of the three crops alongside slavery and the antislavery narrative, inspired by the literary critic Domingo del Monte (1804–1853) and his famed literary salon, which produced the first works to document life on the island, the tension between sugar and tobacco defines the outcome of a process that culminated in the Spanish American War and the formation of the Cuban republic in 1902. But the study of coffee and sugar uncovers the process of an emerging nation struggling with issues of slavery. We know that tobacco is native and coffee and sugar are foreign, and that tobacco relied on free white labor, while coffee and sugar required slaves. However, coffee also pressed for free black workers. By juxtaposing sugar and coffee, Villaverde reconstructed a historical period in which the two crops rivaled for dominance, allowing him to describe two discourses representing different slavery systems, ideological positions, and cultures. The immediate question for planters in the first half of the nineteenth century was not whether Cuba should support slavery or independence, but which kind of slavery was best for the island and its economy, the positions that sugar and coffee represented. This was a period in which European demand for and consumption of Cuban crops increased, and one that celebrated the successes of the French Revolution and its effects in the New World. Certainly support for coffee, which argued for a benevolent form of slavery, implied increased freedom for slaves and a demand for free labor, a direction that history would later record. For the sugar aristocracy, coffee threatened the central control that sugar exemplified.

Coffee and sugar were indeed opposites, and their agricultural systems attested to two competing ideological positions, with implications for the development of culture on the island. Compared to each other, coffee plantations were a metaphorical paradise and sugar an inferno. Sugar plantation owners were absentee landlords. Overseers, who had production schedules to meet, ran the sugar mills, and to do so meant treating slaves brutally. Coffee owners, in contrast, lived on the plantation, interacted with the slaves daily, and managed them with more compassion. They supported free workers, and the technology associated with the crop provided a bridge between large and small property owners.

THE REPUBLIC: 1902–1958

If slavery and independence were nineteenth-century concerns put to rest with the emancipation of slaves in 1886 and the establishment of the republic in 1902, these two fundamental issues did not go away; rather, they would be manifested differently in the twentieth century. Although slaves were legally free, blacks continued to occupy the lower echelon of society. Just as in the nineteenth century, a fear of blacks continued and became a political concern. After the creation of the Republic of Cuba, Afro-Cubans joined the Partido Independiente de Color (Black Independence party). Blacks organized massive demonstrations to protest their promised but unrewarded participation in the Spanish American War, and also the Morúa Amendment to the Cuban constitution. The amendment was named after the Afro-Cuban writer and politician Martín Morúa Delgado (1857–1910), who, under the administration of his friend José Miguel Gómez, became president of the Senate in 1909. Morúa had helped to write the electoral law of 1902, and the Cuban Senate adopted the Morúa Amendment, which stated that political parties could not be organized based on skin color but refused to recognize that white Cubans controlled the other parties. With the formation of the Partido Independiente de Color, many Afro-Cubans stood alongside the party's leaders, Evaristo Estenoz and Pedro Ivonnet, who began to organize Afro-Cubans throughout the island. The Cuban authorities accused the leaders of starting an Afro-Cuban rebellion and choosing the province of Oriente as the site of the uprising. Under the command of General José de Jesús Monteagudo, the Cuban army marched against blacks. On 20 May 1912 General Monteagudo suspended constitutional rights, defeated four thousand accused insurgents, and massacred three thousand of them. He also executed their leaders. Carlos Moore puts the figure of Afro-Cubans killed closer to fifteen thousand, many of whom were lynched or shot without trials, but suspects that the figures are even as high as 35,000 dead. They crushed the rebellion immediately for fear of U.S. intervention, which would also not allow Cuba to become a black republic.

The race war of 1912 was not the first time that whites, whether Spaniards or *criollos* (native-born whites), had viewed blacks as a threat. The actions surrounding the Partido Independiente de Color of 1912 recalled similar events under slavery, during the Aponte conspiracy, one century before. In the ladder conspiracy of 1844, slaves and free blacks were accused of instigating a black rebellion, whipped, and made to confess their participation. Many blacks and slaves were killed. Some critics believe that the captain general fabricated the conspiracy to reduce a growing population of free and successful blacks and mulattos, many of whom had gained considerable economic power and owned slaves themselves.

Cuba became an independent nation, but the economy was tied to the interests of its powerful neighbor to the north, the United States, which had been gaining a foothold on the island as early as the Ten Years' War. Cuba fell prey to a growing and expanding United States, which after the Spanish American War emerged as a two-ocean power with a considerable naval force. U.S. interest in Cuba can be traced to Thomas Jefferson, who wanted to bring the neighboring island into the union to secure the purchase of Louisiana and Florida. Jefferson's was not a lonely voice; other leaders, including John Quincy Adams, supported a similar position. In fact Cuba and the rest of the Americas became the concern of U.S. foreign policy, as expressed by the adoption of the Monroe Doctrine, which essentially opposed European intervention in the hemisphere, proclaiming an America for the Americans. The United States continued to influence Cuban internal and external policies until the middle of the twentieth century, when Fulgencio Batista, the U.S.-backed dictator, fled the country.

Fidel Castro's revolution of 1 January 1959 is the most important event since the nation's birth. Cubans and non-Cubans alike met Cuba's second independence with overwhelming enthusiasm. Castro officials tend to divide Cuban history into two parts: before and after the success of Castro's guerrilla rebels. They also acknowledged that the revolution is a continuation of a nineteenth-century struggle to free the island, first from Spanish domination and later from the grasp of the United States.

Castro's revolution was a response to Batista's coup d'état on 10 October 1952, which ousted the elected president, Carlos Prío Socarrás. In an attempt to challenge Batista's armed takeover of the government, Castro organized an attack on the Moncada barracks in the province of Oriente, on 26 July. After a bloody shootout, Castro and his men were captured and imprisoned.

The uprising against Batista recalls previous protests in the twentieth century, most notably to the Group Minorista (Minority Group), whose members, during the Alfredo Zayas (1921–1925) and Gerardo Machado (1925–1933) periods, demanded reforms and related the arts more directly to the people. This was also a period of dissent among intellectuals. The Minoristas provided the impetus for change at both the political and literary levels. On 18 March 1923 Rubén Martínez Villena (1899–1934), along with a group of writers, artists, and lawyers, left the Academy of Science in protest during the visit of the secretary of justice, Erasmo Regüeiferos. The aim of the "Protesta de los Trece" (protest of thirteen) was to show dissatisfaction with President Zayas's corrupt administration. The social and political concerns of the Grupo Minorista filtered to magazines like *Social* (1916–1933) and *Revista de Avance* (1927–1930).

General Machado suffocated any hope for change. Elected in 1924, he promised the Cuban people an honest government. However, soon after the election he took advantage of a conciliatory Congress, then under the guidance of his friend Sánchez Bustamante, by abolishing the vice presidency and extending his mandate for another six years. The violation of the electoral process led to disturbances that the Great Depression widened. The overall result was civil unrest. Machado answered with violence, and the opposition responded in kind. Discord reached its peak in 1930 with the closing of the University of Havana, the high schools, and the normal schools. On 31 August 1930, Mario García Menocal, Machado's opponent in the 1924 elections, attempted a rebellion. Because of a nationwide strike that paralyzed the island, Machado fled the country on 12 August 1933. The United States was not absent from the negotiations that also contributed to the downfall of the Cuban dictator.

The post-Machado period was characterized by political frustration. After the dictator's fall, Carlos Manuel de Cépedes, with U.S. support, assumed the presidency. Although Machado was gone, the basic structure of his government remained unaltered. Those from the previous administration who were guilty of crimes, went virtually unpunished. The intervention of the U.S. government in the island's international affairs, represented by Ambassador Sumner Welles, compounded the problem. The result was the Sergeants' Coup of 4 September 1933, led by young Fulgencio Batista and supported by students and intellectual allies. The two governments that followed—the

Pentarquía (of Dr. Ramón Grau San Martín, Porfirio Franco, José Miguel Ir-
isarri, Sergio Carbó, and Guillermo Portela) and Grau San Martín's presidency—were doomed to fail due to the marked ideological differences in and
outside the government. Jefferson Caffery, who replaced Sumner Welles as
U.S. ambassador, threatened intervention and thus allied himself with Batista
to defeat Grau's nationalistic and reformist administration.

The cyclical structure of unrest, uprising, and frustration came to a halt
with conservative Colonel Carlos Mendieta, Batista's appointment to the
presidency. The tactics now used to control civil disorder were reminiscent
of the ones Machado had employed. The United States supported Mendieta
through diplomatic recognition, economic aid, and, most important, abolition of the Platt Amendment. Unrest, sparked by the repressive measures of
the new administration, escalated with the general strike of 11 March 1935,
which was reminiscent of the events that had contributed to Machado's
overthrow. Operating under martial law, Colonel Batista violently suppressed
the strike, permanently frustrating the revolutionary fervor that had begun
with the fall of Machado.

When Grau returned to Cuba from exile in 1937, he brought many old
revolutionaries into the Auténtico party (the Cuban Revolutionary party).
He succeeded in forming Cuba's largest party by uniting the noncommunist
left, yet there remained a major difference between his party and that of the
early 1930s. Batista effectively subdued the opposition and forced its members to work within the electoral system. The Auténtico party advocated
democratic reform rather than rebellion. Nevertheless, graft and corruption
plagued the government, defects that also became apparent toward the latter
part of Batista's first administration (1940–1944) and prevalent in the second
Grau (1944–1948) and Carlos Prío (1948–1952) governments.

This apparent change in administrative policy was a decisive blow to those
who expected that once it assumed power, the Auténtico party would carry
out the reforms promised in the early 1930s. Potential revolutionary heroes
turned to gangsterism when they saw how those in office were reaping the
fruits of their work. Grau cleverly used these groups to attain political control
over the predominantly communist unions and the university, a strong political center. In return, he rewarded the gangsters with civil service positions.
Violence had become a way of doing business and acquiring power in Cuba.
The Orthodox party emerged as a possible salvation, but soon lost all of its
hopes when its leader, Eduardo Chibás, committed suicide after a radio
broadcast on 5 August, for not being able to sustain accusations of corruption
he had made against Carlos Prío's minister of education, Aureliano Sánchez
Arango.

THE REVOLUTIONARY YEARS

Castro's revolution can be viewed as a way of rectifying history gone bad. He failed in his initial attack on the Moncada barracks. However, he received a second chance when U.S. administrators pressured Batista into reforming his government, and he released Castro and his men. Batista pardoned Castro and other rebels on 2 May 1955. Castro and his men sought exile in Mexico, where they continued to train for another attack, this time an assault on the island and the Batista dictatorship. This second attempt to oust Batista was decisive. In 1956 Castro and fifty-two men traveled aboard the *Granma* from Mexico to Oriente Province and hid in the Sierra Maestra Mountains. There they succeeded in attacking Batista's army, engaging them in guerrilla warfare.

An overwhelming acceptance of Castro and his 26th of July Movement characterize the initial years of the revolution, which included carrying out Batista's Constitution of 1940. There was genuine enthusiasm by many who had vivid memories of frustrated political reforms. Cubans celebrated Castro as a messianic figure, who would correct history and cause significant change. His supporters wanted change, and Castro took it upon himself to rebuild society from the ground up. However, some of Castro's ideas were not new and appeared to recall the past. One of his first programs was to prevent the reorganization of blacks, which for Afro-Cubans meant disbanding all 256 black societies founded in the republic. Castro's opposition to social and religious organizations affected adversely the Afro-Cubans who, with the exclusion of the Communist party, were the best-organized groups and therefore viewed as a threat. The same also occurred with the Chinese societies, whose records were confiscated. But the same measures were not taken against other organizations with predominantly white members, such as the Confederación de Trabajadores de Cuba (Confederation of Cuban Workers) and the Federación de Mujeres (Federation of Women).

Castro's policies became problematic, especially for the United States; he nationalized property belonging to U.S. citizens and companies. Castro showed himself to be an independent and defiant neighbor and established economic relations with the Soviet Union. Those dissatisfied with Castro's direction fled the island and sought exile, mainly in the United States. The first to leave were middle- and upper-class Cuban professionals, who stood to lose the most. Since that first group of exiles, Cubans of all kinds have attempted to leave the island. Cubans left by the hundreds of thousands in four migratory waves: 250,000 from 1959 to 1961; 400,000 from 1965 to 1972; 120,000 in 1980, because of the Mariel boatlift (Mariel is the Cuban government's designated emigration port); and 45,575 from 1989 to 1994 (a group known as *balseros*, who made their way to Miami on makeshift rafts) (Ackerman 1996, 170). Most Cubans have settled in Puerto Rico, New York, New Jersey, and, above all, Miami, where they have reconstructed a semblance of Cuban life in exile.

U.S.-Cuba relations have been tense from the beginning of Castro's rise to power. In March 1959 Castro traveled to the United States at the invitation of the Press Association. He was a popular figure with Americans, and he played up to African Americans by staying at the Teresa Hotel in Harlem. Although President Dwight D. Eisenhower refused to meet with Castro, Vice President Richard Nixon welcomed him. After a brief conversation, Nixon was convinced that Castro was a communist. Cuban supporters were skeptical until April 1961, one day before the Bay of Pigs invasion, when Castro confirmed that the Cuban revolution was socialist. In so doing he distanced himself from the 26th of July Movement, which brought him to power, and embraced the more traditional but better-organized Communist party.

Soon after Castro's victory, Cuban exile mercenaries (or patriots, depending from where one reads Cuban history), trained by the Central Intelligence Agency, invaded the island. The exiles believed that Cubans on the island were dissatisfied with the direction that Castro had embarked on and would seize the opportunity to rise against and overthrow him; in turn, the victors would receive the exiles as the new heroes. The exile community miscalculated Castro's strength and popularity. With support from all sectors of the country, the Cuban army and militia overwhelmed the invaders and defeated them within a matter of days.

U.S.-Cuba relations came to a head again when the Kennedy administration discovered Soviet missiles in Cuba. The Soviet Union took a hard-line position, refusing to remove the missiles, and reasoned that U.S. missiles in Turkey were directed at Moscow. The Cuban missile crisis, as it was called in the United States, or the Crisis de Octobre in Cuba, created a state of affairs many believed would lead to a third and final world war. Finally, Soviet leader Nikita Khrushchev agreed to remove the Soviet missiles if the Kennedy administration promised not to invade the island. An irate Castro had been left out of the negotiations.

The Cuban missile crisis brought Cuba to the attention of the world. Before the crisis, the interested public had been aware of Castro and his rebel army. After the crisis, a large portion of the world's population acknowledged Cuba's existence. They may have even wondered why superpowers, armed with nuclear weapons, risked annihilating humanity and destroying the planet over a small island in the Caribbean. Castro and the missile crisis nevertheless served to bring much-needed world attention to Cuba, the Caribbean, and Latin America. Castro threatened to spread communism throughout the region, and his actions forced the United States to allocate funds to counteract Cuba's influence and prevent another Cuba in the Americas. John F. Kennedy's Alliance for Progress, an economic aid program to help Latin American countries develop cultural programs, can be viewed as a U.S. government attempt to fight communism. The prevailing belief suggested eradicating poverty and illiteracy to contain communism. Ironically, the Cuban government was also attempting to stamp out the same evils, which it associated with capitalism. A few years later, President Lyndon Johnson sent U.S. Marines to the Dominican Republic and prevented the democratically elected but communist Juan Bosch from resuming his presidency.

Although Khrushchev removed the Soviet missiles aimed at U.S. cities, the Soviet Union continued to be Castro's strongest ally and trading partner. The Soviet treasury subsidized the Cuban economy by purchasing sugar at an above-market price, and selling Castro much-needed oil and other products.

U.S.-Cuban relations may be understood in binary terms, but digesting Cuban domestic affairs has proved to be a challenge. In fact, anyone attempting to grapple with Cuban history since 1959 by concentrating on U.S.-Cuba relations, or the island and the exile communities, will miss the complexity and contradictions taking place in the last forty years. It may be necessary to study occurrences on a monthly or daily basis to come to terms with the unfolding of events. Some contradictions include the Salon de Mai exhibition of surrealist artists in 1967 and the publication of Heberto Padilla's *Fuera del juego* (Out of the Game, 1968), a controversial collection of poems that was awarded the Unión Nacional de Escritores y Artistas de Cuba (Union of Writers and Artists of Cuba) prize but denounced by government officials for its daring criticism of the revolution. It also includes the failure of the 10-million-ton sugar harvest of 1970, which essentially placed into question Castro's ability to govern effectively, offset the Cuban economy and injured the revolution's national pride. In effect, the Castro government became defensive and did not tolerate dissension. The restrictive measures of the period included the detainment of Padilla, followed by a contrived confession, three years after the publication of his poems. (Padilla confessed to conspiring against the government and accused his wife and close friends of doing the same.) Some students of Cuba are tempted to ask, What would have been the outcome of a successful sugar harvest? Similarly, what would have happened had General Francisco Ochoa, the commander of the Cuban Angolan forces, accused of drug trafficking, had not been put to death?

Cuban society and economy experienced a major crisis with Mikhail Gorbachev's reformist policies in the Soviet Union, which led to perestroika, the fall of the Berlin Wall, and the collapse of the Soviet Union. To survive, Castro initiated many changes, some of which returned Cuba to a prerevolutionary period, when Cuba was a tourist paradise. With the disintegration of the Soviet Union and the drop in sugar prices, Russia demanded payment in hard currency. To stay in power, Castro restructured the Cuban economy to take advantage of the island's natural resources: its weather and beaches. The Ministerio de Turismo (Ministry of Tourism) is attempting to attract tourists from all over the world, offering special golf, hunting, fishing, and scuba packages, among others. In fact, Cuba is the fourth most visited country in Latin America. Currently more than 1 million tourists visit the island, and projections indicate that this number will double within the next few years. Italians, Canadians, and Spaniards, in that order, head the tourist list and add millions of dollars to Cuba's economy. However, some capitalist evils that Castro eradicated have reemerged with a vengeance. Castro's policies have made provisions for private ownership, the U.S. dollar to circulate, foreign tourism, and widespread prostitution. Although the Cuban government once proudly claimed that Cuba was a sovereign country, free of Soviet control, Castro considers foreign investment in Cuba's infrastructure a necessity of the new Cuban reality.

For those who knew Cuba in the 1970s and 1980s, the island today appears to be a different society. Earlier, the Soviet presence was evident mainly through products from the Eastern bloc countries. Soviets were not readily visible; they kept to themselves and preferred to remain in their own communities. The dollar did not circulate. In fact, it was considered a crime for Cubans to hold dollars.

Today's Cuba is radically different. New hotels have gone up, under foreign ownership, such as the Meliá Cohíbar, in the Vedado district, owned by Spanish interests. Stores with foreign products, once available only to foreigners and diplomats, are open to anyone with dollars. In fact, the Cuban peso is no longer a viable currency, its worth limited to purchasing scarce items made available through the rationing system. It is also used for public transportation and buying a few necessities. The dollar has become the unofficial currency and has begun to restructure Cuban society and culture.

The Cuban government's move to make Cuba a paradise for tourists will produce a crisis of no small magnitude. Since the economy revolves around the once-prohibited dollar, it has become the currency of choice. Cuba has two economies with two sets of currencies: the dollar and the peso. Those who hold traditional jobs are paid in pesos, and they depend on ration books to purchase needed products. Some who work in tourist-related jobs are paid in dollars, and they have access to supermarkets with products that are available in any developed country. Cubans who possess dollars—those who work with foreigners and those who have relatives living outside the island and receive from them hard currency—are the new privileged group. More than a few professionals are abandoning their jobs to work in hotels so that they can also reap the benefits associated with the tourist industry. The internal flight of professionals, reminiscent of the first wave of Cuban exiles, will undoubtedly affect the society in immeasurable ways.

The most recent economic conditions are affecting all levels of Cuban society and will influence culture. While some Cubans are leaving their jobs to find work in the tourist and tourist-related industry, others are opening their homes to foreign visitors. This is done through the *paladares*, independently owned restaurants in private homes, and families who make arrangements with the government to rent rooms in their home. People who under other circumstances value their privacy are changing their ways in order to survive. Some professionals have had to change their lifestyle and forgo their bedroom with private bath, moving into a smaller room, for the sake of attracting visitors and obtaining hard currency. In many cases, these families have to put up with the same tourist demands known to hotel managers.

Prostitutes seeking dollars are also assaulting Cuban society and culture. However, these are not the prostitutes common in the Havana of the 1950s, or those found in capitalist countries. For the most part, these Cuban prostitutes, commonly known as *jineteras*, are educated women; many of them are students, and even professionals, who venture out into the streets and clubs. Some engage in the profession on a full-time basis, but many do so part time, when their economic situation demands it. It is not uncommon for wives, mothers, and daughters to become the economic head of household. In this respect, women are playing a leading role as breadwinners of their family. Although men compose the majority of tourists, women also vacation in Cuba and look for *jineteros* (male prostitutes).

Cuba's dollar economy has been influenced by the market forces and by the remittances Cuban exiles send to their relatives on the island, which have become the single most important source of revenue for the economy, surpassing tourism and sugar. In 1996 they were estimated to be around 800 million dollars. In this respect, those who have relatives abroad have become members of the nouveau riche with access to dollars, and dollar stores with material goods. Those associated with tourism also participate in Cuba's dollar economy.

As we look into the future, what kind of society will the post-Castro years usher in? Although he continues to enjoy popular support, Castro, born in

1928, is rapidly approaching the end of his career. The title of Gustavo Pérez Firmat's autobiographical novel, *Next Year in Cuba* (1996), has a prophetic effect insofar as it signals a foreseeable return to the island. It is obvious to any student of Cuban history and culture that a post-Castro Cuba will be different from the present society. Raúl Castro, Fidel's youngest brother, who is second in command and chief of the armed forces, does not have the talent or the charisma of his older brother. He will not be able to hold together a society that has an increasing number of dissenters.

The current state of affairs will influence the development of Cuban culture. The breakup of the Soviet Union has produced a move toward democracy. Cuba is among a small group of nations that continue to support communism, but it too shows signs of change. The government has made some token and symbolic gestures, though other changes still need to be made. It has begun to allow freedom of religion, foreign investment, and the formation of a limited human rights organization. Cuban officials also welcome some type of relations with the United States, as demonstrated by the two baseball games in 1999 between the Cuban Nationals and the Baltimore Orioles. The island's geographic location, ninety miles from Key West, compels leaders on both sides of the Florida straits to support some form of diplomatic relations.

Miami Cubans, with their government in exile, continue to prepare for the long-awaited return home. Many will remain in the United States, where they contribute to an expanding U.S. culture. However, a small percentage is preparing to return to the island and resume a life that was once familiar but which has little relevance to today's reality. The U.S. government and exiled communities will do their best to influence the internal affairs of the country, but ultimately Cubans on the island will resolve Cuba's problems.

REFERENCES

Ackerman, Holly. "The Balsero Phenomenon, 1991–1994." *Cuban Studies 26.* Ed. Jorge Domínguez. Pittsburgh: University of Pittsburgh Press, 1996. 169–200.

Faber, Samuel. *Revolution and Reaction in Cuba, 1933–1960.* Middletown, Conn.: Wesleyan University Press, 1976.

Fermoselle, Rafael. *Política y color en Cuba.* Madrid: Editorial Colibrí, 1998.

Guerra, Ramiro. *Manual de historia de Cuba: Desde su descubrimiento hasta 1868.* Madrid: Ediciones R, 1975.

Luis, William. *Literary Bondage: Slavery in Cuban Narrative.* Austin: University of Texas Press, 1990.

Montreal, Pedro. "Las remesas familiares en la economía Cubana." *Encuentro de la Cultura Cubana* 14 (Fall 1999): 49–62.

Moore, Carlos. "Le Peuple noir a-t-il sa place dans la révolution cubane?" *Présence Africaine* 52 (1964): 226–230.

———. *Castro, the Blacks, and Africa.* Los Angeles: Center for Afro-American Studies, University of California, Los Angeles, 1988.

Ortiz, Fernando. *Cuban Counterpoint: Tobacco and Sugar.* Trans. Harriet de Onís. Durham, N.C.: Duke University Press, 1995.

Portuondo del Prado, Fernando. *Historia de Cuba: 1492–1898.* Havana: Editorial Pueblo y Educación, 1965.

Thomas, Hugh. *Cuba: The Pursuit of Freedom.* New York: Harper and Row, 1971.

Valdés, Nelson P., and Rolando E. Bonachea. "Fidel Castro y la política estudiantil de 1947 a 1952." *Aportes*, no. 22 (1971): 26–40.

Villaverde, Cirilo. *Cecilia Valdés.* Ed. Raimundo Lazo. Mexico City: Porrúa, 1972.

2

Religion

LIKE MANY of its sister nations, Cuba is considered to be a Catholic country. This is especially significant under a communist government that according to Karl Marx views religion to be "the opiate of the masses." Certainly the communist government has had an impact on religion and religious instruction on the island. Statistics tell the story. In 1960, 70 to 75 percent of the population identified itself as Catholic, and Protestants were 3 to 6 percent. Twenty-five years later, the numbers had diminished. In 1985 the Catholic church stated that Catholics comprised 38 percent of the total population of 10.5 million and Protestant officials estimated that their followers ranged from 25,000 to 80,000. Fewer than 1,000 considered themselves Jewish. The number of practicing Catholics ranged from 150,000 to 200,000, while that of Protestants increased, and approximately 54 percent of them attend services (Crahan 1989, 217 n.5).

Since the beginning of the economic crisis of the 1990s, many have turned to religion as a source of comfort, and all religions in Cuba have shown a significant increase. According to the CID-Gallup poll of Costa Rica, 20 percent of Cubans said they attended church services. Pope John Paul II's visit to Cuba in January 1998 gave Catholicism much needed support, and more Cubans are expressing their religious beliefs.

Protestant churches support Castro's government and they have been the beneficiaries of growth. The number of Methodist church members has tripled in the last five years. A June 1999 celebration attracted 100,000 Protestants to the same Plaza de la Revolución where the pope had attracted some

500,000 supporters. This most recent celebration was attended by Castro and other government officials.

In addition to Western religions, a high percentage of Cubans are practitioners of Afro-Cuban religions. Afro-Cuban religions mixed successfully with Catholicism, a fusion known as *sincretismo* (syncretism). During the slave trade, slaves brought to the New World their rich culture and religion, which they continued to practice. But slave owners forbade slaves from practicing their religions and forced them to accept Christianity. Slaves saw similarities between Christian saints and African gods, known as orishas, and attributed the characteristics of their gods to their Catholic counterparts. It is difficult to know how many Cubans practice one form or another of the many Afro-Cuban religions. However, it is widely believed that every Cuban president has had a spiritual adviser of African religions and that Castro himself went to Nigeria to become a santero, a priest of the Yoruba tribe.

FREEMASONS

Not everyone living on the island has always embraced a religious affiliation. In the colonial period, French-oriented rationalism led to the development of Freemasonry, introduced in Cuba as a result of the British occupation of 1762. Freemasonry existed legally until the Aponte conspiracy of 1812, when whites and blacks attempted to liberate Cuba from Spain and end slavery. Although some lodges looked to Masonic leadership from Spain, the majority responded to conditions on the island and supported subversive activities. The Cuban patriot and martyr José Martí was a Mason, who was excommunicated by the church. Freemasonry endured clandestinely until Cuba became independent of Spain. In the republic, Freemasons became more conservative in thinking and used their members to influence policy.

PROTESTANTISM

Presbyterianism was the first Protestant religion brought to the island, introduced in 1884 by a Cuban convert working in a tobacco factory. However, not until the Spanish American War was there a noticeable presence of Protestants in Cuba. The leading groups were Southern Baptists, Methodists, Presbyterians, and Episcopalians. Protestant clergy concentrated their efforts among the lower- and middle-income groups and relied on funding from the United States to carry out their mission. The Baptists divided their mission into two geographic areas. The Northern Baptists worked in the eastern part of the island, while the Southern Baptists concentrated their efforts in the western part.

CATHOLICISM

During the period in which Freemasons were prominent on the island, the Catholic church also thrived. Like the Baptists, the church was divided into two ecclesiastical provinces that encompassed the island. The eastern part, set in Santiago de Cuba, was the earlier and dated to 1522; the western one, housed in Havana, dated to 1787. Each was an archdiocese that oversaw two dioceses: the dioceses of Pinar del Río and Matanzas in the west and those of Cienfuegos and Camagüey in the east. Every diocese served more than 200 parishes. One of the most influential forces in the church was the bishop of Havana, Juan José Díaz de Espada y Landa (1756–1832), who was named to the Havana diocese in 1802. A liberal thinker, Bishop Espada was instrumental in introducing a number of reforms, including burials in cemeteries and the development of art on the island.

In the colonial period, the Catholic church relied on the Church of Spain and wealthy islanders for its support and was politically active. For example, it attempted to evangelize the African segment of the population and influence the treatment of slaves. During the fight for independence, the church continued its complicity with the Spanish Crown and sided with the colonial authorities, as represented by a pastoral letter in 1898 issued by the bishop of Havana.

After independence and the founding of the Republic of Cuba of 1902, U.S. authorities imposed a separation of church and state, causing the church to lose its political influence and what little appeal it enjoyed. Furthermore, the church began to lose money. The Cuban constitution deprived the Catholic church of its tax revenue and the privileged status it had maintained during the colonial period. The new constitution also made provisions for secular education. The church lost additional revenue when civil marriage was introduced after 1902 and then made compulsory after 1918. In the republic, the church became an unpopular institution, appealing only to a few and lacking adequate resources, including priests to preach its message.

The 1940 Constitution guaranteed freedom of religion but with certain limitations, ensuring that any position taken by the church could not subvert the public order. Nevertheless, the church did have some successes. Acción Católica (Catholic Action), a lay group, began its activities in the 1930s; the Catholic University of Santo Tomás de Villanueva was founded in 1946;

and by the 1940s, the Christian Social Democrats claimed a significant following.

After Batista's coup in 1952, some church officials began to support the status quo. Archbishop Manuel Arteaga preferred to coexist with the dictatorship and congratulated Batista when he assumed power. However, the archbishop of Santiago de Cuba, Monsignor Enrique Pérez Serantes, and the bishop of Matanzas, Monsignor Alberto Martín Villaverde, opposed the dictator. In fact, the bishop of Santiago became an early Castro supporter and even saved his life after the attack on the Moncada barracks failed. Toward the end of Batista's regime, additional clergy and almost all secular officers criticized Batista and sympathized with the revolutionaries. Father Guillermo Sardiñas was the first priest to join Castro in the mountains in 1957. The religious leaders supported the rebel cause:

> A large number of Catholics and many priests in Oriente were now active members of the 26 July. In the course of the summer, Fr. Guillermo Sardiñas climbed the Sierra to become, with permission of the coadjutor bishop of Havana, chaplain to the rebel army. Another priest, Fr. Chelala, became treasurer of the movement in Holguín. The national treasurer, Enrique Canto, was a leading Catholic layman. Only the bishops and the regular clergy remained suspicious or divided though both the bishops of Santiago and Matanzas never wavered in their hostility to the dictatorship. Protestant pastors such as the Rev. Fernández Ceballos were active in Havana. (Thomas 1971, 946)

Though Cubans consider themselves to be Catholic, only a small percentage of them actually attended church. Prior to the revolution, approximately 10 percent of the island's population were practicing Catholics (Blutstein, Anderson, Belters, et al. 1971, 188). The church catered mainly to a reduced but influential sector of the population—those who were white, middle and upper middle class, and lived in urban areas.

OTHER FAITHS

There were other religious groups in the period of the republic. Chinese, who had arrived on the island as indentured servants in 1847, increased in numbers. Although many accepted Western religions, the Chinese had two Taoist temples by mid-century. The number of Jews also grew in the first half of the twentieth century. There were some 12,000 Jews, and they constructed six synagogues.

REVOLUTION AND BEYOND

With the triumph of the rebel forces, church officials, including Ignacio Biaín, the director of *La Quincena*, the leading church magazine, backed the activities of the new government. However, not everyone in the Catholic and rebel hierarchies thought alike, and both church and government officials viewed each other with suspicion. The churches and synagogues were unprepared for the changes that were to take place.

The government considered the churches to be representative of foreign interests. For example, the vast majority of the 3,000 priests in Cuba were from Spain. Protestants were from the United States and received support for their mission in Cuba. Although the Vatican had recognized the new government, the three dioceses under Spanish leadership were reserved in their support of the new government.

The church attempted to influence the unfolding of events and eventually clashed with rebel leaders. Catholic administrators supported Castro's March 1959 agrarian reform program, but Castro would accuse the Spanish clergy of participating in counterrevolutionary activities. The new government placed restrictions on the island's churches, which included outdoor processions and religious instruction. Moreover, church officials were limited in their travels throughout the island; in particular, they were prohibited from having access to rural communities. Protestants supported the new government, but later assumed a nonpolitical approach.

In 1960 representatives of the clergy, such as Eduardo Bozo Masvidal and Archbishop Pérez Serantes, became openly critical of the government and its move to the left. This was also the case with the Episcopal church, which objected to the government's decision to embrace communism. Toward the end of that year, all the bishops distributed a pastoral letter denouncing Castro's communist policies and his repressive measures against the church. Castro retaliated and accused the church of abandoning its religious responsibilities and participating in politics. The battle between the government and the clergy reached a climax after the Bay of Pigs invasion, when Castro nationalized private schools and buildings.

At the outset of the revolution, the majority of Cubans had identified themselves as Catholics. By 1960, it was believed that approximately 70 to 75 percent of the total population of the island of 7.5 million were Catholics. Between 3 and 6 percent were Protestants (Crahan 1989, 217 n.5).

Some Catholic priests were expelled from the island, and other religious workers became part of early Cuban exodus. By 1965 about 20 percent of the Catholic priests and 90 percent of religious Catholics had left the island, as had 50 percent of Protestant religious and lay leaders, who included more than 200 Protestant pastors and missionaries.

The Jewish community was reduced substantially, from 12,000 to 1,200. The number of Jewish practitioners has since decreased to 150 families. Nevertheless, their congregations continue to function.

Although government officials followed a hard line against religious organizations, they continued to maintain diplomatic relations with the Vatican. In 1963 the government published Pope John XXIII Pacem in Terris. That same year a new papal nuncio, Monsignor Cesare Zacchi, was appointed, and later was made bishop in 1967. Monsignor Zacchi began to rebuild bridges between the church and the Castro government. He believed that the Cuban system provided a means for achieving religious ends and encouraged his followers to work with the government. The church has also benefited from a positive approach to government, offering it material goods to keep up its buildings.

The relationship between the church and the government progressed as religious leaders became more accepting of the limited role that the church could play within a socialist society. Two pastoral letters issued by bishops indicated this position. The first denounced the U.S. blockade of the island and supported government programs that addressed the common good. The second underscored cooperation between Catholics and Marxists in the interest of humanity. However, the reaction to the letters was mixed; not all Catholics supported this newfound position. One group believed that the bishops had made too many concessions to the government, and another felt that they did not go far enough.

Methodists, Presbyterians, and Baptists too sought to benefit from a better relationship with the government. The Cuban Council of Evangelical Churches reflected this position.

In the 1970s, closer relations were established between Castro officials and Catholics, Protestants, and Jews, who wanted to work with the government, thus ensuring their survival and a voice in the construction of the communist state. What some interpreted as a conciliatory position by church officials forced many hard-line leaders to reconsider their stand with regard to institutional religion. This was particularly the case during the Cuban Cultural and Educational Congress of 1971, whose platform considered religion a private matter. Although there was a defense of individual religious beliefs, there was also support for scientific materialism, the position of Marxist officials who question religion and base their observations on a certain understanding of science.

Some Protestant groups were welcomed into the construction of the new society, but Jehovah's Witnesses, Evangelical Gideon's Band, and Seventh Day Adventists were considered to be counterrevolutionaries. The Jehovah's Witnesses and Seventh Day Adventists attempted to convince the government that their religion prohibited them from military service, a requirement for all able men of military age in Cuba. The government's position, which ensured its control over religious groups, was inserted into the Cuban Constitution of 1976. Article 54 was designed to regulate religious activities and make opposition to military inscription illegal: "It is illegal and punishable by law to oppose one's faith or religious belief to the Revolution, education or the fulfillment of the duty to work, defend the homeland with arms, show reverence for its symbols and other duties established by the Constitution."

Jehovah's Witnesses, Evangelical Gideon's Band, and Seventh Day Adventists were persecuted because their beliefs did not coincide with those of the government. But before and after the writing of the Constitution, Catholic and Protestant groups welcomed a clear definition of what the government expected of them.

Those who cooperated with the government stood to benefit. They received encouragement from the Communist party platform of 1978 and the Second Congress of the Cuban Communist party of 1980, which invited all Cubans, whether they believed in God or not, to participate in the construction of a new Cuban society. The government's position reflected that held by proponents of liberation theology, which was spreading throughout Latin America, who did not see any contradiction between Christianity and Marxism. The Nicaraguan revolution became the focus of world attention as it successfully combined revolution with theology. Priest Ernesto Cardenal became minister of education. The new marriage between state and church was a more attractive alternative to Latin America, and the Nicaraguan revolution had replaced the Cuban model. Although Cuban officials were not ready to bring religious leaders into the sanctuary of the Politburo, some church leaders worked within the government, and some government officials even entertained the possibility of being Christian revolutionaries. They recognized that it was in the interest of the church to define a role within revolutionary society and work within imposed limitations.

The relationship between the state and religious organizations has steadily increased, and culminated with Pope John Paul II's visit to Cuba in January 1998. Prior to his visit, significant trips by U.S. religious leaders had set the groundwork for this historic event. In 1984 Rev. Jesse Jackson's visit to Cuba encouraged closer relations between Protestants and the government. After his visit, Protestants had better access to government officials to resolve their needs.

In January 1985 a U.S. delegation that included three Catholic bishops visited Cuba in support of a dialogue between Cuban bishops and the Castro government. The group raised issues that included humanitarian aid to the church, discrimination against practicing Catholics, a scarcity of priests, and declining congregations. In response, Castro defended the revolution and explained that the problems were due more to historical circumstances than to his government's policies.

In December 1989 Castro showed further signs of conciliation with religious leaders. He lifted the ban on the popular pilgrimage to the shrine of Saint Lazarus in the town of Rincón. Once again the road to the church was filled with believers. As in previous times, worshipers made promises to the miraculous saint and were seen crawling or dragging themselves, while others carried heavy objects, to alleviate their sins. Not all who came were Catholics. Others included followers of Santería, an Afro-Cuban religion for whom Saint Lazarus represented their Babalú-Ayé, the patron saint of the sick and the needy.

Finally, Pope John Paul II's much-awaited visit proved to be as exciting as anticipated. Believers and curious were concerned there would be a confrontation between Castro and the pope. It was believed that Castro would use the pope to legitimize his leadership position and that the pope would press Castro to allow more freedom on the island. In effect, the pope asked for Cuba to open itself to the world and for the world to do the same to Cuba.

Prior to the pope's visit, the government wanted to create a hospitable environment for the pontiff. Officials allowed for door-to-door announcements to spread the word of the pope's visit and published the pope's Christmas message to Cubans. In addition, they made provisions for the pope's masses to be televised live.

When the pope arrived, he toured the island, often accompanied by Fidel Castro. In fact, Castro was welcoming. The pope even spoke in Havana's Plaza of the Revolución, the stage for many of Castro's political speeches. Throughout his visit, the pope upheld the position maintained by prisoners of conscience and criticized the lack of political freedom in Cuba; however, he was also critical of the U.S. economic embargo.

The pope's visit had an impact on Cuba's political climate, although it is still too soon to measure its full impact. After the conclusion of the pope's trip, Castro allowed for the celebration of Christmas, which became an official holiday for the first time since 1969; permitted Cardinal Jaime Ortega to deliver a Christmas address; and set free more than 300 political prisoners. Equally important, more Cubans are expressing a newfound faith or are expressing their beliefs more openly. It is no longer uncommon to see well-attended church weddings and other church activities. All religions have benefited, including Santería.

But reforms have not moved as quickly as many had expected. Approval for opening Catholic schools, religious publications, and processions have not been forthcoming. In fact, Cuban officials are careful to explain that the changes that are taking place are due not so much to the pope's influence as to economic forces. Although this may be the case, the impact of the pope's visit on the island cannot be easily dismissed.

The pope's statement to open Cuba to the rest of the world has had positive results for the Castro government. Guatemala and the Dominican Republic have reestablished relations with Cuba, and high-profile figures like the prime minister of Canada, Jean Chretiene, and the king of Spain, Juan Carlos, have made visits to the island. U.S. President Bill Clinton reinstated direct flights to the island, which had been suspended when an airplane of the Hermanos al Rescate (Brothers to the Rescue), an exile rescue group that flies between the island and mainland looking for rafters and other refugees, was shot down off the coast of Cuba in 1997.

African Religions

Many Cubans practice African religions, which in Cuba have combined with Catholicism. According to Lydia Cabrera's classic book, *El monte* (The Wilderness, 1954), Afro-Cubans believe in the spirituality inherent in the woods are inhabited by African divinities and spirits. It is the space of the orishas, the gods, and therefore is sacred. Although slaves were responsible for the emergence of Afro-Cuban religions, these systems of beliefs have gained in popularity and attract adherents from every race.

Santería

Of the Afro-Cuban religions, Santería, also known as Regla de Ocha, has the largest number of followers. Most of the enslaved Africans taken to Cuba were from the Yoruba tribe of Nigeria, and they bought with them the view of the world of their gods. But white masters on the island wanted to exert total control over their slaves; they separated tribes and families, so that members of one linguistic group could not speak to others, and they suppressed their religion. Nevertheless, the Yoruba religion survived clandestinely, and for this reason practitioners of this and other African-based religions were sworn to secrecy, a characteristic that continues today. In slavery, the religion was transformed and mixed with Catholic rituals and practices. The characteristics of African orishas (spirits) were attributed to Catholic saints.

In Santería, Christian saints take on Yoruba characteristics. Olodumare created the earth, the waters, the sun, and the moon. One interpretation of the birth of the orishas is the following:

> Olodumare—God among the Yorubas—is also known as Olofi in Santería. According to one of the legends "patakis" of Santería, Olofi created the orishas by gathering together a number of flat smooth stones "otanes" and projecting some of his aché [divine power] into them. From these otanes, filled with Olofi's divine energy, the orishas were born. Olofi then divided all the various forces of nature among the orishas and gave them dominion over emotions and other transcendental powers. This is why santeros believe that the aché of the orishas is concentrated in the stones that represented them. During the initiation or the *asiento*, when a person "makes the saint," the powers of the orishas are brought down into their respective otanes by means of a special ceremony. Each orisha has a specific number of stones ascribed to him or her. The stones are kept inside colorful tureens *"soperas"* in the colors of the orisha. These stones are "fed" periodically with the blood of the sacrificed animals which are sacred to each orisha. The meat of the animals, which is believed to have the blessings and the aché of the orisha, is then cooked and eaten by the santeros. (González-Whipper 1984, 12)

In Santería, Obatalá, son of Olodumare, is the creator. With some dust given to him by Olodumare, Obatalá began creation in the city of Ilé-Ifé. He worked for four days and rested on the fifth, to give thanks to Olodumare. During a second visit to Earth, Obatalá brought plants, animals, and humans. Other versions show that Obatalá created humans from clay. Since he had been drinking, some of them were ill formed, which he later regretted.

Obatalá is the god of the mind and all thought. Catholic equivalents might be Our Lady of Mercy, Jesus of Nazareth, Saint Joseph, and Saint Manuel. Some of his attributes include his color (white); day of the week (Thursday); precious stones (diamonds and rock crystal); metal (silver); plants (cotton, *ceiba* [silk-cotton tree], jasmine, and night jasmine); animals (spiders, pigeons, and *guabina* fish); and festive day (September 24). These attributes explain the characteristics and powers of the gods and establish a relationship between Santería and other African religions and Christianity.

Another popular orisha is Eleguá, the son of Obatalá and Yemmul. He is the god of the roads and the messenger of the gods; only he can see the past, present, and future without divination. In an offering, he is served before the other orishas. Eleguá's Christian equivalents are the Infant of Prague, Saint Martin of Porres, and Saint Benito. His colors are black and red; his number is three; his precious stones are *azabache* (jet black) and onyx; plants are *hedionda* herb, jurubana, *gua-guao* pepper, and Mastic trees, all of which are Cuban plants; his animals are the rat, chicken, and chameleon; and his festive day is June 3.

Oshún, Our Lady of La Caridad' del Cobre, is the patron saint of Cuba. She is beautiful, sexy, happy, and gracious. She is Yemayá's sister (Our Lady of Regla), with whom she shares the waters. In the Yoruba tradition, she is the goddess of the river. Her color is yellow, and her number is five. She represents Saturday. Oshún's precious stones are topaz, coral, and amber, and her metals are gold and copper. The plants she is associated with are anisette, cinnamon, pumpkin, oranges, sunflower, *cascabelillo, culantrillo de pozo* (maidenhair from a well), and parsley; and animals she is associated with are turkey, caiman (a type of alligator), shrimp, and *aura tiñosa* (urubu [black vulture]). Oshún is the orisha of love and fresh water, and her festive day is September 8. She rules the abdominal area, and for this reason women who desire children pay homage to her.

Other orishas are Changó, the god of thunder and fire, identified with Saint Barbara, and Oggún, the god of metals, identified with Saint Peter.

The santero or santera is a spiritual guide or consultant who communicates with the other world through spirits or gods who advise him or her. Often a spirit who helps to see the past and foretell the future possesses the santero. The religion makes other provisions for uncovering the mysteries of life. Divination is an important aspect of Santería, which establishes communication between this world and the next one. There are four types of divination: the cowry shell, the coconut, the Table of Ifa, and the Okuele. The first is read by the patterns and color of the shells; the second by the way four coconut rinds fall (whether they face up or down); the third by a round wooden board carved with African designs through which Orula (Saint Francis of Assisi) speaks; and the fourth by the position of eight medallions joined by an iron chain. The last two methods can be used only by the Babalawo, the high priest of the religion. The santero keeps a shrine or an altar, with saints or orishas, to whom he prays and makes offerings or gives food. Usually the santero makes an *ebbó*, a sacrifice, to obtain the orishas' *aché*. The offering can be in the form of an animal, flowers, candles, fruits, or any of the foods associated with the orishas. Offerings are also made during ancestor worship, an important element of Santería.

A student is initiated into Santería by a Santero or a Babalawo. The teacher becomes a godfather, a *padrino* or *madrina*, to the initiate, the *ahijado*, and instructs her or him in the ways of Santería and is responsible for this person's well-being. The ceremony is elaborate, and sacrifices are offered to the orishas. The initiate takes on the mysteries of the orisha under whom he or she is initiated.

The orishas make appearances at festivities known as Fiestas de Santos or Tambores. The African drums have a special function; their sound is a way of communicating with the orishas. There are three drums—Iyá, Okónkolo, and Itótele—each of which speaks with a different tone and to a particular orisha. Possessions, offerings, and food, as well as singing, dance, and divination, characterize the fiestas.

Regla Conga

Another Afro-Cuban religion is the Regla Conga. It is well known and respected in Cuba, though not as popular as Santería. The Regla Conga originated with the Kongo o Bakongo people from the areas of Cameroon, Angola, and Mozambique and whose language is Kikongo. In Cuba, however, the religion is associated with the Bantu people. The Congo people lack a complex system known to the Lucumí pantheon, and therefore have accepted the Lucumí world view as their own. For example, Changó, which is Saint Barbara, becomes Nsasi, Siete Rayos (seven lighting); Obatalá, Our Lady of Charity, becomes Mamá Kengue, Tiembla-Tierra (earthquake); and Eleguá, the Infante of Prague, becomes Nkuyu Nfinda, Lucero Mundo (world lighthouse).

There are different branches of the Reglas Congas, and these include Regla de Palo Monte, the Regla Kimbisa, the Biymba, the Musunde (or Musundí), and the Brillumba (or Vrillumba). Although the Congos have a supreme being, whose name is Nzambi Mpungu (Sambi), he does not receive any special treatment. He created the world, with its orishas and spirits, and humans, and he taught them both good and bad magic and how to reproduce their species. After his creation, Sambi left these dynamic forces behind. The practitioners believe in a relationship between humans, the dead, and the gods. The spiritual leaders are called Ñgangulero or, in Cuba, Paleros or Mayomberos, and they pay tribute to the deceased—that is, the spirits and the power that they embody. The spiritual force can be harnessed in statues or medicinal pouches known as *macutos* that can be transported from one place to the other. The iron pot now serves the same purpose. The practitioner makes a pact with the dead spirit, which also possesses him. The spirit, in effect, carries out the orders given to it. For the Congo, the most common rituals are those associated with initiation of practitioners and those of sacrifices and funerals.

Abakuá

The Abakuá or Ñáñigo Secret Society is a brotherhood that dates to the colonial period, specifically to the Havana port of Regla in 1836, and is practiced mainly in the provinces of Havana and Matanzas. Originally its members were from the region of Calabar, a province in Nigeria; in Cuba they were members of either Apapa Efo or Brícamo Apapa Efi societies, corresponding to the Ekol or Ibibio African tribes. They are divided into *naciones*, and each "nation" has seven leaders, who are descendants of African chiefs or priests, with its own system of beliefs and rituals. Although the early membership was limited to blacks, others were allowed to participate. Their ranks included mulattos, whites, and Chinese.

The Carabalí belief system is similar to those of the Yoruba and Congo people. Its main god, Abasí, who resembles Olodumare and Sambi, is also distant and receives little attention. Like the Congo, the Carabalí borrows many of its intermediary gods from the Yoruba religion. For example, the Yoruba Obatalá is the Carabalí Obandío; Babalú-Ayé, which corresponds to Saint Lazarus, is Yiniko; and Changó, Saint Barbara, is Okún. Like other Bantu groups, the Carabalí believe in good and evil. Abasí had an evil and envious brother, Nyógoro, who is associated with the devil.

The Carabalí practice magic, and each ceremony is initiated with a ritual of purification, which includes magical elements. In all ceremonies, communication is established with the dead ancestors, the world of the spirits, and that of the group's origin. Rituals pertaining to initiation are elaborate. They start at midnight and end at sundown. Because it is a secret society, its mysteries are well guarded. Nevertheless, some practices are public. For example, the dances of the spirits, the deities, represented by Íreme, Diablitos, Ñañas, or Ñáñigos (devil-like figures), are public. The Ñáñigos dress in colorful straw costumes and hide their identity behind masks with a cone-shaped hat. According to the believers, the spirits are attracted to the burlap and then pass on to the Íreme. This transference occurs without the usual spiritual possession. The devil-like figures make appearances during special religious occasions, like the one that celebrates Three Kings Day on 6 January.

The Isué, similar to a Catholic bishop, is the main spiritual leader. In him resides the power, and he plays an important part in baptisms and initiation rituals. He is the owner of the *sese* or *seseribó*, a drum with the same significance as the cup that holds the host in Catholicism. Ancestral worship is an essential element of the Ñáñigo ritual. The spirit of the dead or the ancestors is present at these ceremonies.

Because of their secrecy, the Ñáñigos are feared. Historically they have been persecuted by authorities and have been considered dangerous thieves and killers, who carry knives, blades, and other weapons. In literature, the Ñáñigos have been depicted as being primitive and savage. In fact, the Abakuá Society is a religious and mutual aid organization that works in the interest of its members.

REFERENCES

Blutstein, Howard I., Lynne Cox Anderson, Elinor C. Betters, et al. *Area Handbook for Cuba.* Washington, D.C.: U.S. Government Printing Office, 1971.

Cabrera, Lydia. *El monte.* Havana: Eds. CR, 1954.

Castellanos, Jorge, and Isabel Castellanos. *Cultura afrocubana.* 3 vols. Miami: Ediciones Universal, 1992.

Constitution of the Republic of Cuba. Havana: Instituto Cubano del Libro, 1975.

Crahan, Margaret. "Freedom of Worship in Revolutionary Cuba." In *The Cuba Reader: The Making of a Revolutionary Society.* Ed. Philip Brenner, William M. LeoGrande, Donna Rich, and Daniel Siegel. New York: Grove Press, 1989. 211–219.

"Cuba, su pueblo y su iglesia de cara al comienzo del tercer milenio" (Material de trabajo que sirvió para un encuentro de presbíteros de las diócesis de Santiago de Cuba, Holguín, Bayamo-Manzanillo y Guantánamo). *Encuentro de la Cultura Cubana* 15 (1999–2000): 203–215.

Cuervo Hewitt, Julia. *Aché, presencia africana: tradiciones yoruba-lucumí en la narrativa cubana.* New York: Peter Lang, 1988.

Cuesta, Leonel-Antonio de la. "The Cuban Socialist Constitution: Its Originality and Role in Institutionalization." *Cuban Studies* 6 (1976): 18–20.

González-Whipper, Migene. *Rituals and Spells of Santería.* New York: Original Publications, 1984.

Matibag, Eugenio. *Afro-Cuban Religious Experience: Cultural Reflections in Narrative.* Gainesville: University Press of Florida, 1996.

Partido Comunista de Cuba. *Plataforma programática: Tesis y resolución.* Havana: Editorial Ciencias Sociales, 1978.

Thomas, Hugh. *Cuba: The Pursuit of Freedom.* New York: Harper and Row, 1971.

3

Social Customs

SOCIAL CUSTOMS in Cuba have been determined by the ethnic and racial composition of its inhabitants and the historical period in which they interacted. With the practical extermination of the Amerindians, the inhabitants of the island were all foreigners. Spaniards and West Coast Africans interacted, though not on equal terms, along with Chinese, who arrived in the mid-nineteenth century, to create customs and behavior patterns associated with Cuban culture. Each group arrived with its own system of belief, and their coming together produced a uniquely Cuban culture. The customs formed during three distinct moments in Cuban history: under Spanish rule, in the republic, and during the Cuban revolutionary period. Throughout these periods, Afro-Cubans have found themselves at the bottom of the social and economic scale, first as slaves and later as discriminated Afro-Cubans. Their status, however, has not diminished the impact of their contribution to Cuban culture.

The Cuban revolution altered life on the island. With Castro's proclamation of a socialist revolution, the entire capitalist economy, which supported and complemented certain social behavior, was turned upside down. International businesses were nationalized, and private property confiscated. Existing social rituals were eliminated or severely altered. For example, debutante parties became a thing of the past.

Revolutionary leaders sought to replace the past with the New Man—someone dedicated to the construction of a new society, willing to sacrifice himself or herself for the success of the revolution. This new individual is selfless, works for moral incentives, and rejects materialism. Although voluntarism was encouraged, the government has not been totally successful in instituting moral incentives. A significant number of youths rejected the concept of the New Man. Their dissatisfaction became evident when many decided to flee the island during the Mariel boatlift in 1980. The rejection of moral incentives became especially evident in the Special Period, when the dollar began to circulate in the Cuban economy.

Cubans have had to do without many of the comforts and customs they enjoyed prior to the revolution. Although Cuban women like to dress fashionably and make themselves up, they have had to become accustomed to wearing uniforms or what little they are able to purchase at government stores. Cosmetics are hard to buy. Whereas Cubans followed U.S. and European fashions prior to 1959, they have become more informal in their dress, which responds more to tropical climatic conditions. The suit, tie, and white shirt, no longer part of the business dress code, have been replaced by the *guayabera*, a Caribbean shirt.

Castro himself has become a mythical figure in his own life. He enjoys popular support, and on a short moments notice can bring large numbers of people together, as he recently did with the case of Elián González, whose mother drowned while escaping on a boat to Miami in November of 1999. Castro made this an international crisis, with demonstrations demanding the return of the child to his natural father, who lives in Cuba. Though Castro's popularity has waned, as a whole Cubans still support this charismatic figure. Many still have his photograph in their home with the popular phrase "Fidel, esta es tu casa" (Fidel, this is your home). Since Castro opened Cuban society to all Cubans, when someone received something for free, it was customary to respond by saying "Gracias Fidel" (Thank you Fidel). As time passes, Cubans are more apt to complain about their economic situation, but they tend to blame someone other than Castro for the island's problems. This was also the case with the much-loved charismatic leader, Camilo Cienfuegos, who died in a mysterious airplane accident in the early years of the revolution or with the execution of General Ochoa in the 1980s, who was accused of trafficking in drugs. However, there are those who claim that nothing happens in Cuba without the approval of Castro himself. No one will ever have the same impact on the Cuban people that Castro enjoys, certainly not his younger brother Raúl, who has been named his successor.

With the collapse of the Soviet bloc and the beginning of the Special Period, Cuban customs seem to be returning to those of the prerevolutionary period. A shift to a dollar economy has brought back some habits prevalent in prerevolutionary Cuba.

Mass Organizations

Castro has been able to stay in power because of the help of mass organizations, which provide an avenue for individuals to become involved in politics. There is considerable pressure to join one or more mass organizations and thus show support for the government. They engage the individual and fall into two categories: supportive and communal. Although there are many modes of participatory activities, the three most important activities have been identified as follows: "Voluntary labor campaigns (usually in agriculture at harvest time), work on community improvement projects (such as adult education, public health classes, vaccination campaigns, blood donation drives, school improvements, etc.), and socialist emulation (contest between individuals or groups to see who can fulfill or over fulfill their work plans most quickly)" (LeoGrande 1989, 191).

Of the many organizations, the Comité de Defensa de la Revolución (Committee for the Defense of the Revolution) plays an important and supportive role. During the early 1960s, the CDR came into existence with the purpose of defending the revolution against internal opposition. Although the CDR renders public services, such as vaccination programs, it remains the ears and eyes of the revolution and through this informant role can exert control over individuals. For example, members can provide information about someone's activities that may facilitate permission to travel abroad and regularly denounce those who do not conduct themselves in a revolutionary manner.

Cuba has become a public society in which individuality is sacrificed for the common good. However, it is also a secretive one. Although the doors are opened to neighbors and friends, many Cubans are guarded. No one knows whom to trust, or to confide in, for fear of reprisal. This idea is conveyed in Sara Gómez's *De cierta manera* (In One Way or Another, 1974), a film in which one of the characters confides in the protagonist that he will not be at work because he will be with his lover. In the interest of the revolution and the common good, the friend denounces his friend in a public meeting.

Identity

With the publication in 1940 of his *Contrapunteo cubano del tabaco y el azúcar* (Cuban Counterpoint: Tobacco and Sugar), the anthropologist Fernando Ortiz (1881–1969) used the term *transculturation* to define Cuban culture. He meant the dynamic process in which cultures come together and interact with each other. Ortiz explains the richness of Cuban culture.

Among all peoples historical evolution has always meant a vital change from one culture to another at tempos varying from gradual to sudden. But in Cuba the cultures that have influenced the formation of its folk have been so many and so diverse in their spatial position and their structural composition that this vast blend of races and cultures over-shadows in importance every other historical phenomenon. Even economic phenomena, the most basic factors of social existence, in Cuba are almost always conditioned by the different cultures. In Cuba the terms Ciboney, Taino, Spaniard, Jew, English, French, Anglo-American, Negro, Yucatec, Chinese, and Creole do not mean merely the different elements that go into the make-up of the Cuban nation, as expressed by their different indications of origin. Each of these has come to mean in addition the synthetic and historic appellation of one of the various economies and cultures that have existed in Cuba successively and even simultaneously, at times giving rise to the most terrible clashes. (Ortiz 1995, 98–99)

Cubans are avid consumers of their national and export products: sugar, coffee, and tobacco. At the beginning of the nineteenth century, the three crops rivaled each other for supremacy, a struggle that sugar ultimately won. Each of the three crops points to a certain custom that contributed to the development of Cuban spirit and society. Sugar is associated with monoculture, large extensions of land, central authority, and slavery; tobacco, which grows in smaller parcels, requires specialized workers and argues for independence and freedom. Like tobacco, coffee is grown in smaller parcels. The growers often lived on this land and established a more personal relationship with their slaves. They supported a more benevolent type of slavery but also believed in freedom. Coffee plantations were intellectual centers, where leisure life was enjoyed and the works of liberal thinkers were read. Coffee, which was consumed in coffee houses throughout the world, inspired thinking, conversation, and the spread of liberal ideas. Cuban customs and cultures are influenced by what the three crops represent. They tend to encompass the extremes of sugar's central authority and tobacco and coffee's freedom and independence.

CITIES

Although Cuba during the republic had a number of important cities, such as Santiago de Cuba, Trinidad, and Matanzas, Havana, the capital, became synonymous with island identity. Aspiring dancers, musicians, and professionals, as well as those wanting to improve their lives, traveled to Havana with high hopes for the future.

There are distinct differences between Havana and interior cities such as Santiago de Cuba, located in the easternmost province. For example, if Havana looked to Europe and the United States, Santiago de Cuba is more of a Caribbean city. It is through this city that French influence from Haiti entered the island, and still has a considerable population of Afro-Haitian descent.

In order to create a better-balanced society, the revolutionary government has emphasized the development of towns and cities. Between 1959 and 1971, 246 new settlements were constructed, many of them around work centers. In addition, the government restricts mobility, controlling housing and jobs, and has improved conditions in the countryside, thus making it more attractive to residents. One of the most impressive projects was that of Alamar, built by *microbrigadas* (small groups of workers) on the outskirts of Havana in 1971. It is a self-sufficient community, with schools, day care facilities, theaters, health care, and sports facilities to serve 130,000 people.

The island's politico-administrative units have changed as well. From 1878 to 1976, the island was divided into six provinces: Pinar del Río, La Habana, Matanzas, Las Villas, Camagüey, and Oriente, each with its own capital city. In 1976 these provinces were subdivided. They are now Pinar del Río, La Habana, Ciudad de La Habana, Matanzas, Villa Clara, Cienfuegos, Sancti Spiritus, Ciego de Ávila, Camagüey, Las Tunas, Holguín, Granma, Santiago de Cuba, Guantánamo, and the municipality of the Isla de la Juventud.

WOMEN

With the advent of the women's movement, Cuban women have become more independent and assertive, and they now work in jobs once considered to be the traditional domain of the man.

In 1960 the Federación de Mujeres Cubanas (Federation of Cuban Women) was formed to mobilize women and institute governmental, societal, and behavioral reforms. It sought to free women from their traditional roles and encourage them to make economic, political, and social decisions about their own lives. These measures were to take place by opening the educational process and allowing women to pursue all careers, including professional ones. Since then, women have participated in the militia, worked as sugarcane cutters, and undertaken other tasks that were once not considered befitting of their sex. Equally important reforms were to be instituted by eradicating machismo and changing the family structure, as indicated by the Family Code of 1975, which gave equal responsibilities to both husband and wife, including the rearing of children and household duties.

The women's movement has had varying success, as many women and men were unprepared for the changes. For the most part, decisions did not originate with women but were rather made from the top and imposed. The Cuban Constitution limits the types of jobs that women may perform. Article 43 limits them to tasks that are in line with their physical makeup. Other resolutions reserved some jobs for women and others for men, and protected women from taking jobs for which they were not prepared and others deemed harmful to their health. Other changes include an increase of divorces, particularly high for men between the ages of 20–24 and women between 15–19, and the number of single parents.

RACE RELATIONS

Blacks have been feared since slavery, especially after the Haitian uprising in 1791 and the establishment of the black Republic of Haiti in 1804. After emancipation, blacks did not fare any better. Miguel Barnet's *Biografía de un cimarrón* (Autobiography of a Runaway Slave, 1966) shows that Esteban Montejo's life changed very little in slavery and in the republic.

In the period of the republic, blacks continued to be feared. Martín Morúa Delgado's amendments to the Electoral Reform Law of 1910 made illegal the formation of political parties by race, thus essentially outlawing the Partido Independiente de Color (Black Independence party). In the aftermath, thousands of party members were killed. After the dictator Gerardo Machado's defeat in 1933, the Ley de Nacionalización del Trabajo (job nationalization law) essentially excluded blacks from many jobs, including salesmen in department stores, tramway or railway conductors, and nurses. Those open to blacks were menial jobs, such as shoeshine boy, or those that were physically demanding. Although the mulatto Batista brought about some changes during his presidency (1940–1944), his complexion excluded him from the Havana Yacht Club, an upper-class club.

When Castro took power, one of his early speeches admitted to the racial discrimination against blacks. Some changes have improved the lives of blacks as Castro moved forward to eradicate the vestiges of capitalism and establish an egalitarian society. For example, recreational areas have been opened to all Cubans, and with the goal of eliminating illiteracy by providing education for all, blacks have been able to move into professional areas once held exclusively by whites. Certainly measures to redistribute resources and reforms such as those pertaining to housing have helped those who historically were at the bottom of the societal ladder. And the racial composition of the National Assembly has improved.

Nevertheless, racial discrimination persists. Currently, there is no black political leader with significant power. And the social situation of blacks may get worse. As Cuba moves to a market economy based on tourism, whites more likely than blacks will occupy jobs that will have direct contact with foreigners. Even now, blacks are conspicuously absent in hotels, restaurants, and bars. However, black women are visible in areas frequented by European men, who favor Afro-Cuban women.

EDUCATION

Education has been one of the crown jewels of the revolution. Prior to the revolution, only about half of the island's primary school children attended any formal education, and the figure was even lower in the rural areas. Twenty-five years after the revolution, more than 3.5 million people attend school. This figure includes almost all children between the ages of six and twelve enrolled in primary schools and 84 percent between ages thirteen and sixteen in secondary schools. During the 1982–1983 school year, more than 250,000 teachers worked at all levels of the educational system (Leiner 1989).

Early in the revolution, the government made a commitment to eliminate illiteracy and provide universal education, especially for those living in rural areas. With this end in mind, it nationalized all schools and reorganized the school system. In 1961 the government embarked on a campaign to eradicate illiteracy. Students as young as fifth grade were sent to the countryside to teach peasants to read and write. The aim was to provide everyone with a minimum of a first-grade education. With a 96.1 percent literacy rate, Cuba has become one of the most literate countries in the world, and certainly the most literate in Latin America (Leiner 1989).

The next goal became the "Battle for the Sixth Grade." Over twelve years, more than 500,000 adults completed a sixth-grade education. These educational goals were achieved with strong moral conviction, volunteers, and financial investment. Prior to the revolution, the government had invested 12 pesos per student; by 1980, the figure was 137 pesos per student.

The government has built many new schools throughout the country at all levels, including day care centers. There has also been an emphasis in building *escuelas en el campo* (schools in rural areas); these are boarding schools where both students and teachers live in dormitories. The first one was built in 1971; by the mid-1980s, there were 384 junior high and 183 senior high schools, serving 37 percent of junior high students and 47 percent of senior high students. Between 1975 and 1980, enrollment increased from 277,000 to 478,000 at the junior high level. Students attend school part of the day and work the rest of the day, usually in agriculture.

Prior to the revolution, there were only three university centers. Since then, the number has increased to forty. Women have been one of the beneficiaries of the educational reforms. They now represent 46 percent of the university population. In 1983 Cuba was ranked twelfth in the world in percentages of women enrolled in university studies, ahead of all the Latin American countries.

One year after the 1975 party congress, the government put into effect plans designed to improve the educational system; the recommendations had emerged from the 1971 Primer Congreso Nacional de Educación y Cultura (First National Congress on Education and Culture). In the five-year Perfeccionamiento (Perfection, 1976–1981), education would be increased by one year to thirteen, and all children would be guaranteed one year of kindergarten. The new plan divided the elementary school program into two stages: children in grades 1–4 would remain with the same teacher, and grades 5–6 would offer special subjects. Three years of junior high and three years of senior high school would follow.

Nevertheless, it has not been smooth sailing for the Cuban educational system. First, schools have had to deal with a shortage of teachers, many of whom left as exiles. Also, there have been shortages of books, and the quality has been lacking. Testing has been used to measure the acquisition of knowledge, but this has led to widespread cheating. However, Cuba has moved ahead of its Latin American neighbors in the field of education. As one researcher puts it, "In the case of Cuba, we have the one Latin American country that has overcome the lockstep of school failure, the absence of educational opportunity, and poverty. Cuba has gone a long way toward fulfilling the educational needs of children at all school levels and has adopted broad measures to provide sound health care and proper nutrition, indispensable ingredients in a comprehensive effort to achieve victory over a history of neglect" (Leiner 1989, 455).

HEALTH

Half of Cuba's 6,300 physicians left the island and sought exile abroad within the first five years of the revolution. As a result of this shortage of medical staff, the Cuban medical system and its education had to be re-vamped in order to avoid crisis. Within a relatively short time, the Cuban health care system has been able to serve much of the population.

Prior to the revolution, Cubans who had access to health care were treated by a private physician or participated in a health maintenance program called *mutualista*. But the majority of Cubans, especially those living in the countryside, did not receive significant medical attention. Although there were fifty-eight hospitals in Cuba, which were in private or religious hands, most of the beds were in Havana.

The government now provides medical care free of charge. The health care system is under the auspices of the Ministerio de Salud Pública (Ministry of Public Health), which oversees all the clinics, hospitals, nursing homes, medical schools, pharmacies, and any other services associated with health. It also employs all the doctors.

In 1965 polyclinics were created as the principal facility for health care. In an urban setting they can serve as many as 20,000 to 30,000 people and in a rural setting as few as 7,500. Their staff can include pediatricians, obstetricians-gynecologists, psychologists, ophthalmologists, and even dentists.

The number of hospitals has increased to 256, and these are mainly in rural areas. In 1959 there were 28,563 beds; by 1983 the number had increased to 47,327, and it continues to grow. There are specialized hospitals for pediatrics, cardiology, ophthalmology, and psychiatry, to name a few. One of the largest hospitals is the Hermanos Almejeiras located in central Havana. Its staff of 2,500 serves a population of more than 250,000.

Cuba is plagued with shortages. Its pharmacies can provide only about 83 percent of the drugs consumed on the island. The others are obtained from other countries like Sweden, Mexico, and some are even smuggled from the United States.

Students who want to study medicine must be at the top of their class when they complete their secondary education, though others who want to study medicine are given an opportunity. Students enter medical school directly from high school, and instead of taking the Hippocratic oath, they swear to abide by revolutionary principles. The government places further demands on them upon graduation: "All graduates, upon earning their degrees, are required to perform rural service, practicing community medicine in the countryside. Soon after the revolution, young doctors were sent to the mountains and to the farms for 14 months. But as the number of physicians increased, so did the period of rural duty. In 1968 it was increased to two years, and the current three-year period of service was introduced in 1974" (Ubell 1989, 441). After their duty, physicians can further their education. The number of women doctors has dramatically increased; at Havana's medical school, they make up slightly more than half of the student body. Salaries range from 250 pesos for residents to over 700 pesos for full professors.

Cuba has overcome many of the diseases that plague developing countries. Ironically, now it is susceptible to those that affect industrial ones, like cancer, heart disease, and stroke. Life expectancy is close to that of the United States. Infant mortality has been reduced by more than half, from 38.0 to 17.3 per 1,000 live births (Ubell 1989, 435). There were more than 5,000 cases of tuberculosis prior to the revolution. By the mid-1970s that number was down to fewer than 100.

Following an internationalist ideology, Cuban doctors and other health providers serve abroad, in countries like Angola, Nicaragua, Vietnam, South Yemen, and Ethiopia, for a period of one to two years.

Cuba suffers from HIV (Human Immunodeficiency Virus); some believe this virus was brought to the island by some of the 400,000 Cuban troops fighting in Africa, and others uphold that foreign visitors have also been responsible for the spread of disease. The majority has been infected on the island. As of December 1994, a reported 342 people had contracted AIDS (Acquired Immunodeficiency Syndrome), and of these 218 died from the disease; of the 1,099 Cubans who tested positive for the HIV virus, 783 were male and 316 female. The numbers have continued to increase slowly. Three years later, there were 1,678 cases of HIV, and 609 diagnosed with the AIDS virus. There are as many homosexuals as heterosexuals infected, although the number of infected homosexuals is on the increase. In Cuba, the disease is generally transmitted through sexual intercourse; drug use and blood contamination are almost unheard of (Holtz, 1997).

The government promotes a policy that tests everyone for the HIV virus. The initial tests were not obligatory, but political and social pressures forced many to submit to them voluntarily. By 1993, more than 13 million Cubans had been tested.

Except in a few cases, HIV medication is not available. The government relies on a controversial HIV/AIDS program that places infected patients in sanitariums like Los Cocos. AIDS is considered a health problem with human rights dimensions. The policy, which began in 1986, places the virus in the category of infectious disease. In 1993 the policy was modified to treat patients in sanitariums or at home. Approximately 70 percent of patients live in sanitariums. Because sanitarium patients are provided with food and other necessities, some desperate youths have elected to infect themselves with the virus to live few years in comfort, rather than many years with struggling to find the bare necessities. This idea is portrayed in León Ichazo's *Azúcar amarga* (Bitter Sugar, 1996).

NIGHTLIFE

In spite of difficult economic and social conditions, Cubans remain a lively and friendly people who enjoy music and dance, which are available in small clubs, but also at large public gatherings on festive occasions. The evenings are much cooler than daytime temperatures and more enticing for enjoying the late hours. Cuban nightlife is best captured in Guillermo Cabrera Infante's novel *Tres tristes tigres* (Three Trapped Tigers, 1967), which opens at the famed Tropicana, a cabaret that continues to be popular. The open-air club attracts entertainers like those found in Las Vegas. There are other clubs as well at major hotels in Havana, such as the Havana Libre (formerly the Hilton), the Nacional, the Presidente, the Riviera, and the recently built Meliá Cohíbar, just to name a few. Equally important are after-hours clubs, such as Montmatre, San Souci, and El Chori, where Cabrera Infante's protagonist La Estrella, whose real name was Freddy, often sang. Zoé Valdés' *Te di la vida entera* (I Gave You All I Had, 1997) also exposes the reader to popular night clubs.

Gambling and prostitution were prevalent in the prerevolutionary period, and the U.S. mafia was very much involved in these aspects of Cuban life. Although these evils associated with the capitalist system were eliminated when the rebel army came to power, a different form of prostitution has returned. This one is related to the difficulties caused by the need to obtain dollars and includes women who are well educated; some are even married.

In spite of the resurgence of petty crime, Havana and other Cuban cities continue to be among the safest in Latin America. It is possible to walk the streets at any time without fear.

SPORTS

Since the triumph of the revolution, Cuba has built one of the most competitive sports programs in the world, certainly the most successful one in Latin America. Its athletes have excelled in the sports where Cuba has had a long-standing tradition, like boxing and baseball, but also in others that have not been associated with Cuban athletes, like track and field, judo, volleyball, water polo, and weightlifting. Cuba's system of sports closely follows the Soviet model, which considered sports an activity and a social act, reinforcing the bond that exists between the individual and society. However, for Cuban officials, it also meant universal access to sports facilities, and an investment in their athletes. In addition, sports became another way of challenging and rivaling its powerful and capitalist neighbor to the north.

As a colony of Spain, Cuba followed in the sports tradition of its mother country. By the mid-nineteenth century, primarily two sports dominated the public sphere: bullfighting and Jai Alai. During this period the Plaza de Toros was constructed in Havana, which featured bullfights on Sundays in the winter months. Bullfighting was popular only among Spaniards, and as a sport it ceased to exist after Spain lost control over the island. Unlike bullfighting, Jai Alai survived the end of colonial rule and was played during the period of the republic. In 1901 the Palacio de los Gritos was inaugurated in Havana, and in the following year, the Jai Alai Company was organized. However, the sport attracted gamblers and involved professional players.

At the beginning of the twentieth century, soccer, a sport played throughout Europe and Latin America, became popular in Cuba. The Hatuey Sport Club was established in 1909, and by the 1920s a number of clubs competed, including the Unin Racing-Fortuna Sport Club, Iberia, Cataluña, Vigo, and Olimpia. Cuba was a member of the international soccer federation, and in 1938 it played Rumania in the World Cup match. Cuba became the world champion and defeated its opponent by one goal.

If soccer appealed to club members, cockfighting was a sport that attracted the average person and was practiced throughout the island, in towns and villages alike. In the colonial period it was approved by the government and was played on Sundays and public holidays. The fights—which were held in pits with roosters that were bred for fighting—were accompanied by gambling, and large amounts of money changed hands. Cockfighting survived the War of Independence and the sport continued in the republic, becoming a component of Cuban culture.

Although these sports were limited to a local audience, Cuba did have its international figures. One of these was José Raúl Capablanca (1888–1942), who became Cuba's national chess champion at the age of twelve, when he defeated Juan Corza, then Cuba's master player. He moved to the United States in 1904, where he became an overnight star and received wide press coverage. His record was extraordinary during one month of a tour sponsored by Manhattan's Rice Chess Club: 703 victories, 10 ties, and 12 defeats (Sánchez 1999–2000). He was also victorious against Frank J. Marshall, the best U.S. player. Capablanca became world chess champion in 1921, with the defeat of Emmanuel Lasker in Havana, and held that title until 1927 when he triumphed over Alexander Aleckline in New York by two and one-half points. He is the only chess player to have won the world title by defeating his opponent without losing a match; he only lost one match in his impressive career. Above all, Capablanca is remembered for his masterful endgames. Many present-day champions, like Bobby Fischer and Anatoly Karpov, recognize Capablanca for the influence he had on the way they learned to play chess. Capablanca died of a cerebral hemorrhage in New York in 1942 and was buried in Havana.

The overwhelming majority of Cubans are dedicated fans of baseball and boxing, two sports that also provide some economic mobility to their participants and brought Cuba much world attention. Cuban boxers and baseball players are equal if not superior to their counterparts in more developed and industrial countries.

Boxing had a rocky start in Cuba, and was plagued with corruption. The first professional boxing match was held in Havana in 1909. By 1912 boxing was abolished due to public disturbances between whites and blacks related to the massacre of blacks in the race war of that same year. Boxing was driven underground for nine years until 1921, when it was legitimized and the National Commission of Boxing and Wrestling was created. The sport already had gained international attention in 1959, when Jack Johnson fought Jess Willard in a forty-five round bout. To the public's surprise, Johnson, the superior boxer, lost to the inferior Willard in the twenty-sixth round. In spite of the questionable match, Havana emerged as one of the world's boxing capitals.

Cuba would produce an extended list of world-class boxers. Kid Chocolate (Eligio Sardinas) was the first Cuban boxing champion, and he was king of the ring during the 1920s and 1930s. He had won 100 amateur fights, 86 by knockouts, and was undefeated in 21 professional fights.

Chocolate traveled to the United States in 1928, where he continued to triumph over fighters like Joe Scalfaro, Benny Bass, Lew Feldman, and Jack Kid Berg. He retired from the ring in 1938, after his fight with Nick Jerome in Havana. In honor of this great figure, Nicolás Guillén wrote "Pequeña oda a Kid Chocolate" (Short ode to Kid Chocolate, 1929), which emphasizes the boxer's skin color. If Kid Chocolate became the undisputed king of the ring during his prime, Gerardo González, Kid Gavilán, would do the same in the 1950s. He held the impressive record of winning 143 bouts and losing only 30, all by decision. These included two with Sugar Ray Robinson, the best welterweight boxer of all time. Kid Gavilán retired in 1958—the same year that the sports facility Coliseo de la Ciudad Deportiva was inaugurated, which attracted world champions to the island. Kid Gavilán was successful in the ring for eleven years.

Like his predecessors, Benny Kid Paret became an international celebrity in the ring. However, toward the end of his career, in the early 1960s, he was brutally beaten by Jimmy Fullmer. A few months later, Emile Griffith convincingly defeated him in Madison Square Garden. Out of shape and not fully recovered from his bout with Fullmer, Paret was unable to protect himself. The arbiter did not stop the fight, and Paret died shortly from the beating he sustained in the ring.

As in the United States, baseball is Cuba's national pastime. In Cuba baseball can be traced to the nineteenth century, when Nenesio Guillo returned from a U.S. college in 1864, during the U.S. Civil War, bringing with him the first ball and bat (González Echevarría 1999). The first baseball stadium, Palmar de Junco, was inaugurated in Matanzas in 1874. Baseball was also played after the Spanish Cuban-American War, when U.S. soldiers stationed in Cuba played against the islanders. One scholar proposes that the game represented the modern spirit of the Creole elite in opposition to the past of the mother country. He adds that the U.S. influence in the game was not evident until 25 February 1947, in a contest between Dolfo Luque (Almendares) and Mike González (Havana), in which the Almendares won. The game regularized Cuban baseball; it eliminated its chaotic style and brought the sport closer to the way it was played on the mainland (González Echevarría 1999).

Baseball has brought greater contact between Cuban and U.S. cultures. Major-league players traveled to Cuba during the summer and played on the island; island players did the same on the mainland, looking to make a future for themselves and better their economic conditions. More than a few played in the major league. Some of these great players include Mike Cuellar, who first played for the Havana Sugar Kings, and later played for Baltimore, where he won the Cy Young Award in 1969, and in 1970 held Cincinnati scoreless to win the 1970 World Series. Tony Pérez played for the sugar factory, and later signed with the Cincinnati Reds in 1960. Seven years later he helped the National League All-Star Team defeat the American League, and became the Reds' Most Valuable Player. In 2000, for his outstanding performance, Pérez was the first Cuban to be elected to the Baseball Hall of Fame. Pedro Oliva played for Minnesota in 1963. The following year, he established the rookie hit record and won the batting title. He led the American League in hits from 1965 to 1970. Dagoberto Blanco Campaneris played semipro in

Costa Rica, and was signed by Kansas City. In 1965 he became the first major-league player to play in all nine positions in one game. He also led the league in stolen bases, was a member of the All-Star team, and helped the A's to three World Series victories. Luis Tiant, Jr., who like his father was famous for his spitball, pitched for the Cleveland Indians, where in 1968 he threw four consecutive shutouts. As a member of the Boston Red Sox, he led the American league in 1972. The game initiated contacts that influenced both U.S and Cuban cultures.

In spite of Cuba's success with boxers and baseball players, the majority of Cubans did not have access to a variety of sports. Sports were relegated to the wealthy and played in private clubs. The nation invested little in its citizens, in spite of Law 409, passed in November 1935, which made physical education a requirement in all schools. Outside of private schools, little if anything was done to uphold this law. There was also a lack of government support for international competition; Batista did not want to back the 1955 Pan-American games because they were not profitable. Between 1900 and 1956, Cuba sent 197 athletes to six Olympic games. As a group they won thirteen medals: six gold, four silver, and three bronze. A considerable number of them were awarded to Ramón Fonst, who won a gold medal in fencing in the 1900 Paris Olympics, three individual goals, and one team gold in the 1904 St. Louis Olympics. He and other successful athletes lived and trained abroad. Cuban officials preferred to send island athletes to Central American and Pan-American games, where there was less competition.

The lack of commitment to amateur sports changed when the Rebel Army gained power in 1959. In 1961 the National Institute of Sports, Physical Education and Recreation (INDER) was founded for the purpose of providing physical education for all children as part of their education. According to one scholar, Law 936 was created to remedy the past. It states: "this institution is to promote and stimulate the participation of the masses in this development process through the creation of Voluntary Sports Councils. These councils, created in workplaces, schools, and peasant areas, are composed of people who have a talent for sports and want to contribute something to and work in sports" (Ruiz Aguilera 1989, 431). Though the intent was to offer sports to as many Cubans as possible, Ruiz Aguilera admits that the government has not been able to reach all the elementary schools, especially those in the rural areas, where there is a lack of facilities and professors. However, he believes that more than 1.5 million individuals participate in some sport. On 19 March 1962, Resolution 83-A officially eliminated professional sports in Cuba.

In today's Cuba, students who show talent for a particular sport are sent to the intermediate-level Escuelas de Iniciación Deportiva Escolar (Schools for the Initiation of Sports). Although the emphasis is on athletics, students continue to attend academic classes. Those who excel at the intermediate level are then sent to an Escuela Superior de Perfeccionamiento Atlético (School for Athletic Perfection), where they receive more specialized training. Successful athletes reside there anywhere from six to ten years.

Cuba is now a powerhouse in the sports arena. Boxing superstar Teófilo Stevenson won an unprecedented three gold medals in the 1972, 1976, and 1980 Olympics. Known for his power and jabs, Stevenson defeated formidable opponents like Duane Bobick in Munich, John Tate in Montreal, and Michael Spinks in Moscow—opponents who went on to become professional champions.

Much had been said about a possible bout between Stevenson and Muhammad Ali, two undefeated champions in their respective amateur and professional fields. It was rumored that there would be a five-bout match, so that Stevenson would not lose his amateur status. Many in the boxing world believed that Stevenson would defect to the United States and become a professional boxer. None of the above occurred, though Stevenson was in his prime and Ali, who was four years his senior, was still a worthy opponent. Regardless of what might have happened, Stevenson will be remembered as the best amateur boxer in history, and Ali as the best professional boxer. Such a rivalry will give boxing fans much to speculate if indeed the match had taken place.

Stevenson was the most recognized of Cuban athletes during the 1970s, but he was not alone. In 1976, when Stevenson made his second Olympic appearance, Alberto Juan Torrena won gold medals in the 400 and 800 meters in track and field, an event usually dominated by U.S. athletes. Cuba and the United States did not meet in the Olympics during the 1980s. Cuba boycotted the 1984 and 1988 Olympics, and the United States did the same in 1980. Cuba did participate in the 1989 World Cup meet in Rome, where Javier Sotomayor established the world high-jump record and Ana Fidelia Quirot finished fourth in the 400-meter race. Sotomayor went on to become the dominant force in the world for the high jump.

The 1990s proved to be successful for Cuban sports. The 1991 Pan American Games were hosted in Cuba, and they placed a strain on the Cuban economy. Twenty-one installations were built, forty-six sites were renovated, and fifty-five buildings were constructed for the athletes, at a cost of $24 million in hard currency and another 100 million in pesos. Although the United States beat Cuba in total medal count, 353 to 265, Cuba had more gold medals, 140 to 130. In addition, Cuba's baseball team beat its northern neighbor 3 to 2, and in boxing it walked away with 11 of the 12 gold medals and 29 of 30 gold medals in weightlifting.

Cuba and the United States met again in the 1992 Olympics held in Barcelona, Spain. Cuba ranked sixth in total medals and fifth in gold medal counts, winning 14 golds, 6 silvers, and 11 bronzes. The Cuban boxing team won 7 of the gold medals, and the baseball team had the distinction of being the first to win the first gold medal awarded in an Olympic game. Cuba's exceptional position is clear in numerous fields: "On a medals-won-per capita basis, Cuba has long been the best performer in the Western Hemisphere, and in amateur baseball, Cuba remains king. Cuba has dominated Pan-American baseball, losing its first game since 1967 at the 1987 games. Despite losing six medals at the 1983 games due to drug use, Cuba proved to be a weightlifting stronghold by winning all the weightlifting medals at the 1987 Pan-American Games. Cuban boxers also dominated these games, winning a record ten medals in 1987. By 1991, with the demise of the GDR [German Democratic Republic] as an independent country, Cuba became the world's best sports performer on a per-capita basis" (Pettavino and Pye 1994, 216).

Certainly baseball has not been without its political ramifications and may prove to be a formidable diplomat. It is the national passion of the two rivaling countries. Like Ping-Pong diplomacy that opened China to the Western world, baseball between Cuba and the United States has the potential to serve a similar purpose. Following the example established with boxing in 1977, in which the Cuban and U.S. federations agreed to yearly exhibits, the Baltimore Orioles and a selection of Cuban all-stars agreed to a two-game exhibition. As diplomats would have wanted it, the Orioles won the first game, held in Havana on 28 March 1999, and the Cubans the second, held in Baltimore on 3 May. The games featured Cuban stars such as third baseman Orestes Kindelan and slugger Omar "El Niño" Linares.

Cuban baseball has had to make several changes to meet the current political situation. For example, a ticket to a baseball game costs only ten cents (though only strong government supporters got tickets for the Cuban-Orioles games). Moreover, in 1977 the Cuban team switched to the use of aluminum bats because they break less often than wooden bats do. Perhaps more detrimental to the Cuban team has been the defection of its star players. Iván Hernández joined the Florida Marlins in 1996 and one year later became the team's Most Valuable Player in the 1997 World Series. One year later, his half-brother, Orlando "El Duque" Hernández, who was the ace pitcher for the Cuban national team for many years, defected. In 1998 he went to play for the New York Yankees, where he contributed to the team's victories in the 1998 and 1999 World Series.

HOLIDAYS AND HOLY DAYS

The most important holiday of the revolutionary period is 26 July, which commemorates the attack on the Moncada barracks. For this holiday, Cubans gather at the Plaza de la Revolución in Havana to hear Castro speak. It is not unusual for the plaza to be full of Castro supporters, who listen to him speak for three to four hours about the success of the revolution. A similar event is celebrated on 1 January, which commemorates the day Batista left the island and the rebel forces, represented by Ernesto Che Guevara, entered Havana.

Prior to the revolution Cubans celebrated 20 May, the day of independence, and 10 October, when Carlos Manuel de Céspedes led an armed insurrection against the Spanish colonial forces. Other festive days are 7 December, the day of national mourning, commemorating the death of Antonio Maceo, and 19 January, commemorating José Martí, who died in action fighting the colonial government.

Although not all are devout Catholics, Cubans celebrate 6 January, Día de Reyes (Three Kings Day). During the colonial period, Afro-Cuban organizations were given permission to celebrate the Epiphany. They used the opportunity to parody the colonial establishment, practice their religion, and play their drums. A nineteenth-century Spanish observer, Pérez Zamora, described the event within the framework of his culture:

> Countless groups of *comparsas* [street dance with drumming and singing] of African Negroes go through the streets of the capital; the crowd is huge; its aspect horrific. . . . The noise of the drums, horns and whistles is everywhere deafening to the ear of the passerby; here is to be seen a mock *Lucumí* [Yoruba] king amidst his Negro phalanx, there a *Gangá* or *Carabalí* [from Calabar] all kings for a day, they chant in disagreeable monotone, in African language, the memories of their peoples; and hundreds of voices some shrill, some hoarse, all wild, respond in chorus to the African king, forming a diabolical concert that is difficult to describe. In addition to the groups mentioned so far, there are others no less rabble-rousing, whose individuals dance like ghosts in the night or the shadows of hell, screeching, gesticulating, moving to the noise of the drums and the whistles around a negress they have proclaimed queen. They are all the children of Africa's ardor in their frenzied January 6 celebrations in the capital of Cuba; they all commemorate the tradition of their homeland; and, as they commemorate them every year, each slave is free . . . but for a single day! (Bettelheim 1993, 14)

Before Lent, Cubans celebrated carnival, with spectacular floats, music, and *comparsas* (street dancing with African drumming). The celebrations in Havana and Santiago de Cuba were the biggest and best attended. In fact, Santiago de Cuba celebrated two carnivals—one before Lent, known as Winter Carnival, mainly for whites, and the other in July, known as Summer Carnival, for blacks. The latter was held after the sugar and coffee harvests. Winter Carnival in Santiago was abandoned in the 1920s. Since the revolution, carnival has taken place in July, to coincide with the end of the sugar harvest and the 26 July celebration.

There are other festive holidays in Cuba. On 8 September Cubans celebrate the day of La Caridad del Cobre, the island's patron saint. Many make the pilgrimage to El Cobre near Santiago de Cuba to honor her. (Afro-Cubans revere Oshún, the Yoruba deity.) Other popular saints and their Afro-Cuban equivalents are celebrated: Saint Lazarus, or Babalú-Ayé, on 17 December; Our Lady of Mercy, or Obatalá, on 24 September; Saint Anthony, or Eleguá, on 3 June; Saint Barbara, or Changó, on 4 December; and Our Lady of Regla, or Yemayá, on 7 September.

FESTIVALS

Cuba is known for its many cultural festivals that attract many visitors to the island. Some go to show solidarity with the Cuban government; others attend out of curiosity or professional convictions. One of the most widely attended festivals is the Festival Internacional del Nuevo Cine Latinoamericano (International Festival of the New Latin American Cinema), held every December. The festival attracts directors, producers, and aficionados. Some of the celebrities have included singer Harry Belafonte and movie director Spike Lee. The festival premiers films from Latin America, but also from other regions and countries, including the United States.

Other festivals include the Festival of Caribbean Culture, sponsored by Santiago de Cuba's Casa del Caribe (Caribbean House), which focuses on Caribbean identity. It takes place in the eastern part of the island, since this is the most Caribbean area. Immigrants from other Caribbean islands like Hispaniola, Jamaica, Guadalupe, and Saint Kitts have made Santiago de Cuba a uniquely Caribbean city.

Festival Mundial de la Juventud y Estudiantes (Youth and Student World Festival) is another widely recognized and attended international event. In 1997 it hosted more than 11,000 delegates from around the world. The Festival Nacional de Aficionados Campesinos (National Farmers Amateur

Festival) gives amateur peasants the opportunity to perform and show their artistic talents.

FOOD AND DRINK

Cubans like to eat meat. Many Cuban dishes come from the colonizing culture, but Africans and Chinese have modified others. For example, *ropa vieja* is a popular Afro-Cuban dish that transforms beef brisket with *sofrito* (sautéed onion, green bell pepper, and garlic). Another dish of mixed cultures is the Cuban *ajiaco* (a stew of meat and vegetables) which mixes many different items. María Josefa Lluriá de O'Higgins explains the Cuban *ajiaco* in the following manner: "Cuban Ajiaco is made principally with *viandas*, or root vegetables. It was created by African slaves for their Spanish masters using local roots that were like African tubers, combined with meats available in Cuba, especially the precious jerked beef, tasajo. A meal in itself, ajiaco usually was served in Cuba for almuerzo (lunch) because it was too heavy for the evening meal. Like all recipes containing tasajo, this one requires planning ahead because the jerked beef must be soaked and desalted" (1994, 25). The *ajiaco* can include jerked beef, pork, beef brisket, corn, plantains, yucca, and other local vegetables.

The *lechón asado* (roast suckling pig) is another dish associated with Cuban cuisine. In Cuba before the revolution, it was the traditional Christmas Eve dinner. The pork was marinated with sour orange juice, ground pepper, oregano, garlic, cloves, and vegetable oil and covered with leaves from a guava tree, then cooked in a pit or spiked above a fire.

There are other dishes distinctly related to Cuban cuisine. A taste for white rice is one of the contributions to Cuban cuisine made by Chinese Cubans. White rice and black beans are an accompaniment to any meal, but so are *moros y cristianos* (Moors and Christians), rice with black beans mixed together, and *congrí*, the same as the *moros y cristianos* except that it is prepared with red beans. The *congrí* is typical of the eastern regions, where black beans were not eaten. In this respect, Cuba's eastern region has more in common with other Caribbean countries, such as Puerto Rico and the Dominican Republic, where red beans are a favorite dish. Other side dishes include yucca garnished with chopped parsley and onion with lemon, *malanga* (corn fritters), fried bananas, and tomato salad with lettuce. Cubans usually eat everything together on the same plate. A typical desert is guava marmalade served with yellow cheese.

Rum is associated with Cuban culture. In fact, Barcardí, which since the revolution has been manufactured in Puerto Rico, was known throughout the Western world. It is the only rum that Cuban exiles drink. After the departure of Barcardí, Cuba produced the famed Havana Club rum. And there are other fine-quality rums such as Ron Palmas Paticruzado, and others from other provinces, such as the Ron Matusalem and Caney from Santiago de Cuba. A number of well-known drinks are prepared with rum. One is the Cuba Libre (Free Cuba), prepared with Coca-Cola and an optional lime wedge. The daiquirí clásico, writer Ernest Hemingway's favorite drink, is prepared with crushed ice, rum, freshly squeezed lime juice, and sugar, shaken vigorously in a cocktail shaker. The *mojito* is made with rum, freshly squeezed lime juice, sugar, sprigs of fresh mint, seltzer or club soda, and finely cracked ice. Cubans also enjoy drinking beer, usually Cristal or Bucanero.

CUBAN CIGARS

Cuban cigars have always been considered the best in the world. The cigars are handmade and come in different sizes, from the smallest *cigarritos*, which are commonly enjoyed by women and take no more than fifteen minutes to consume, to the slightly larger *panetelas*, and the largest torpedoes, which last well over one hour. The brands include the Montecristo, Corona, H. Upmann, Hoyo de Monterrey, and Partagas. There are other brands that have disappeared like Henry Clay, La Corona, María Guerrero, Cabañas y Carbajal, Don Candido, and Don Alfredo. Although Castro no longer smokes, in the past the brand he smoked was Cohíbar, which became one of the most recognized cigars of the contemporary period. They were sold in colorful, well-designed boxes or in metal or crystal tubes. A cedar leaf protected some, like the Super Coronas.

The Cuban cigar has become the choice of cigar connoisseurs, who are careful to select a particular brand, in the same way as one chooses a fine wine. A connoisseur describes the experience as a sublime total and sensual experience: "Like all oral experiences, smoking a Havana appeals to all the senses. Sight, firstly, allows us to appreciate the cigar's amber hue as well as its quality and craftsmanship. Touch then evaluates the degrees of softness and smoothness that indicate the life of the cigar. Of course, the sense of smell comes into play by detecting woody, fruity, or spicy notes even before lighting, and fully savors these aromas during burning. Hearing also 'savors' the cigar: the rustling of the embers that precedes the sound of the lighting. Finally, and most importantly, is taste—which when combined with a Havana produces a supremely pleasurable sensual encounter" (Pere 1997, 8).

Cuban cigars have also influenced literature and have been the subject of Fernando Ortiz's *Contrapunteo cubano del tabaco y el azúcar*, and Guillermo Cabrera Infante's *Holy Smoke* (1985), among others.

Cubans are accustomed to drinking coffee with plenty of sugar and smoking a cigar.

CUBAN EXILES

Some Cubans have always lived abroad. Some emigrated in the nineteenth century to Europe, among them the writers Condesa de Merlín and Gertrudis Gómez de Avellaneda, but the vast majority of them sought exile in the United States. These included authors Cirilo Villaverde and José Martí, Cuba's national hero. However, the Castro revolution produced the largest number of Cuban exiles ever. Some live in Spain, France, Puerto Rico, Mexico, and other Spanish American countries, but the overwhelming majority reside in the United States, particularly Miami.

Cuba exiles have turned Miami into a prosperous city and sections of that city into a replica of Havana. In fact, Miami's Calle Ocho (Eighth Street) is known as Little Havana, and the names of some of the establishments come straight from Cuba. In one sense, Little Havana represents time standing still. Cubans who live there follow the same customs and traditions familiar in the prerevolutionary period, including the celebration of religious and secular holidays. In the early spring, Little Havana celebrates its own carnival, in which exiled singers, like Celia Cruz, the queen of Salsa, and younger Cuban-American ones, like Gloria Estefan, have participated.

The first generation of exiles believed that their stay in the United States would be temporary; it was just a matter of time until they returned to the island. For this and other reasons, they maintained their language and culture intact and have attempted to pass their values down to the next generation. However, the next generation, born or raised in the United States, speak Spanish but mainly English, and some have married North Americans. Although this generation belongs to Cuban culture, it also conforms to that of the United States. Gustavo Pérez Firmat's *Life on the Hyphen: The Cuban-American Way* depicts the two parts of the hyphen to which Cuban Americans belong. This and later generations of Cubans are a part of a larger phenomenon of Latinos, which includes Chicanos, Puerto Ricans, and Dominicans, who are born or raised in the United States. The culture of the parents and that of their adopted country come together in the same time and space and can be expressed as a dance between two cultures.

REFERENCES

Atlas demográfico de Cuba. Havana: Empresa de Geodesia y Cartografía de Ciudad de La Habana, 1979.

Azicri, Max. "Women's Development Through Revolutionary Mobilization." In *The Cuba Reader: The Making of a Revolutionary Society.* Ed. Philip Brenner, William M. LeoGrande, Donna Rich, and Daniel Siegel. New York: Grove Press, 1989. 457–471.

Barnet, Miguel. *Autobiography of a Runaway Slave.* Trans. Jocasta Inness. London: Bodley Head, 1966.

Bettelheim, Judith. *Cuban Festivals: An Illustrated Anthology.* New York: Garland Publishing, 1993.

Cabalé Ruiz, Manolo. *Teófilo Stevenson: grande entre los grandes.* Havana: Editorial Orbe, 1980.

Cancio Isla, Wilfredo. "Kid Chocolate y los otros." *Encuentro de la cultura cubana* 15 (1999–2000): 113–123.

Carbonel, Walterio. *Crítica cómo surgió la cultura nacional.* Havana: Ediciones Erre, 1961.

Casal, Lourdes. "Race Relations in Contemporary Cuba." In *The Cuba Reader: The Making of a Revolutionary Society.* Ed. Philip Brenner, William M. Leo-Grande, Donna Rich, and Daniel Siegel. New York: Grove Press, 1989. 471–486.

Castellanos, Jorge, and Isabel. *Cultura afrocubana.* 3 vols. Miami: Ediciones Universal, 1992.

Del Pino, Willy. *Enciclopedia del boxeo cubano.* Miami: Talleres de Continental Printing, 1988.

Domínguez, Jorge. *Cuba: Order and Revolution.* Cambridge, Mass.: Belknap Press of Harvard University Press, 1978.

Eckstein, Susan. "The Debourgeoisment of Cuban Cities." In *The Cuba Reader: The Making of a Revolutionary Society.* Ed. Philip Brenner, William M. Leo-Grande, Donna Rich, and Daniel Siegel. New York: Grove Press, 1989. 419–429.

González Echevarría, Roberto. *The Pride of Havana: A History of Cuban Baseball.* New York: Oxford University Press, 1999.

———. "Cuban." *Encuentro de la Cultura Cubana* 15 (1999–2000): 103–112.

Holtz, Tim. "Summary of Issue of HIV-AIDS in Cuba." *Alpha Cuba Tour*, August 1997.

Leiner, Marvin. "Cuba's Schools: 25 Years Later." In *The Cuba Reader: The Making of a Revolutionary Society.* Ed. Philip Brenner, William M. LeoGrande, Donna Rich, and Daniel Siegel. New York: Grove Press, 1989. 445–446.

LeoGrande, William M. "The Role of Participation in a Revolutionary Ideology." In *The Cuba Reader: The Making of a Revolutionary Society.* Ed. Philip Brenner, William M. LeoGrande, Donna Rich, and Daniel Siegel. New York: Grove Press, 1989. 186–198.

Lluriá de O'Higgins, María Josefa. *A Taste of Old Cuba*. New York: HarperCollins, 1994.

Luis, William. *Dance between Two Cultures: Latino Caribbean Literature Written in the United States*. Nashville, Tenn.: Vanderbilt University Press, 1997.

Méndez, Adriana. *Cubans in America*. Minneapolis: Lerner, 1994.

Montreal, Pedro. "Las remesas familiares en la economía cubana." *Revista Encuentro de la Cultura Cubana* 14 (Fall 1999): 49–62.

Moore, Carlos. *Castro, the Blacks, and Africa*. Los Angeles: Center for Afro-American Studies, University of California, Los Angeles, 1988.

Ortiz, Fernando. *Cuban Counterpoint: Tobacco and Sugar*. 1940. Trans. Harriet de Onís. Durham, N.C.: Duke University Press, 1995.

Pere, Gérard, et Fils. *Havana Cigars*. New York: Barnes and Noble, 1997.

Pérez Firmat, Gustavo. *Life on the Hyphen: The Cuban-American Way*. Austin: University of Texas Press, 1994.

Pérez-Stable, E. J. "Cuba's Response to the HIV Epidemic." *American Journal of Public Health* 81 (1991): 563–567.

Pettavino, Paula J., and Geralyn Pye. *Sport in Cuba: The Diamond in the Rough*. Pittsburgh: University of Pittsburgh Press, 1994.

Portes, Alejandro, and Robert L. Bach. *Latin Journey: Cuban and Mexican Immigrants in the United States*. Berkeley: University of California Press, 1985.

Ruiz Aguilera, Raudol, "The Cuban Sports Program." In *The Cuba Reader: The Making of a Revolutionary Society*. Ed. Philip Brenner, William M. Leo-Grande, Donna Rich, and Daniel Siegel. New York: Grove Press, 1989. 430–34.

Sánchez, Miguel Ángel. "Capablanca en Nueva York." *Encuentro de la Cultura Cubana* 15 (1999–2000): 124–129.

Ubell, Robert. "Twenty-five Years of Cuban Health Care." In *The Cuba Reader: The Making of a Revolutionary Society*. Ed. Philip Brenner, William M. Leo-Grande, Donna Rich, and Daniel Siegel. New York: Grove Press, 1989. 435–445.

4

Broadcasting and Print Media

PRINT MEDIA

CUBA HAS a rich history of print media. The country's writers and publications are among the best in Latin America.

The first newspapers in Cuba emerged two years after the British takeover of Havana in 1762. The British presence was short but important; it opened Cuba to a non-Spanish-speaking world. The *Gazeta* (Gazette) was the idea of Spanish Captain General Ambrosio de Funes y Villapando, the Conde de Ricla, and began publication on Mondays, but disappeared after a two-year period during his government. It provided political and commercial news, as well as government dispositions and a list of ships entering and leaving Havana harbor. That same year Gabriel Beltrán de Santa Cruz and Ignacio José de Urrutia y Montoya published *El Pensador* (The Thinker) with a similar content as the *Gazeta*.

Cuba's first newspaper is considered to be *The Papel Periódico de la Havana* (Havana Newspaper), which came into existence on 24 October 1790 at the insistence of Don Luis de las Casas, governor general of the island. Later it was acquired by the powerful Sociedad Económica de Amigos del País de la Habana (Friends of the Country's Economic Society). It ceased publication in 1828. The newspaper contained commercial news and offered cultural news of the capital, literature, and literary criticism. It represented the interests of the emerging *criollo* bourgeoisie.

The first newspapers were published in Havana, but other cities had their own newspapers. For example, in the eastern city of Santiago de Cuba Matías

Alqueza published *El Amigo de los cubanos* (Cuba's Friend, 1805–?), owned by the Sociedad Económica de Amigos del País of that city. Mariano Seguí introduced the first newspaper to Puerto Príncipe in 1812, believed to be called *Espejo de Puerto Príncipe* (Mirror of Puerto Principe). However, it is also believed that Antonio Guerra y Gordo had already distributed a manuscript of *Espejo de Puerto Príncipe* in 1810. In 1819 that same city published the *Gaceta de Puerto Príncipe* (Puerto Príncipe's Gazette), in which Gaspar Betancourt Cisneros, writing under the pseudonym of El Lugareño, made his debut and created a reputation with his articles on customs. Sancti Spíritus had *El Fénix* (The Phoenix) in 1834, but it was owned by the Diputación Pariótica de la Sociedad Económica de Amigos del País of Havana.

These publications and others from Havana, such as *El Regañón de la Havana* (The Havana Scolder), *El Criticón de la Havana* (The Havana Gossip), *El mensajero político-económico literario de la Habana* (The Politico-Economic Literary Messenger of Havana), and *El Patriota Americano* (The American Patriot), all published before 1812, were subject to ecclesiastical censorship, which ended with a decree that allowed freedom of expression. Spain was undergoing its own transformation, and experienced the success of the liberals in power, who introduced the liberal constitution of 1812.

A number of quality newspapers were published in the 1830s, a period that coincided with the beginnings of a national literature and Domingo del Monte's famed literary circle. Del Monte was the most important literary critic of his time and the adviser of a generation of writers. In an 1846 issue of *La Aurora*, Cirilo Villaverde, author of *Cecilia Valdés*, Cuba's national novel, and a member of del Monte's literary circle, recognized a literary explosion that offered wonderful opportunities to young writers, but also a decline in the quality of works published. They include *La Moda; o, Recreo Semanal del Bellos Sexo* (The Fashion; or The Beautiful Sex's Weekly Entertainment); *El Nuevo Regañón de la Habana* (The New Havana Scolder), which gave Cuban literature a push by opening its pages to incipient writers; *El Álbum* (The Album); *La Siempreviva* (The Everlasting Flower); and *El Plantel* (The Staff). Villaverde published his short story "Cecilia Valdés" in *La Siempreviva*, which he later inserted into the final version of his novel published in New York in 1882. The compositions by slave poet Juan Francisco Manzano appeared with some regularity in a *Diario de la Habana* (Havana Daily, 1831, 1838, 1841), *Diario de Matanzas* (Matanza Daily, 1830), *La Moda o Recreo Semanal del Bello Sexo* (1831), *El Pasatiempo* (The Entertainment, 1834–1835), *El Aguinaldo Habanero, El Álbum* (1838), *Faro Industrial de la Habana* (The Havana Industrial Beacon, 1843), and *La Prensa* (The Press, 1842). Other contributors included the mulatto poet Gabriel de la Concepción Valdés (better known as Plácido), Anselmo Suárez y Romero, Ramón de Palma, and José Zacarías González del Valle, all members of del Monte's literary salon.

The most important publication of the colonial period was Mariano Cubí y Soler's *Revista y repertorio bimestre de la Isla de Cuba* (The Island of Cuba's Bi-monthly Magazine and Repertoire, 1831–1834, 1910–1959), later known as the *Revista Bimestre Cubana* (Cuban Bi-monthly Magazine). After the second issue, the *Revista* was handed over to the Sociedad Económica de Amigos del País and edited by José Antonio Saco, one of the intellectual figures of the period. In a short period, the *Revista* became one of the most notable publications published in the Spanish-speaking world. It exposed readers to the most meritorious cultural events in Cuba as well as in Europe and the Americas and documented the activities of the Sociedad Económica de Amigos del País and those of its Sección de Educación. Although readers relied on the *Revista* for news about matters pertaining to culture, it ceased to exist in 1834 when Saco was exiled for his political beliefs. The *Revista* reappeared in 1910, again under the auspices of the Sociedad Económica de Amigos del País, this time edited by two turn-of-the century intellectuals, Fernando Ortiz and Ramiro Guerra. Under the ruthless dictator Gerardo Machado (1927–1933), Elías Entralgo directed the *Revista* in 1931, though Ortiz continued to be listed as director. The editorial board continued to change throughout the following decades.

Faro Industrial de la Habana (1841–1851) was one of the first defenders of Cuban national interests on the island, and its critical position within the colony may explain why it was shut down ten years after its first issue. The same year in which it appeared, *La Presa* was published, representing the interest of Spaniards on the island. Of more importance is the publication of the *Diario de la Marina* (Marina Daily) in 1844, derived from *El Noticioso y Lucero de la Habana* (The Havana Knower and Star), which was born after *El Lucero de la Habana* (The Havana Star) and the *Noticioso Mercantil* (The Mercantile Knower, 1813) were combined. The *Diario de la Marina* has the distinct history of being the longest-running newspaper in Cuba; it was characterized by a pro-Spanish position in the early period, and an anti-communist stance in the later one. Among its exceptional contributors were the essayist Jorge Mañach, who figured prominently in the republican period.

Newspapers also played a crucial role during the national uprisings against the Spanish governments. During the Ten Years' War (1868–1878), the leader of the insurgents, Carlos Manuel de Céspedes, founded *El Cubano Libre* (Free Cuban) on 18 October 1868; it was edited by José Joaquín Palma. This and other insurgent newspapers, some of which had a short life span like *La Patria Libre* (Free Country) and *El Diablo Cojuelo* (The Lamed Devil), played supportive roles during the war. *El Cubano Libre* and other newspapers kept their readers informed of rebel activities and provided them with pertinent news, such as speeches from rebel leaders, and government decisions and maneuvers.

One of the leading journalists at the end of the nineteenth century was the Afro-Cuban Juan Gualberto Gómez, who published *La Fraternidad* (The Fraternity) and later *La Igualdad* (Equality, 1892–1895). Although he did not embrace a Spanish nation, Gómez was not a revolutionary. Rather, he considered himself to be a separatist and preferred to work within the constitution, which made provisions for his position, and not against it. In an article entitled "Por que somos separatistas" (Why we are separatists; *La Fraternidad*, 23 September 1890), he affirmed his separatist thesis. Gómez favored separation from Spain and recognized that each country had a different history and destiny. But he was denounced by General Polavieja and was imprisoned for eight months. He was released on appeal before the Tribunal Supremo of Madrid. His success precipitated the publication of a number of separatist newspapers.

Gómez also became a spokesperson for Afro-Cubans at a time when they lacked representation and a voice. His position was made clear in "Lo que somos" (What We Are) published in *La Igualdad*, on 7 April 1892, which stated that although the newspaper supported all the issues that affected Cuba, it was particularly interested in those pertaining to race. In fact, he said, its main concern was the equality of all Cubans: white, black, and mulatto.

As the national culture struggled with identity, one independent from those of Spaniards and the mother country, *criollos* ventured to voice their political views in the print media. There was wide dissatisfaction with the colonial government, but the opposition did not represent a unified position. It was divided into reformists, who supported colonial rule with more freedom; annexationists, who believed the island should be part of the United States; and independents, who fought for a sovereign nation. These positions were made clear both at home and abroad, where an increasing percentage of politically active *criollos* lived. Those in exile lived mainly in the United States, in cities such as New York, Philadelphia, Tampa, and New Orleans, where they continued to organize and oppose the colonial power. New York became the center of activities and of armed insurrection against the colonial government, which continued until Cuba became independent from Spain as a result of the Spanish American War.

Cuban exiles living in the United States, well organized and informed, developed an effective system of organization and communication through the print media. Félix Varela's *El Habanero* (1825–1826) is the most important of these publications, not only because of the status of its publisher as an educator and a writer, but because it was published in Philadelphia and New York and initiated a long tradition of newspapers published by Cuban exiles and emigrants in the United States. *El Habanero's* message was political and anticolonial, and for those reasons it was not read in Cuba. Of a different persuasion was Miguel Teurbe Tolón's *La Verdad* (The Truth, New York, 1848–1853; New Orleans, 1854–1860), which supported the annexationist position.

José Martí's *La Patria* (The Country, 1892–1898), under the auspices of the Partido Revolucionario Cubano, supported armed insurrection as a means of obtaining independence for Cuba and Puerto Rico. Martí, who had written poetry and narrative, was also a well-known journalist who wrote for *La Nación* (The Nation) of Buenos Aires, *La Opinión Nacional* (The National Opinion) of Caracas, and *El Partido Liberal* (The Liberal Party) of Mexico; he also contributed to New York papers like *The Sun* and *The Hour*, and Spanish ones published in New York, like *El Economista Americano* (The American Economist), *El Avisador Hispanoamericano* (The Hispanic American Informer), and *La América*.

The Spanish American War and the founding of the Republic of Cuba in 1902 represented a major political and historical shift for the nation. However, some newspapers published during the colonial period continued. Of these the *Diario de la Marina* maintained a consistently conservative position. Founded under the direction of Nicolás Rivero, it was passed down from father to son, to José Ignacio Rivero, and later to his son. The newspaper published an important literary supplement, directed by José Antonio Fernández de Castro, which publicized the literary vanguard movements, to which many internationally known figures contributed.

There were other newspapers born with the republic. *El Mundo* (The World) began publication on 11 April 1901, first under the direction of Rafael Govin and shortly after under José Manuel Govin. It ushered in a new era in Cuban journalism by introducing innovations into Cuba's print media, including mechanical printing, the eight-column page, social chronicles, and color presentations. In 1904 it published a Sunday literary supplement, *El Mundo Ilustrado*.

A number of influential magazines were published during the period of the republic. *El Fígaro* (1885–1933; 1943–), subtitled *Semanario de sports y de literatura. Órgano del baseball* (Literary and Sports Weekly. Baseball Organization), publicized all sports, but baseball in particular; it survived the transition from colony to republic. The combination of literature and baseball should be no surprise: "It was no coincidence that *El Fígaro* was published by a group of literati who were also baseball enthusiasts. Modernista literature was a social affair that took place in salons, cafés, and theaters" (González Echevarría 1999, 97). In the nineteenth century, *El Fígaro* and *La Habana Elegante* (Elegant Havana, 1883–1891), which became *La Habana Literaria* (Literary Havana, 1891–1893), provided space for the *modernista* movement, which placed aesthetics above all else and catered to a small elite. These magazines published *modernista* writers like Julián del Casal, Juana Borrero, and Federico Uhrback of Cuba and Rubén Darío, Manuel Gutiérrez Nájera, Salvador Díaz Mirón, José Santos Chocano, and Amado Nervo of Spanish America. At the turn of the century, *El Fígaro*, subtitled *Revista Universal Ilustrada* (Universal Illustrated Magazine), attracted both young and established writers. It continued to publish literature, but broadened its pages to include social, political, and cultural problems evident in Cuba and abroad.

Another early magazine was Miguel Ángel Quevedo's *Bohemia* (1908, 1910), perhaps the most popular magazine with the widest Spanish circulation. It began as an illustrated magazine that emphasized literature and art, and claimed to be the first to publish the work of Cuban artists in color. During the Machado period, *Bohemia* became more political, and its editorials were critical of the government. During the Castro government, the magazine continued its illustrations but became more informative. In 1960 Quevedo left the island and founded *Bohemia Libre* in exile in the United States.

Conrado W. Massaguer's *Social* (1916–1933, 1935–1938) deserves special recognition. Its original intent was to move away from the political sphere regarding all news, from home and abroad, and information about crime and delinquency. Instead it highlighted social and cultural life, with photographs and social notes. *Social* left its mark in literature. In 1918 Emilio Roig de Leuchsenring became the director of the literary section, and he welcomed to the magazine writers and artists of the period, in particular those belonging to the Grupo Minorista, Cuba's political and intellectual vanguard. *Social* published the latest fashions and social chronicles as well as short stories, poems, literary criticism, art, and movie and book reviews. It had an impressive list of contributors who included, from Cuba, Alejo Carpentier, Nicolás Guillén, Juan Marinello, and Fernando Ortiz and, from abroad, Federico García Lorca, Horacio Quiroga, José Vasconcelos, Diego Rivera, Vicente Alexandre, and Paul Valéry. The second period of *Social* included important writers like José Lezama Lima and Onelio Jorge Cardoso, but it never reached the importance it had achieved during its initial period and focused more on social news. Later, Lezama Lima went on to publish magazines that were detached from political and social concerns, and underscored the aesthetic and the metaphor in particular. He edited *Vérbum* (1937), *Espuela de Plata* (Silver Spur, 1939–1941), *Nadie Parecía* (No One Seemed, 1942–1944), and, with José Rodríquez Feo, *Orígenes* (Origins, 1944–1956).

Revista de Avance (Advance Magazine, 1927–1930) emerged as the vanguard magazine of the period. If *Social* catered to the interests of the bourgeoisie, *Revista de Avance* publicized literature, art, and music. Its first editorial board was made up of Francisco Ichaso, Jorge Mañach, Juan Marinello, Alejo Carpentier, and Martín Casanovas; José Zacarías Tallet and Félix Lizaso replaced the last two. Those associated with the *Revista de Avance*, like Carpentier and Marinello, protested the Machado dictatorship and were persecuted by his police force.

By the time Castro came to power, there were more than fifty newspapers published throughout the island. These were manipulated by the Batista government through some form of subsidy; only a handful were self-sufficient. However, after 1959, the numbers diminished rapidly and were replaced by government-controlled newspapers. Ramón Vasconcelos's *Alerta* (Alert), José López Vilaboy's *Mañana* (Tomorrow), Rolando Masferrer's *El Tiempo* (Time), Alberto Salas Amaro's *Ataja* (Attack), F. Valdés Gómez's *Pueblo* (Town), and *El Mundo* were expropriated by the government. José Zayas' *Avance*, José Ignacio Rivero's *Diario de la Marina*, and Sergio Carbo's *Prensa Libre* (Free Press) were considered to be antirevolutionary and taken over by their unions.

In the early period of the revolution, journalists became more aggressive about their position to support the rebels and intolerant of any criticism of them. Newspapers began to append statements known as *coletillas* (little tails), disapproving of news stories. Since not everyone was in agreement, the *coletillas* produced tension between workers and management. Jorge Zayas, the publisher of *Avance*, disagreed with his workers' use of the *coletilla*, but eventually was forced to seek refuge in the Ecuadorian embassy because he was viewed as an enemy of the people. The day Zayas arrived in Miami, the Ministry of Recovery of Stolen Property confiscated the newspaper. By April 1960 the seventeen newspapers publishing in the republic were reduced to four: *Diario de la Marina*, *Prensa Libre*, *El Crisol* (The Crucible), and *Información* (Information). The traditional and oldest newspaper, *Diario de la Marina*, developed problems with the *coletillas* and was confiscated in May 1960. The progressive and popular *Prensa Libre* got into trouble when it came to the defense of the *Diario de la Marina*. It was taken over in May.

El Crisol could not make ends meet, and it closed in November 1960. *Informacion* ceased to exist the following month. There were two other newspapers. Clarence Moore's *The Times of Havana*, an English paper read by English speakers living in Cuba, did not survive the inhospitable climate. The Roman Catholic magazine, *La Quincena* (The Fortnight), published its last issue in January 1961.

Of this early period *Revolución* (1959–1965), the official newspaper of the 26th of July Movement, is the most important. Founded by Carlos Franqui during the clandestine period, *Revolución* supported the rebel cause and provided news of the events and changes that were transforming the Cuban nation. When the change in government occurred, *Revolución* took over the offices of *Alerta* (Alert). And after the intervention of *Prensa Libre, Revolución* moved into its modern facilities.

The newspaper also offered literary and artistic information in a page entitled "Nueva Generación" (New Generation), recalling the title of a periodical that Franqui had published during the republic, and later "R[evoulución] en el arte/en la literatura." These two literary pages were replaced when, in March 1959, *Revolución* published a weekly literary supplement, *Lunes de Revolución* (Monday of Revolution) edited by Guillermo Cabrera Infante. The first issue contained six pages, and the last one, in 1961, listed sixty-four. *Lunes de Revolución* was distributed with *Revolución*, starting with a circulation of 100,000 and surpassing 250,000, greater than other comparable publications of larger countries, including the *New York Review of Books* in the United States. *Lunes de Revolución* was daring for its time, as made evident by the magazine's designers, and its content was varied, though none of the articles supported an antirevolutionary position. The magazine was the most significant and most widely read literary supplement in the history of Cuban and Latin American literatures. As Castro shifted his allegiance away from the 26th of July Movement and toward that of the Communist party, *Lunes de Revolución* and its editorial staff fell from grace. Franqui, who once belonged to Castro's inner circle of advisers, could not save them. A shortage of paper was the official reason for closing the magazine, but in reality *Lunes de Revolución* stood for a liberal position that members of the Communist party believed was antithetical to their position and cause. The last *Lunes* issue appeared in November 1961. Significantly, it was dedicated to the cubist artist Pablo Picasso. In 1965 *Revolución* and the communist newspaper *Noticias de Hoy* (Today's News) were combined to produce *Granma*, named after the boat that Castro and his men had used to invade the island in 1956. It became the official newspaper of the Communist party. *Granma* represented only one view, that of the government, and published all of Castro's speeches. Weekly editions of *Granma* became available abroad in French, English, and Spanish.

Diario de la Tarde (Afternoon Daily) was transformed into *Juventud Rebelde* (Rebel Youth), the newspaper of the Unión de Jóvenes Comunistas (Communist Youth Organization). Unlike *Granma*, it was an evening newspaper and provided an outlet for young readers to be critical of the inner workings of the government. In 1969, *Juventud Rebelde* became available on Sunday mornings. That same year *El Mundo* ceased to exist. Like *Revolución* and *Noticias de Hoy*, it was merged into *Granma*.

Each Cuban province publishes a newspaper that provides mainly local news. Camagüey has *Adelante* (Forward), Holguín has *Ahora* (Now), Matanzas has *Girón*, Santa Clara has *Vanguardia*, Santiago de Cuba has *Sierra Maestra*, and Pinar del Río has *Guerrillero*. In 1966 the Chinese community published *Kwong Wah Pao*, which espoused the ideas of the Chinese Communist party.

As with newspapers at the outset of the revolution, the government consolidated existing magazines into a few that were controlled by Castro functionaries and favored one point of view: that of the Castro government. After the demise of *Lunes de Revolución*, *Casa de las Américas* (House of the Americas), published by the namesake institution, became internationally known. After issue number 30, it became associated with its editor, Roberto Fernández Retamar. *Casa de las Américas* was successful in breaking the cultural blockade imposed by the United States and informed the Spanish-speaking world of the heroic feats of Cubans and the accomplishments of the revolution. It published a variety of materials, in particular literature, literary criticism, and historical, political, and philosophical essays. The periodical accepted contributions from many of the best Cuban writers and others from Spanish-speaking countries, like Julio Cortázar, José María Arguedas, Ernesto Cardenal, and Rafael Alberti. After the events of the Padilla affair of 1971, when the poet was arrested for conspiracy against the government, *Casa de las Américas* became even more political in its editorial decisions. Roberto Fernández Retamar published his *Calibán* in a 1971 issue of *Casa de las Américas*. The essay takes the basic ideas of Castro's speech delivered before the Consejo Nacional de Educación y Cultura in which he denounced critics of the revolution and developed them within the context of Shakespeare's *The Tempest*.

If *Casa de las Américas* catered to the outside world, *Unión*, of the Unión Nacional de Escritores y Artistas de Cuba (UNEAC, National Union of Cuban Writers and Artists) emphasized the national. Its motto became "Defender a la Revolución es defender la Cultura" (To defend the revolution is to defend culture). *Unión* published work by its members and information about the organization's activities. Also, special issues were dedicated to other countries and literatures, like those pertaining to Vietnamese, Rumanian, Soviet, and Algerian literatures. The UNEAC also publishes *La Gaceta de Cuba* (1962), a tabloid about art and literature. Its first director was Nicolás Guillén, the president of the UNEAC, and editor Lisandro Otero, and stressed the quality of the work over all other considerations. Contributors to *La Gaceta de Cuba* included members of the UNEAC and those of the once-socialist countries. The publication's title was later changed to *La Gaceta*.

In 1966 *Juventud Rebelde* published a literary supplement, *El Caimán Barbudo* (The Bearded Caiman), geared to Cuba's youth, born or raised in the revolution. It published fiction, and essays in literature, sociology, politics, art, music, theater, film, and other fields, written by its members, and others of the same generation living in Latin America. Its first editor, Jesús Díaz, encountered early problems with the government after he invited Heberto Padilla to comment on the 1964 Seix Barral award given to Cabrera Infante's *Vista del amanecer en el trópico* (View of Dawn in the Tropics). Although Cabrera Infante was considered an enemy of the revolution, Padilla, who had belonged to *Lunes de Revolución*, favored his book over *La pasión de Urbino* (Urbino's Passion), by the revolutionary but less talented writer Lisandro Otero. This event sparked the Padilla affair, which culminated in his arrest in 1971.

There are other specialized magazines associated with particular organizations. (In fact, it would not be an exaggeration to say that most organizations in Cuba have their own publication.) Those of wide circulation include *Verde Olivo* (1959), of the Fuerzas Armadas Revolucionarias (Revolutionary Armed Forces), and *INRA*, of the Instituto Nacional de la Reforma Agraria (National Institute of Agrarian Reform), which later became *Cuba*. Like the *Caimán Barbudo*, *Verde Olivo* also became involved in the Padilla affair. Leopoldo Ávila, a pseudonym for Luis Pavón, then director of the National Council of Culture, used its pages to attack Padilla.

Although the majority of magazines and periodicals are published in Havana, there are others in the provinces that merit some attention. They play a crucial role in providing a forum for writers and critics who may not have access to Havana publications. For example, *Islas* (Islands), published by the Universidad Central de las Villas, became associated with its editor, Samuel Feijóo. Its mission is to publicize the folklore of the province of Las Villas. *Santiago*, associated with the Universidad de Oriente, plays a similar role for its province. And *Signos* (Signs) belongs to the Departamento de Investigaciones de la Expresión de los Pueblos of the province of Las Villas (Department of Research of the Expression of the Towns of the Province of Las Villas).

Other magazines and periodicals even more specialized than the ones mentioned above have a limited circulation and life span. Since the Special Period went into effect after the fall of the Soviet bloc, the island has experienced a shortage of paper. Some newspapers and magazines have disappeared, and others appear infrequently.

BROADCAST MEDIA

Cuban radio was born in the 1920s, a time when Cuban music, and the *son* in particular, began to spread throughout the island and abroad. In Oriente the Trío Matamoros, with Siro, Cueto, and Miguel, was a regional success, and in Matanzas, the Sonora Matancera, with Valentín Cané as director, was popular.

Theaters in the 1920s featured the same singers and orchestras heard on the radio. The Teatro Alambra offered *sainetes*, reviews, and *zarzuelas* with scripts by Sergio Acebal and Pepe del Campo. Works such as "Flor de té" (Tea Flower), "La isla de las cotorras" (Island of Parrots), "La patria en España" (The Nation in Spain), "La casita criolla" (The Native Hut), "La danza de los millones" (The Million Dollar Dance), and "El cierre a las seis" (The Six O'clock Closing) were among the most successful representations. Upon the works' conclusion at the Alambra, they were performed in the Teatro Payret, but with a more polished language. The Cuban cinema also came into its own, showing both foreign films and national ones, such as *El traficante* (The Trader, 1925), starring Chirito Campoamor. This was also a period in which many Cuban artists recorded for U.S. and R.C.A. Victor phonographs were selling for $1,500 pesos.

Cuba was the first country in Latin America to broadcast (and among the first in the world to do so). Only the United States, France, Great Britain, and the Soviet Union had broadcasting stations. Cuba's first radio program was broadcast in 1918 by the brothers (Guillermo and Manuel) Salas. Humberto Giquel and composer and band director Luis Casas Romero were also pioneers of Cuban radio.

Casas Romero began regular evening broadcasts in 1922. His daughter, Zoila Casas, the first woman announcer, read meteorological reports. The first station in the provinces were Rafael Valdés and Pedro Nogueras' station in Camagüey and Frank H. Jones' in Santa Clara, both inaugurated in 1923.

The official date for the first Cuban broadcast was 10 October 1922, commemorating the start of the Ten Years' War, with a broadcast by President Alfredo Zayas. His speech, in English, was meant to be heard in the United States, since Cuba had fewer than 100 radios at that time.

In 1922 the radio station PWX, better known as La Cubana Telephone, began broadcasting; its first artists included violinist Joaquín Molina, pianist Matilde González de Molina, singer Rita Montaner, tenor Mariano Meléndez, soprano Loal de la Torre, and baritone Néstor de la Torre. After each song or musical composition, the announcer mentioned the name of the singer or the orchestra, or the name of the song. That same year, the radio station Cuban Telephone, a subsidiary of International Telegraphy and Telephone, hailed as its first announcers Raúl Falcón and Remberto O'Farrill. In 1923 Gonzalo Roig debuted on the station with his Gigante orchestra.

To make ends meet and stay on the air, radio stations begin to sell commercial announcements. The corrupt political situation on the island allowed radio stations to play a social role, and newspapers were read over the air. There was no uniformity of opinion or presentation, and everyone expressed his or her own interpretation of events. In March 1933 a portable station announced the fall of the Machado dictatorship, sparking celebration. Participants were disappointed when they found out that the broadcast was a hoax. The dictator did not fall until August of that year.

Radio fever spread, and in 1924 A. Martínez's CMC, at the Loma del Mazo, and Autrán's CMCY in the Vedado, and the Rodríguez brothers' CMCJ were on the air. In the province of Camagüey, the station CMJA began broadcasting. By the following year, when Machado assumed the presidency, the incipient radio stations were already in competition. Typically they were housed on the first floor of two- or three-story *criolla* houses made of cement and tiles. In the entrance was usually a marble staircase. The studio was in the living room, with a grand or upright piano, and other musical instruments. The equipment was in one room and the announcer and his records in another. Other rooms housed the archives and other radio phonic artifacts.

The two most important radio stations of the period were the CMQ and the RHC. The CMQ was housed at 20 and H. It was originally located in Monte y Prado, property of José Fernández Suviaur. Miguel Gabriel and Ángel Cambó purchased the facilities on 11 March 1933 and it was later moved to 20th Street and H. Opponents of the dictatorship, they used the station as a means for expressing opinions and began to attract capital from small businessmen. After Machado's fall, the CMQ was hailed as a revolutionary radio station and gained in popularity.

By 1934 there were twenty-six radio stations in Havana and another twenty-five spread throughout the rest of the country. This placed Cuba behind the United States (625), Canada (77), and Russia (68), and ahead of Sweden (31), Australia (30), Germany (29), France (28), and England (22) in number of stations. In Latin America, Uruguay had 25 stations, Brazil had 22, and Argentina had 17. That same year Radio Guía outlined programming as follows: forty-six newscasts; twelve hours given to political parties; ten to comedies, zarzuelas, and dramas; nineteen to political opinions or commentaries; thirty-six to music slots for songs and tangos; twenty-six to instrumental and classical music; sixty-nine to dance music; four to religious programs; and two to those of humor.

The most successful program of the period debuted in 1937, one year after writer, composer, and journalist Féliz B. Caignet left his native Santiago de Cuba to work in Havana. His detective serial, *Chan Li Po*, aired over CMK, owned by Félix O'Shea. This and other programs were sponsored by soap advertisements and other toiletries directed more to the poor than to rich people (who comprised only about 5 percent of the population).

In May 1939 Amado Trinidad Velazco, who with his brothers Ramón and Diego in 1921 created the tobacco company Trinidad y Hermanos, founded two radio stations—the long-wave CMHI and the short-wave COHI—in the city of Santa Clara. With the CMCF of Havana and the CMKO of Santiago, these stations controlled most of the broadcast business in the island. During the 1940s, the radio became the ideal means for reaching large numbers of people at a time when political corruption, gangsters, and U.S. interests reached new heights.

The radio soap opera was born within a reprehensible political climate; it offered an alternative to Cubans who desired to escape their immediate situation. The programs allowed listeners to flee into their imagination and dream about the extravagance of high society. On 26 August 1939 the soap opera *Pepe Cortés*, about a Robin Hood type who robs the rich and gives to the poor, was aired; it became an instant hit in the central and western regions of the country. The actors, who were well paid, were secretly bought by the CMQ, and their salaries jumped from sixty to three hundred pesos monthly. This forced Amado Trinidad, who had contracted the series, to move to Havana and compete effectively.

There was fierce competition among radio stations in this period. "La Hora Multiple" (Multiple Hour) for example, was transferred to at least eight stations. In 1940 Amado Trinidad became the largest stockholder of RHC (Radio Habana Cuba), begun the previous year by O'Shea, with stations in the central and eastern parts of the island. He added other local stations and extended telephone wires, making the RHC-Cadena Azul a national broadcasting company, to compete with the CMQ. After this business venture, radio stations that wanted to survive were obligated to attract large sums of capital.

The Guerra del Aire (air war) was launched between the CMQ and RHC. In 1942 they offered similar programming. The RHC had three adventures, three radio soap operas, ten musical slots, seven giveaways, seven newscasts, and one sports program. The CMQ had three soap operas, thirteen musical slots, one giveaway, ten newscasts, and four comedies. By 1946 the CMQ was winning the war. Its programs were popular and widely listened to. These included "Radioteatro argentino" (Argentine Radio Theatre), "Tarzán el hombre mono" (Tarzan, King of the Jungle), "La novela radial Candado" (The Radio Novel Candado), "El collar de lágrimas" (The Tear Necklace), "Frente a la vida" (Facing Life), "La novela Pilón" (The Pilón Novel), "La novela de las cuatro" (The Four O'clock Novel), "La historia de Julia Sandoval" (The Julia Sandoval History), "Un romance en la tarde" (An Afternoon Romance), "Tamaré," "El folletín Hiel de Vaca" (The Serial Hiel de Vaca), "La novela Palmolive" (The Palmolive Novel), and "Mariana." RHC combated the CMQ's success by buying out its actors and technicians, luring them with high salaries. Nevertheless, the CMQ continued to triumph. In 1948 it built Radio Centro, the first radio center of its kind in Latin America. In addition, Goar Mestre, who was backed by U.S. interests, was elected president of the Asociación Interamericana de Radiodifusión (Inter-American Association of Radio Broadcast).

The war between the two companies was also a war between owners Amado Trinidad and Goar Mestre. Trinidad was flamboyant and held wild and well-attended parties by the press, and members of panels conferring awards, of which his staff received top honors—and more than their share. Mestre, a graduate of Yale University, was more reserved but energetic in presenting his progressive agenda and his ties to U.S. interests. During the inauguration of Radio Centro, four vice presidents of the National Broadcasting Company attended the event. His programmers and technicians studied in the United States, and his company had the most advanced offerings available anywhere, similar to those available in the United States.

As the two companies went head-to-head in programming, RHC took top honors in its dramas, "La novela del aire" and "Lo que pasa en el mundo" (What Happens in the World). But CMQ controlled the afternoon programming with tear-jerking stories and others that included violence, which kept an overwhelmingly female audience fixed to the radio. The CMQ became a financial success as advertisers bought up large blocks of time. For example, in a twelve-hour programming period, ten and one-half hours were reserved for direct or indirect commercials, many of them jingles done in such a tasteful manner that the audience was unaware that they were commercials. The sponsors used audience surveys systematically to understand the audience and boost ratings. Some of these were done by Sabatés S.A., Crusellas and Co., Sterling Products Ink, Domingo Menéndez and Sons, Ramón Rodríguez S.A., Marton Dosal and Co., Nueva Fábrica de Hielo S.A., and Laboratorios Gravi.

The war between Trinidad and Mestre influenced the other's efforts to bring television to Cuba. Trinidad gave it a try in 1948, to no avail, and found out that RCA Victor and General Electric had backed Mestre. But the biggest news at that time was Mestre's success in signing Félix B. Caignet, the most successful scriptwriter in the history of Cuban radio and in Latin America and author of the popular television program *El derecho de nacer* (The Right to Be Born), which set new highs for ratings. Trinidad made an unsuccessful attempt to buy CMQ's best actors, but Mestre had better results in luring away RHC's comedians Leopoldo Fernández (Trespatines), Aníbal de Mar (Don Pancracio), and Mimi Cal (Nananina), and later acquiring the entire program "Pototo y Filomeno." The competition between the two rivals reached international proportions when Mestre, through the Asociación Internacional del Aire, denounced Argentina's Juan Domingo Perón's government interference in the radio and print media. In addition, the CMQ identified Trinidad as an agent of Perón, who received campaign contributions from the Argentine strongman.

Mestre was also involved in national issues. As the important owner of a successful radio empire, he had disagreements with the government, in particular with the minister of communications, Carlos Maristany, for supporting Eduardo R. Chibás, the leader of the Partido Cubano del Pueblo (Orthodox party). The issues were such that other broadcast media, like *Diario de la Marina* and *Prensa Libre*, stepped forward to defend democracy and freedom of expression.

Of more importance than the melodramas, directed at women, were the contests promoted by radio stations. Critics of the contests believed they were of questionable nature since at first it was not clear if there were any winners, and that with high product prices the consumer was paying for the gifts. However, the public did not object; a 1950 survey showed that 92.82 percent of the audience agreed with product prices, to the delight of the commercial detergent companies like Colgate-Palmolive International (González 1988, 210).

Other programs professed to perform miracles. One of them was "El buzón de 'Clavelito' " (Clavelito's Mailbox). "Clavelito" revealed his supernatural powers and offered miraculous remedies for sicknesses and ailments to millions of listeners, and for whom the rivaling CMQ and RHC had no answer. Listeners had so much faith in his powers that they placed a glass of water on the radio to receive his mental transmissions. "Clavelito" was finally forced off the air in August 1952, but not without fan protests that included a writing campaign directed at Batista. Nevertheless, the radio companies returned to their regular program, but this time with much more control over their actors, making them sign contracts.

Eduardo Chibás, a presidential candidate of the Orthodox party, made the most dramatic use of the radio waves with his weekly Sunday night programs in which he denounced government corruption and gangsterism. An exceptional orator, practically the entire country flocked to their radios to listen to him speak. In June 1951 Chibás accused the minister of education, Aureliano Sánchez Arango, of corruption and stealing money for timber in Guatemala. The minister insisted he was innocent and said he had ample evidence to show it. But Chibás committed himself to showing proof on the air. There was no proof. On 5 August Chibás walked over to the CMQ, gave a short speech, and as he was going off the air shot himself. He died ten days later.

On 11 August 1955 Amado Trinidad Velasco, commonly known as the "Guajiro," committed suicide, thus bringing an important stage of radio to an end. However, three years before, he had sold the RHC to other interests, which included the Columbia Broadcasting System, which also looked to create a television station. The name changed to Circuito Nacional Cubano (Cuban national circuit). By the time Trinidad passed away, there were five national radio networks: CMQ, Union Radio (October 1947), Radio Progreso (December 1929), Cadena Oriental de Radio, and Circuito Nacional Cubano. Gaspar Pumarejo, who had become dissatisfied with Mestre, founded Union Radio, and would play a role in Cuban television. During that period, radio declined and television became the most important broadcast medium as middle-class Cubans began to purchase television sets.

TELEVISION

The history of television in Cuba began with the competition that existed among the radio stations CMQ, RHC, and Union Radio and other interested parties, like the *Diario de la Marina*, though there have been reports of the existence of a crude television station in 1928. Gaspar Pumarejo, of Union Radio, inaugurated the first television station, CMUR-TV, on 24 October 1950, a few months after Mexico and Brazil established theirs. The first programming included singers, music, and odd shapes (probably test patterns).

Pumarejo, who began broadcasting from his home, failed to raise the necessary capital for a television station, so in August 1951, he announced that he was selling Union Radio's radio and television to Manolo Alonso, a successful producer of Cuban films and newsreels. It was rumored that President Carlos Prío was behind the purchase, fostering suspicions of government attempts to control and manipulate the media.

CMQ, which received its license in 1949, did not begin broadcasting until 18 December 1950. In a short period of time, it became the most important station. The station recreated the nightclub atmosphere. *Cabaret Regalías* (Royal Cabaret) and *Casino de la Alegría* (Casino of Joy) were among the island's highest-rated programs. Under the direction of Mario Barral, the CMQ also ventured into television soap operas and produced *Senderos de Amor* (Love Paths), starring Armando Bianchi and Adela Escrín. By 1951 CMQ had three of its eight-station network. A year later, Cubans were rushing to purchase more than 100,000 television sets, ranging in price from $350 to $2,000. In 1954, Havana, with a population of 1 million, was home to five of Cuba's stations: CMQ-TV channel 6; CMUR Televisión Nacional channel 4; CMAB Telemundo channel 2; CMBF, second CMQ station, channel 7, which played foreign films; and Televisión del Caribe, channel 11. By 1959, Cuba led Latin America with sixteen stations and 275,000 receivers (Salwen 1994, 78).

If the Mestres competed with Trinidad for supremacy over radio, a similar competition developed over television, this time between Mestre and Amadeo Barletta, co-owner of *El Mundo*. In 1952 Mestre sold his shares in Union Radio and acquired Telemundo. Soon after, he wanted to construct an eight-station empire to compete against CMQ's dominion.

Gaspar Pumarejo was the most popular personality of television of the period. He leased one hour from Televisión Nacional for his *Escuela de Televisión* (Television School), a variety program that first aired in January 1953. In 1955 Pumarejo and Barletta signed a five-year contract to offer the variety program to Telemundo. The programming included *Queen for a Day*, *This Is Your Life*, and *The $64,000 Question*, similar to their counterparts in the United States. Another popular top-50 program was the children's *Pumarejo y sus amigos* (Pumarejo and His Friends). Pumarejo is also credited with introducing the first color television station. In 1956 he obtained permission from Batista's Ministry of Communications to use channel 12, Tele-Color, the first color television in the world. In that year, there were only 509 color sets on the island, and Pumarejo also saw the opportunity to sell color televisions. Some believed that Pumarejo had support from Batista, an accusation he always denied.

When Batista took over the government in 1952, he attempted to silence his critics. The censorship increased after Castro's 26 July attack on the Moncada barracks and reached its peak in 1957. Mestre went into self-imposed exile and remained abroad until Batista fled the country on New Year's Eve 1958. Although members of the mass media were punished severely, and some were even imprisoned, criticism against the dictator continued. The program *El Dictador del Valle Azul* (The Dictator of the Blue Valley) was a parody of Castro and his men fighting to overthrow the dictator and was aired because the government did not understand that it was being parodied.

RADIO AND TV DURING AND AFTER THE REVOLUTION

The radio became one of the weapons used by rebels. Radio Rebelde (Rebel radio) was inaugurated on 24 February 1958 to break Batista's censorship of the airwaves. The station pronounced: "This is Radio Rebelde! Transmitting from the Sierra Maestra, in the free territory of Cuba." The station offered a variety of programming. An increasing number of Cubans tuned into the station to listen to the progress made by the rebel army—their victories and manifestos—but also music and even poetry. Carlos Franqui, a member of the 26th of July and a friend of Castro, wrote its news bulletins.

When Batista fled the country, most broadcast owners were not at their stations, and station employees did the work. Although there was skepticism about the initial news of the dictator's flight, the first credible report came from Telemundo's well-responded political reporter, Carlos Lechuga. The CMQ Radiocentro became the headquarters of the 26th of July Movement information center, providing uncensored information. Stations associated with the dictator were confiscated, as was the case with Circuito Nacional Cubano, an eleven-station network. Pumarejo became a target of the revolutionary government and was accused of business dealings with the dictatorship. When he left the country, his programs were confiscated.

After the revolutionary leaders came to power, rebel leaders saw the broadcast media as a way of reaching the entire population, particularly those in rural areas, where reception was poor or nonexistent. The clandestine Radio Rebelde became the most important and largest station in the country. As events began to move rapidly, even those who supported Castro were in danger. For example CMQ's Conte Agüero began a campaign to warn Castro of the communist presence in his government. This led to the confiscation of CMBF-TV, because it turned out that Batista had an interest in the station. On March 1960 Goar Mestre abandoned the island and headed for New York. Toward the end of the month, Castro denied that Conte Agüero was his friend, and Conte Agüero sought refuge in the Argentine embassy. Abel Mestre, Goar's brother, stayed in Cuba to oversee CMQ's business, but on 1 April he also left the country. CMQ and Radio Progreso later were taken over by the government. Even Castro's popular commentator, José Pardo Llada, who believed that there was room for the Communist party in the revolution, defected in March 1961, recognizing that an independent position was no longer possible. By the time of Pardo Llada's defection, the government had gained control of radio and television. All were consolidated into the Frente Independiente de Estaciones Libres (Independent Front of Free Stations), made up of over 100 radio stations and 28 television stations.

By 1975 there were some 115 radio broadcasting stations throughout the island, reaching 1.5 million radio receivers. The major five national networks were Radio Rebelde, Radio Progreso, Radio Liberación, Radio Musical Nacional, and Radio Reloj, and five provincial networks, CMHW of Las Villas, Cadena Agramonte of Camagüey, Cadena Oriente CMKC, Radio Veintiseis for Matanzas, and Radio Guama for Pinar del Río.

The radio stations were set up for cultural and educational programs to foster the goals of the revolution. For example, Radio Rebelde offered Russian-language instruction as well as literary and political commentary. Cuban stations had to compete with those broadcasting from Miami, to which many Cubans from the island listened. For this reason, island stations began to offer U.S. and British musical programs that also played in the United States. Cuban radio stations were set up for the domestic audience, but Radio Havana was envisioned to reach an international one, in particular that of Latin America. This it did with eight short-wave transmitters. Of the 154 hours of broadcasting weekly, most programs were in Spanish and directed to Spanish America. Eighty hours were in English, and of these, seventy-nine were directed to the United States; thirty-three hours were in French and fourteen hours in other languages such as Arabic, Portuguese, Guaraní, Quechua, and Haitian Creole.

There are now three television stations in Cuba—two in Havana, named Televisora Nacional, and one in Santiago de Cuba, named Tele-Rebelde. One of the Havana stations is deemed educational; it broadcasts programs in science, language, mathematics, and other subjects. The other one is also cultural and educational, but includes entertainment. It is not uncommon to see old movies and recent melodramas from Cuba and other countries. Recently, as a consequence of the Elián González affair, the government has begun to confiscate powerful antennas that receive U.S. programs.

CUBAN MEDIA ABROAD

Cubans have been publishing outside Cuba since 1824, when Félix Valera published *El Habanero* in Philadelphia and New York. In the contemporary period, all major cities with large Cuban and Hispanic populations enjoy Spanish newspapers. Writers who have left Cuba since the Mariel boatlift have made great efforts to continue to write and publish abroad. Some of them have felt a need to publish journals so that others with similar interests have a way of expressing common ideas. Noteworthy are Heberto Padilla's *Linden Lane Magazine* (1981) and Reinaldo Arena's *Mariel* (1986), each with its own publishing house. They have provided space for exiles that may not be readily available through other literary means. Of a much broader interest is Jesús Díaz's *Encuentro de la Cultura Cubana* (Meeting of Cuban Culture, 1996). Once the editor of *El Caimán Barbudo*, the literary supplement of *Juventud Rebelde*, when Padilla voiced a critical opinion about Lisandro Otero's *La pasión de Urbino* (Urbino's Passion, 1967) and a favorable one of Guillermo Cabrera Infante's *Tres tristes tigres*, at a time when the latter had already abandoned the island. A strong supporter of the government, Díaz lives in Madrid and has produced a high-quality journal open to all who desire some form of reconciliation. *Encuentro de la Cultura Cubana* is widely read in Cuba and is highly regarded.

Cuban exile groups have also used the airways as a medium for combating Cuban communism. There are regular broadcasts from hidden or mobile transmitters. Some of these are Radio Trinchera (Trench Radio), La Voz Cristiana de Cuba (Christian Voice of Cuba), La Juventud Progresista Cubana (Cuban Progressive Youth), La Voz de Alpha 66 (a terrorist organization), Radio Abdala, Radio Libertad Cubana, and La Voz de Cuba Independiente y Democrática (Cuban Democratic and Independent Voice). The last broadcasts from five transmitters located outside the United States.

The U.S. government has also been involved in broadcasting to Cuba. Voice of America transmits to Cuba and other countries in the Americas, on medium and short wave, five hours per day all week. Programming includes news and commentary, science and the economy, and sports programs. The United States became more aggressive with its broadcast with the creation of Radio Martí. Radio Martí was conceived under the Reagan administration by an executive order in September 1981. Castro fiercely protested this new attack on the island's sovereignty and retaliated by jamming the radio waves. In its final form, Radio Martí did not become another "Radio Free Europe," as Reagan had envisioned. As part of Voice of America, Radio Martí began broadcasting in May 1985. It consists of one AM and two short-wave bands. Like Radio Liberty and Radio Free Europe, it attempted to undermine the government's policies on the island. Its purpose was to offer another interpretation of Cuba's domestic and international policies, which could not be obtained on the island. Although the station was not going to destabilize the government, it represented for Castro an act of aggression.

Univisión and Telemundo are television broadcasting companies that serve the Cuban and Hispanic communities in the United States and Puerto Rico, offering news, sports, soap operas, commentaries, children's programming, musical specials, public affairs programs, game shows, and other programming familiar to U.S. audiences. Univisión offers its affiliates twenty-four-hour programming. Its affiliates include Miami's WLTV channel 23, New Jersey's WXTV channel 41, Philadelphia's WXTV channel 42, and most recently Boston's WVNI channel 27. Its popular programming features *Sábado Gigante* (Giant Saturday), *Cristina*, *Primer Impacto* (First Impact), and *Despierta América* (Wake Up America). Equally popular is Telemundo, with sixteen stations and cable connections serving over 7 million customers in the United States. Some of their East Coast affiliates are New York's WNJU channel 47, Hialeah's WSCU channel 51, and Puerto Rico's WKAQ channel 2. These stations use television personnel from Cuba and other Spanish-speaking countries. The Hispanic community in the United States brings together all of Spanish America.

REFERENCES

Brenner, Philip. "United States–Cuban Relations in the 1980s." In *The Cuba Reader: The Making of a Revolutionary Society*. Ed. Philip Brenner, William M. LeoGrande, Donna Rich, and Daniel Siegel. New York: Grove Press, 1989. 316–331.

Casanovas, Martín, ed. *Órbita de la Revista de Avance*. Havana: UNEAC, 1965.

Collazo, Bobby. *La última noche que pasé contigo: 40 años de farándula cubana*. San Juan, P.R.: Editorial Cubanacán, 1987.

de la Pezuela, Jacobo. *Historia de la isla de Cuba*. Madrid: Imprenta de Bailly-Bailliere, 1878.

Diccionario geográgico, estadístico, histórico, de la isla de Cuba. Madrid: Imprenta del Establecimiento de Mellao, 1863. Vol. 3.

Frederick, Howard H. *Cuban-American Radio Wars: Ideology in International Telecommunications*. Norwood, N.J.: Ablex, 1986.

Friol, Roberto. *Suite para Juan Francisco Manzano*. Havana: Editorial Arte y Literatura, 1977.

Gómez, Juan Gualberto. *Por Cuba libre*. Havana: Editorial Ciencias Sociales, 1974.

González, Reinaldo. *Llorar es un placer*. Havana: Editorial Letras Cubanas, 1988.

González Echevarría, Roberto. *The Pride of Havana: A History of Cuban Baseball*. New York: Oxford University Press, 1999.

Nichols, John Spicer. "The Press in Cuba." In *The Cuba Reader: The Making of a Revolutionary Society*. Ed. Philip Brenner, William M. LeoGrande, Donna Rich, and Daniel Siegel. New York: Grove Press, 1989. 219–227.

El periodismo en Cuba. Havana: Retiro de Periodistas, 1944.

Ripol, Carlos. "*La Revista de Avance* (1927–1939), vocero de vanguardismo y pórtico de revolución." *Revista Iberoamericana* 30 (1964): 261–282.

Salwen, Michael B. *Radio and Television in Cuba: The Pre-Castro Era.* Ames: Iowa State University Press, 1994.

Thomas, Hugh. *Cuba: The Pursuit of Freedom.* New York: Harper & Row, 1971.

5

Cinema

CUBANS ARE avid moviegoers. Prior to 1959, of Cuba's 7 million population, approximately 1.5 million living in Havana and other large cities went to the movies weekly, mainly to see Hollywood films. Cuban movie aficionados were a significant sector of the population ready to be educated or influenced by whomever controlled by movie industry. The Cuban revolutionary government has considered cinema to be an important and necessary medium for reaching large numbers of Cubans. Fidel Castro and other leaders support Lenin in considering cinema the most important art form.

Shortly after assuming power, Castro created on 25 March 1959 the Instituto Cubano de Arte e Industria Cinematográficas (Institute for Cinematographic Arts and Industries, ICAIC), Cuba's movie industry, to oversee the production, distribution, and exhibition of films. The ICAIC's first director was Alfredo Guevara, one of Castro's university student friends. A member of the Partido Socialista Popular, Cuba's Communist party, Guevara and allies sought to influence the direction of Cuban cinema at the expense of other competing interests. Large movie houses were nationalized, smaller ones were incorporated into government cooperatives, and a mobile cinema, consisting of trucks and mule teams, made available a variety of films to those living in remote parts of the island. The ICAIC also exposed the public to foreign films. The majority of them were filmed in Eastern bloc countries (the Soviet Union, Czechoslovakia, Yugoslavia) and the People's Republic of China. Others were imported from Western Europe (England, Spain, and France), Japan, and Latin America, in particular Mexico. Twenty-four years after its creation, the ICAIC has produced 112 full-feature films, over 900 documentaries, and more than 1,300 weekly newsreels.

For economic and ideological reasons, the emphasis has been on the documentary, which has been directed to audiences in Cuba and Latin America. Documentary production can be divided into five categories:

> Films which deal with domestic politics promote governmental policies and encourage popular participation and mass mobilization. Historical films chart various aspects of the formation of national identity through the five centuries of the island's recorded history. Documentaries of a cultural nature may be either national or international in their focus. Films which take international relations for their theme might focus on Cuba's role in international affairs, analyze the developed sector, or express solidarity with other Third World nations. Finally, "didactic" documentaries, highly technical or scientific in nature, are generally produced by specific agencies rather than ICAIC. (Burton 1997, 128)

The lack of economic resources has forced directors to become experimental and creative with whatever they have available to reach their intended audience.

The early part of the twentieth century was a period in which movie theaters began to spread. The first movie theater was Diorama, and it was destroyed by the hurricane of 1846. The next one was built in 1913, and it was located in the gardens of the Trocha Hotel in the Vedado district. It showed shorts four times a week by Max Linder. The numerous movie theaters in and outside Havana showed Cuban, but also U.S., French, Russian, German, and Italian movies. During the silent period, movie houses contracted musicians to accompany the films.

Cuba's native cinema began shortly after the establishment of the republic. It can be traced to Enrique Díaz Quesado, who constructed a studio on the roof of his house located on 356 Monte Street, in the Víbora district. His first film was *Manuel García, el rey de los campos de Cuba* (King of the Cuban Countryside, 1913), with a script from Federico Villoch. He also directed movies about Havana: *La Habana en agosto 1906* (Havana in August 1906), *El parque de Palestino* (Palestino Park, 1906), and two years later, *Un turista en la Habana* (A tourist in Havana, 1908). And he is credited with making others with social themes, such as *Arrollito* (Stream) and *La zafra* (Sugar Harvest).

In the 1920s, Ramón Peón filmed *El veneno de un beso* (The Poison of a Kiss) and *La virgen de la caridad* (Our Lady of Charity, 1930), with commercial interests. The talkies arrived in Cuba after the fall of Machado. The first motion picture was attributed to Ernesto Caparrós, who in 1937 completed *La serpiente roja* (The Red Snake). During this period Peón made many movies, including some with nudity like *Tierra, amor y dolor* (Earth, Love and Distress, 1934) and *El bastardo* (The Bastard, 1937) and musicals like *Sucedió en La Habana* (It Happened in Havana), *El romance del palmar, Cancionero*, and *Siboney*. The following decade was characterized by a strong Mexican influence, in which films from Mexico were distributed. Cuban directors attempted to copy Mexican and Argentine films, but without success. Only Manuel Alonso's *Siete muertos a plazo fijo* (Seven Dead at a Fixed Time, 1949), merits attention. In effect, Mexico and the United States, through Columbia's Mexican interests, controlled and influenced Cuban cinema. Emilio Fernández's *La rosa blanca* (The White Rose) was co-produced with Mexico, and Tulio Demichelli's *Un extraño en la escalera* (A Stranger on the Stairs), with Argentina, also belongs to this period.

After World War II, a small group of young directors began experimenting with short films. Tomás Gutiérrez Alea, who became Cuba's most important director, produced *La caperucita roja* (Little Red Riding Hood, 1946) and *Un fakir* (1947) and, with Néstor Almendros as cameraman, *Una confusión cotidiana* (An Everyday Confusion, 1948). While Gutiérrez Alea was making his first films, Germán Puig and Ricardo Vigón founded the Cine Club of Havana, around 1948 and 1949, which showed classic films and considered cinematography to be an art. The club's early members included Guillermo Cabrera Infante, Gutiérrez Alea, and Almendros. Later the Cine Club was renamed Cinemateca de Cuba and produced short films such as Carlos Franqui and Puig's *Carta a una madre* (Letter to a Mother), *El guante* (The Glove), *Pintura* (Painting), and *Hamlet*. By this time, the Cinemateca de Cuba was incorporated into the film department of the society Nuestro Tiempo. This private society, which Franqui help found, was taken over by members of the Cuban Communist party, who imposed their ideology on the others.

Early in the 1950s, two members of Nuestro Tiempo, Gutiérrez Alea and Julio García Espinosa, studied film at the Centro Sperimentale de Cinematografía di Roma, and neorealism, which had become popular after World War II. Upon their return and with the help of Jorge Haydú, they produced *El megano* (The Charcoal Worker, 1954–1955), a neorealistic short film about Cuban coal miners in the Zapata region. However, not all agreed with this cinematic orientation. Almendros, arguably the best cameraman of all time, explained the tension that erupted early on in the foundation of Cuban cinema: "It was then that we decided to abandon Nuestro Tiempo and continue our sessions on the side. The Communists wanted to impose their political points of view. We didn't. We were interested in defending cinema and nothing more. We defended a good Russian film as if it were a good film from any other country, including the United States. This Marxist Cine Club, which was originally ours and later Nuestro Tiempo's, then divided" (Luis 1987, 17).

The early competing interests between members of the Cinemateca of Cuba and the Marxist group continued when Batista fled the island and Castro became the new leader. Franqui and other members of the 26th of July Movement expressed their ideas through *Revolución*, the official newspaper of the Rebel army, and its literary supplement, *Lunes de Revolución*. Members of the Communist party took over key positions within the Dirección de Cultura and the ICAIC. Working for the Dirección de Cultura, García Espinosa scripted and Gutiérrez Alea directed in 1959 *Esta tierra nuestra* (This Land of Ours), about the agrarian reform, and García Espinosa directed *La vivienda* (Housing), about urban reform. In that same year, this time under the banner of the ICAIC, García Espinosa directed *Sexto aniversario* (Sixth Anniversary), about the invitation to farmworkers to go to Havana and help commemorate the attack on the Moncada barracks, and Humberto Arenal directed *Construcciones rurales* (Rural Constructions), about the improvement in rural construction. Guillermo Cabrera Infante became vice president of the ICAIC, but resigned his position when he realized that freedom of expression was being curtailed in the new Cuba.

The ICAIC has been responsible for promoting Cuba's image both at home and abroad and for educating the viewing public. Since 1960 it has published a film magazine, *Cine Cubano*, and since 1979, it had sponsored the International Festivals of the New Latin American Cinema, which gathers movies and directors from all over the world, including the United States. Four periods can be identified in the ICAIC's history:

1959–1960, marked by a sense of nationalism, openness, and optimism. The first films supported the rebel cause and criticized the previous regime.

1960–1969, a period of declining artistic liberty and increasing pressure for directors to become militants of the revolution. Cuba's style became more eclectic; the documentary, through the works of Santiago Álvarez, and full-feature fictional films, received international attention.

1970–1974, influenced by the failure of the 10-million-ton-sugar harvest. Artistic liberty continued to decline. There was emphasis on less experimentation, more documentary efforts, and reaching the average person.

1975–1983, when the ICAIC was reorganized and incorporated into the Ministry of Culture. Julio García Espinoza replaced Guevara. (Burton 1997, 131–133)

The Special Period, initiated by perestroika and the fall of the Soviet Union, has been characterized by relative freedom and tolerance. During this recent stage, Armand Hart, minister of culture, was replaced by Abel Prieto, and Alfredo Guevara returned to occupy his position as president of the ICAIC.

The first years of the revolution and the creation of a national cinema were characterized by a plurality of opinions in which different groups competed for public opinion. These were turbulent years in which history was turned upside down. The United States went from being a friend to an enemy, and the Soviet Union from an enemy to a friend. Cuban cinema reflected a similar shift, as Cubans were exposed to films sympathetic to the changing society. In this early period, cinema became a battleground between *Lunes de Revolución* and the ICAIC, reminiscent of the tension that erupted in the 1950s between members of the Cine Club and those of Nuestro Tiempo. *Lunes de Revolución* and the ICAIC represented two different cinematography orientations. Members of the ICAIC supported the neorealist ideas of the Italian school, which Roberto Rossellini and Vittorio De Sica originated, and Cesare Zavattini represented. The ICAIC had invited Zavattini to the island to teach seminars to its students. Members of *Lunes* rejected neorealism and supported a broader position that included Hollywood cinema, and the English Free Cinema or French *cinéma vérité* in vogue at that moment. This new current did not transform reality to make it what it should be. On the contrary, the camera eye captured reality in the making. Almendros himself had put this technique into practice with his film *Cincuenta y ocho cincuenta y nueve* (Fifty-eight Fifty-nine, 1959), in which his camera recorded the New Year's Eve celebration in New York's Times Square. In the film, the happy faces of the celebrants were juxtaposed with that of a man begging for food, who was invisible to all but the camera.

The tension between supporters of the two competing positions was best captured in a *Lunes de Revolución* issue dedicated to movies ("Lunes va al cine," 94 [6 February 1961]), prepared with the help of Fausto Canel and Néstor Almendros, who also contributed an article on Spanish films. The entire issue focused on movies and included material pertinent to the *P.M.* (Past Meridian) controversy that followed. Emilio García Reira opened the debate with what could have been *Lunes de Revolución*'s position, in support of the New Wave in filmmaking. For him, movies did not reflect reality; they recreated it. He also considered neorealism a thing of the past; the present belonged to the New Wave. He appraised the two as not only different but opposites.

For García Reira, the New Wave, which was not exclusively French, was open to the ideas and styles of the filmmaker. Neorealism, on the other hand, offered a failed recipe. He claimed that Zavattini was a part of history and orthodox neorealism. He favored Luchino Visconti, Roberto Rossellini, Michelangelo Antonioni, and Federico Fellini, Italian filmmakers who began their careers with neorealism but moved on to give birth to a new cinema.

García Reira's essay also stressed the importance of liberty, especially when commenting on the commercial and decadent movie industry. Although he recognized its downfall, García Reira also realized that the talent of a Fritz Lang (a German director) could be instructive, revealing, and create an appreciation for all films. He also underscored form, which he believed moviemakers should develop, but without surrendering to commercial interests. García Reira ended his essay by stating that the problem of creation is one of liberty.

Julio García Espinosa's "El neorrealismo y la nueva ola francesa" (Neorealism and the French New Wave) represented the position associated with the ICAIC. He studied the two most recent currents: the Free Cinema and neorealism. García Espinosa remembered that prior to 1959, many thought that neorealism was the future of movies. More than a style, it was an attitude toward reality and a weapon against dictatorship and imperialism.

García Espinosa believed the Free Cinema derived from the camera eye of the Russian director Dziga Vertov. But the French New Wave, which some claimed to be similar to neorealism in content, differed in cinematic language. It emphasized style rather than attitude, which García associated with the petit bourgeoisie. Unlike the New Wave, neorealism took its subject matter from the popular sectors of society (i.e., the lower classes). The former projected the attitude of the artist, while the latter remained distant from it. Although García Espinosa was not willing to say that one form was better than the other, for him neorealism deepened an understanding of the masses. Later García Espinosa developed his ideas further in the often-cited "Por un cine imperfecto" (Toward an Imperfect Cinema, 1969). In this essay he proposed a cinema antithetical to the perfect cinema of the elite—one that is imperfect and contributes to class struggle. The active spectators will become involved in transforming their own reality.

Alfredo Guevara's essay, "Realidad y deberes de la crítica cinematográfica" (Reality and Duty of Cinematography Criticism), was overtly political. It started out by attacking the bourgeois sentiments that had dominated the movies. Guevara claimed criticism had been controlled by opportunism and ignorance, but also by the U.S. embassy's financial and political interests. The revolution represented change, and critics could not ignore the changes. They must reflect on the act of writing and ask the following questions: For whom is the writer writing? Why? For which period and society? And, above all, why write? In answer to those questions, the critic should ask others— such as about how to write, what to write, and when to write.

If the first part of the *Lunes* issue captured the debate between neorealism and Free Cinema and contained articles about film in Poland, Czechoslovakia, France, and Spain, the second part initiated another debate, representing a different tradition in movies, eroticism. "El erotismo en el cine" (Eroticism in the Movies) contained pictures of the sexiest women of the times: actresses Theda Bara, Gloria Swanson, Virginia Bruce, Greta Garbo, Jean Harlow, Carole Lombard, Marlene Dietrich, Rita Hayworth, Sophia Loren, Kim Novak, and Hedy Lamarr. In "Técnica del erotismo" (Techniques of Eroticism), Lo Duca explored the commercial movies and their insistence on sex or eroticism, even in films that did not call for such scenes, such as *Bernardetti* and *Joan of Arc*. The second half of the issue also featured an article on Marilyn Monroe by Arthur Miller and another on Brigitte Bardot by Simone de Beauvoir, in which innocence, child woman, and breasts are these women's salient qualities.

Although Cabrera Infante did not write in "Lunes va al cine," his position was well known. He supported a broad-minded attitude toward film and was known as a connoisseur of Hollywood films. This may help to explain the presence of the second section in *Lunes*, which certainly infuriated members of the Communist party. As a film critic for *Carteles*, he had already taken a position regarding Zavattini and De Sica in his review of *El oro de Nápoles* (Naples's gold) dated 15 January 1956. The version that appears in *Un oficio del siglo 20: G. Cain 1954–60* (A Twentieth Century Job, 1963), and whose title recalls the Hollywood film giant 20th Century Fox, was preceded by an epigraph: "Cain had already warned us of Zavattini's decadence (and De Sica's)." In this review, Cain (Cabrera Infante's nom de plum) claimed that this film, which attempted to represent Neapolitan reality, was not one of their best pictures and the worst of the series. Cabrera Infante seized the opportunity to undermine neorealist ideas, which divided Italian criticism, and at that time were not important to the organizers of the famous Cannes Festival. He went to great lengths to point out that in Naples, De Sica, Marotta, and Zavattini deceived the people into believing they were making a glorious film about Naples, but instead showed pizza vendors and prostitutes. Naples's mayor even classified De Sica alongside Curzio Malaparte, Naples' number one enemy.

Cain dedicated more time and space to his review of *El último disparo* (The Last Shot), which showed that the greatest problems of the century were not political but those related to love. This is a theme Cabrera Infante would develop in some of his later novels. In the film, the two protagonists, representing two distinct political systems and ideologies, fall in love. But Isolda's shooting of Oleg, before being rescued by his men, indicates that socialism has triumphed over eternal love. And tears over her lost love suggest the film's ambiguity—that is, the hero is not totally good and the villain is not totally evil. This he considered a triumph for the Soviet movie industry.

Cabrera Infante ended his review of *El último disparo*, and consequently the cycle of Soviet films, by referring to them but also by alluding to the current debate unfolding in Cuba. He took the opportunity to take a pot shot at the communists. He explained that he did not want to answer questions about the film's double meaning, or about someone who suggests that, like Isolda with her final gunshot, the communists have killed in Russia all that was subtle and elegant. From Cabrera Infante's perspective, love was not spontaneous but subject, like other aspects of society, to communist control.

P.M. CONTROVERSY

The ICAIC and members of the Communist party elected to have a show-down with Cabrera Infante and followers of *Lunes de Revolución* over Sabá Cabrera Infante and Orlando Jiménez-Leal's *P.M.* (Past Meridian, 1961), a short film that features the nightlife of blacks within the backdrop of a changing society. Filmed in the style of the New Wave, the camera eye crosses Havana's harbor on a ferry and moves from one location in Havana to another, from bar to bar, where Afro-Cubans are dancing, drinking, smoking, and having a good time. Although the film had an initial showing, the censors did not consider it an appropriate expression of the revolution at a time when the Cuban government was assuming a more defensive position with regard to the United States. The festive attitude of the Afro-Cubans in the film may have been considered antithetical to the ideological one that white leaders of the revolution wanted to impose on the rest of the population. Writing for *Bohemia*, Almendros provided the following review of *P.M.*:

> And, what is "Past Meridian"? Simply, it is a short film (of some fifteen minutes), which captures faithfully the atmosphere of the nightlife of the popular bars of a large city. The camera-scalpel travels like an untiring noctambulant from Regla, in a water taxi to the port of Havana, to the cafes of Cuatro Caminos, and ends in the small bars of the Playa

de Marianao, and back to Regla. The process could not have been simpler. It belongs to the spontaneous movie, the "free cinema" which is in vogue in the world. Never impertinent, the hidden camera gathers images without the awareness of those being filmed. Reality is captured as is, without actors, without additional lighting like in the studios, without a director ready to falsify things advising and deciding each of the movements or the dialogues. There is no film script a priori, without the scenes developed in life, without "fixing" them. Essentially, this is a documentary movie, which selects and extracts from reality, surrounding the elements used to compose the film. "Past Meridian" is a visual and musical document, but one in which a poetic transfiguration of common daily events take place. "P.M." is immensely realistic, but it is also immensely poetical.

Almendro's review and *P.M.* came into conflict with the ideological orientation of the ICAIC. In some respects, *P.M.* became a New Wave response of sorts to García Espinosa's neorealistic *Cuba baila* (Cuba Dances, 1960) the first film completed by the ICAIC. Although Almendro's review of *Cuba baila* was cautiously positive, he nevertheless described the film's defects. But there was a major difference between *P.M.* and *Cuba baila*: García Espinosa had the support of the official movie industry (ICAIC), while Sabá Cabrera and Jiménez-Leal were young aficionados who belonged to *Lunes de Revolución* and had received a modest sum from the magazine to finish the film. In spite of the monetary and artistic resources available to García Espinosa, Almendros gave *Cuba baila* three stars (which meant it was a good film) and awarded the amateur filmmakers four stars (an excellent film). Luis Orticón who, in *Bohemia*, claimed that *P.M.* accomplished something absent in other Cuban films, supported Almendros's review.

P.M. was censored for portraying a decadent aspect of Cuban life, which officials in power, acting on behalf of the revolution, wanted to eliminate. The censorship was also an attack on *Lunes de Revolución* and its possible influence on the direction of the film industry, which the communists wanted to control. *P.M.* and *Lunes de Revolución*, in their attempt to give culture a new direction, became victims of a transition that gave the Cuban Communist party an increasingly powerful voice in the new government. Castro's speech "Palabras a los intelectuales" (Words to the Intellectuals) of 1961 would determine present and future policy toward culture in Cuba and supported the ICAIC's decision to censor films. "Within the revolution everything, against the revolution nothing," signaled a commitment that all writers and artists were expected to assume. *P.M.* became a casualty in a long-standing struggle between opposing political and artistic currents. Its suppression indicated that the ICAIC was in firm control of cinema in Cuba and would not tolerate any film or criticism not sanctioned by the official industry. "Lunes va al cine" may have been considered a daring affront to the ICAIC and Cuban government. It may have been interpreted as *Lunes de Revolución*'s attempt to influence the direction of movies in Cuba, and the magazine was a formidable enemy that had to be eliminated. For the communists, *P.M.* was a sign of what was to come from the *Lunes* group. The ICAIC was not willing to share its new-found power, and *P.M.* proved to be an important field of battle.

After the elimination of *Lunes de Revolución*, the ICAIC emerged as a unified movie industry. One of its missions was to document events unfolding in the new Cuba. With this in mind, a series of documentaries was produced, including Manuel Herrera's *Girón* (Bay of Pigs, 1972), which was also televised, and Jorge Fraga's *Me hice maestro* (I Became a Teacher), about the literacy campaign of 1961. Santiago Álvarez has been recognized for his newsreels and documentaries. In 1967 he produced eleven documentaries, which included *Hanoi, martes 13* (Hanoi: Tuesday December 13), a documentary about life in Vietnam to arouse anti-U.S. sentiments, and *Abril de Girón*, about the Bay of Pigs invasion. That same year Octavio Cortázar directed *Por primera vez* (For the First Time), about those in rural areas watching cinema for the first time, and *Acerca de una persona que unos llaman San Lázaro y otros Babalú* (About a Person Some Call St. Lazarus and Others Babalú), on the subject of Afro-Cuban religion.

Many of the ICAIC's films have won national and international prizes in the most prestigious film festivals. The success of the ICAIC and the films it produces have inspired a younger generation to consider film as a medium of communication. Some of these have had the opportunity to exhibit their works at the International Festival of the New Latin American Cinema. For example, at the eleventh festival, held in December 1989, Elio Ruiz and Lizette Vila presented *Los que llegaron después* (Those Who Arrived Later), a documentary video consisting of interviews with youths born and raised under the guidance of the revolution. The youths offer an extraordinary testimony in which they refer to their isolated and marginal positions within the revolution and question the government's educational and social policies. The video reflects a situation that Ruiz experienced when he was asked to leave the university for candidly but naively stating that the Soviet Union had replaced U.S. dominion over the island. The documentary was awarded two Corales at the film festival. Ruiz also received recognition for his next work, *¿Quién baila aquí?, la rumba sin lentejuelas* (Who Dances Here? The Rumba Without Sequence), which obtained the Premio Caracol Especial del Jurado of the UNEAC (the UNEAC Jury's Special Caracol prize), the Premio Pitirre de Documental del IIdo Festival de Cine San Juan, Puerto Rico (the Pitirre Documentary Prize of the Second Festival of Cinema of San Juan, Puerto Rico), and the Premio Coral de Documental del XIImo Festival Internacional del Nuevo Cine Latinoamericano (the Coral Documentary Prize for the 12th International Festival of New Latin American Cinema). In this documentary, Ruiz traces the history of the rumba, whose origins are found in the Afro-Cuban religions of the Yorubas and Congolese. He looks at the rumba from a uniquely, but not exclusively, Afro-Cuban perspective, and its impact on contemporary music, from Chano Pozo's collaborations with Dizzy Gillespie, to Pablo Milanés's Nueva Trova songs, to those of the popular group Van Van. In spite of his rising career, Ruiz had problems in Cuba. *Los que llegaron después* was too problematic for some government officials, and Ruiz was forced to leave for Mexico, where he has resided since 1991.

Ruiz's case is not an isolated incident. Even established filmmakers from the ICAIC have been subjected to varying degrees of criticism from government officials. This dogmatic scrutiny can be traced to the sectarian period at the outset of the revolution, when Communist party member Aníbal Escalante worked with the Organizaciones Revolucionarias Integradas (Integrated Revolutionary Organizations), created in 1961 to bring together the old Communist party, the 26th of July Movement, and the Directorio Revolucionario. In the spring of 1962, Castro attacked sectarianism as a warped sense of Marxism. Guevara echoed Castro's words before the First National Cultural Congress and defended artistic autonomy. In 1964 the ICAIC resisted pressure from hard-liners writing in the Communist party newspaper *Hoy* and affirmed the public's right to see Federico Fellini's *La Dolce Vita*. It is ironic that Guevara, who had denounced the liberal expressions of writers and artists affiliated with *Lunes de Revolución*, found himself having to defend filmmakers but also writers and artists attempting to experiment with content and form.

After the closing of *Lunes de Revolución*, the ICAIC took on the responsibility of creating the appropriate environment for creative artists to develop their talents. In the early period this was the case with graphic artists and poster designers, and in the contemporary with painters. The ICAIC also provided a safe haven to Silvio Rodríguez, Pablo Milanés, and other members of the Nueva Trova. Some, like Mario Daly and Carlos Varela, have collaborated with the ICAIC and brought their music to the cinema. The ICAIC's impact also extends to literature. It has protected writers such as Jesús Díaz, Senel Paz, Ambrosio Fornet, Osvaldo Sánchez, Zoé Valdés, and many others from political bureaucrats looking for one narrow interpretation of reality, which supports their cause.

On some occasions orthodox government officials have not tolerated even criticism that is "within the revolution." For example, some films have been totally misinterpreted. This is the case with García Espinosa's *Las aventuras de Juan Quinquín* (The Adventure of Juan Quinquín, 1967), based on Samuel Feijóo's *Juan Quinquín en Pueblo Mocho*, a fragmented but entertaining comedy that parodied the heroic actions of guerrilla fighters. Some revolutionaries interpreted the film as making a mockery of them.

Guevara himself had his own problems. He was the only gay man to occupy a significant position within the government. His opponents, whom he described as conservative Catholics masked under the cloak of Marxism, used the filming of Humberto Solás's *Cecilia* (1983) to force him out of office. He was accused of contributing more than the annual allocation for films to making *Cecilia*, and at the expense of other projects. Moreover, the film deviated from the narrative of Cirilo Villaverde's *Cecilia Valdés* (1882), Cuba's national novel, and insinuated an Oedipus complex not present in the original masterpiece. The making of *Cecilia* had direct bearing on Guevara, who lost his job as president of the ICAIC and left the country to become Cuba's representative to the UNESCO in Paris.

García Espinosa replaced Guevara as the new president of Cuba's film industry. Nine years later he resigned amid protest against a proposed idea to merge the ICAIC with the television studio and the armed forces studio, thus weakening its original structure. In 1991 Guevara returned to occupy the presidency of the ICAIC. Most recently, he has had to defend filmmakers like Gutiérrez Alea from Castro's own criticism. In his 24 February 1998 inaugural address before the new session of the National Assembly, Castro chastised filmmakers who were critical of Cuba's social and economic conditions and classified them as counterrevolutionaries. Although Guevara accepted Castro's criticism, he suggested that the commander might not have been provided with the correct interpretation of the films.

REVOLUTIONARY PERIOD FILMS OF NOTE

Regardless of the revolution's internal problems and pressures from abroad, Cuba has produced some of the best directors and motion pictures in the hemisphere. Among the directors, Gutiérrez Alea is the most important filmmaker of the revolutionary period. He came into prominence as the director of *Memorias del subdesarrollo* (Memories of Underdevelopment, 1968), based on Edmundo Desnoes's novel, *Memorias del subdesarrollo* (1965). The film reproduces the life of a bourgeois who decides not to flee the island with his family at the outset of the revolution and remains in Cuba. He struggles between his own cultural development and the country's underdevelopment. The German character Hanna becomes a symbol of an ideal partner, and he tries to find her in his many lovers. All of his relationships with women are doomed to fail. While the revolution was made for the common person and it expropriated Sergio's property, he experiences revolutionary justice, much to his surprise. Sergio is accused of raping a minor of humble origins but is exonerated by the court when the prosecutor revealed her background as a prostitute. Desnoes and Gutiérrez Alea made some important changes to the script of novel and added political essays, with footage of the Bay of Pigs invasion of May 1961 and the Cuban missile crisis of October 1962. These essays make the film less ambiguous than the novel and more in line with a revolutionary cause.

Gutiérrez Alea also directed the *La última cena* (Last Supper, 1977), a film based on a late-eighteenth-century count who was torn between his Christian beliefs and his economic interest in meeting sugar production. The film parodies Christ's Last Supper; the count invites twelve of his slaves to dine with him. As the night unfolds and all have consumed wine, the master reveals a human side, and the slaves noticed that they and the master are not that different. In a moment of weakness, the count concedes that the slaves should rest and not work on Good Friday. However, the next day, the overseer, who was not privy to the conversation, forces the slaves to work, which causes the slaves to protest and rebel. All who dined with the count are found and killed, except for Sebastián, who with the help of African religion, lives to continue the fight against slavery.

Other full-featured films have been well received in and outside the island. For example, Humberto Solás's *Lucía* (1969) acknowledges the role women play in the island's history and therefore responds to the women's movement. The film reproduces the character Lucía during three distinct moments in Cuban history: the war for independence in 1895, the uprisings against Machado in 1933, and at the outset of the Cuban revolution. All the Lucías, and by inference other women, have played crucial and decisive roles in the development of Cuban society. In the present, she is politically and socially active and helps combat the structures of machismo prevalent in the revolution. In this film, Solás explores the changing role of women and their dynamic relationship with men within the historical context in which they live.

The idea of associating the revolution with slave uprisings was first made popular by Sergio Giral's *El otro Francisco* (The Other Francisco, 1975), based on Anselmo Suárez y Romero's *Francisco* (1839, published 1880). The film is divided into two parts. The first reconstructs the novel's narration about a black house slave who falls in love with a mulatto slave. However, the master also desires the slave. Although he promises to free her in exchange for her love, she prefers the slave Francisco. The outraged master, rejected for a black slave, punishes Francisco without mercy, until the mulatto slave Dorotea finally gives into him and saves the slave's life. Francisco discovers Dorotea's betrayal and commits suicide. The second part of the film proposes a different and more revolutionary unfolding of events. In this version, Francisco does not commit suicide but rebels against his master and kills him. There were indeed nineteenth-century slave rebellions, but the film imposes a contemporary and even revolutionary call to action on the past. The film director proposes that Suárez y Romero and the literary critic Domingo del Monte only had their class interest in mind. Although the novel does not report a killing of a white by a black, a narrative strategy that was not available during the time of writing, Francisco did propose radical ideas, and it was censored. It exposed the white master as an evil person, and Francisco as a human, who follows Christ's sacrificial example. In addition, the mulatto Dorotea rejects freedom and racial whitening, symbolized by her master, and elects to remain with the black Francisco.

The theme of Afro-Cubans and marginality within a revolutionary setting was the subject of Sara Gómez's *De cierta manera* (In One Way or Another, 1974). Gómez was the only female Cuban director of her time. The film is controversial insofar as it proposes that Afro-Cuban religions are associated with a past of ignorance and superstition, and they should be abandoned for a revolutionary present. This is conveyed though the protagonist, Mario, who is considering joining an Afro-Cuban secret society, and his lover, Yolanda, a schoolteacher of humble origins. She is a symbol of progress, education, and women's rights—the present and future of Cuban society. The strong images of a wrecking crane destroying old buildings suggest that the past must also be erased. The destruction of an essential element of Cuban society and culture is problematic: however, the viewer will never know if this is the film Gómez wanted to present, since she died before its completion. Gutiérrez Alea and García Espinosa completed and edited the film, and may have altered aspects of it to conform to revolutionary ideology. This may be the case since Gutiérrez Alea introduced changes to the cinematic version of Desnoes's *Memorias del subdesarrollo*. Gómez had close ties to Afro-Cubans and may have presented them in a different light. According to Carlos Moore, she had participated in Afro-Cuban study groups that the government had attempted to suppress.

Pastor Vega's *Retrato de Teresa* (Portrait of Teresa, 1979), with Ambrosio Fornet's script, confronts the issues of the traditional role of women and men in the face of a changing society. Filmed in the style reminiscent of neorealism, the audience is exposed to Teresa's daily life. A wife with three sons and a full-time job, Teresa takes on the added responsibility of being cultural secretary at her factory. This new position causes her traditional husband to become jealous, which makes her feel inadequate. Finally, she throws him out of the house, and he is forced to live with his mother. The new Cuban woman will not mother her husband.

FILM IN THE SPECIAL PERIOD

The Special Period marks a new stage in Cuban politics. Perestroika and the fall of the Berlin Wall forced the Cuban government to open its borders to Western ideas, forced directors to seek support from abroad, and nudged the government to become more tolerant. Gutiérrez Alea and Juan Carlos Tabío tackled the sensitive subject of homosexuality in *Fresa y chocolate* (Strawberry and Chocolate, 1993). Once considered to be taboo, homosexuals were imprisoned in detainment camps known as Unidad Militar de Ayuda a la Producción (UMAP). Based on Senel Paz's "El lobo, el bosque y el hombre nuevo" (The wolf, the woods, and the new man), *Fresa y chocolate* dramatizes the relationship between men in the most recent stage of the revolution. The revolutionary David meets and becomes friends with the homosexual Diego. As his revolutionary duty, the main character accepts the friendship and advances of a homosexual, deemed to be an enemy of the government. Once the distance between the two diminishes, David understands more clearly the life of the other. However, he continues to be loyal to the ideas of the revolution, represented by his very good-looking friend, and a sexual encounter with Diego's female neighbor. Although David represents a sign of tolerance for gays in the revolution, Diego chooses to leave the country. Critic Francine A'Ness argues that "Alea's film is actually an allegory of the nation—not only as it is now, but as it was and as it could be, with some effort, in the future." The film was set in 1979, thus suggesting that David's attitude was already present before the 1980 Mariel boatlift. The production of the film also speaks to the current state of affairs. It could not have been made without Spanish and Mexican support, and released in the United States without Robert Redford's assistance. *Fresa y chocolate* has been well received by the national and international communities. According to Gutiérrez Alea, "*Strawberry and Chocolate* may hold the record for the greatest number of Cuban viewers. I don't know. But at any rate, it is the film which has attracted the greatest number of viewers in the shortest period of time." *Fresa y chocolate* received most of the top prizes at the 1993 International Festival of the New Latin American Cinema in Havana, was shown at the 1994 New York Film Festival, and the following year was nominated for an Academy Award as the best foreign-language film.

Gutiérrez Alea and Juan Carlos Tabio's *Guantanamera* (1994) is perhaps the most controversial of Gutiérrez Alea's films. It tells the story of the famous singer Yosita, who returns from Havana to her native Guantánamo, and after fifty years is still anxious to see her former lover, Cándido. During their reunion, Yosita is overwhelmed, suffers a heart attack, and dies. The film journeys back to Havana, as Cándido, Yosita's niece, Georgina, and her husband, Adolfo, accompany Yosita's coffin. This second journey uncovers the difficulties of Cuban society under communism, which include Mariano, the womanizer, and Adolfo, the schemer who wants to be considered a creative and successful administrator by saving gasoline. After so many years living under a revolutionary government, Cubans have not assimilated a revolutionary conduct and continue to do whatever is necessary to survive. Gutiérrez Alea did not hear Castro's denunciation of films like *Guantanamera*. He died two years before, in Havana on 15 April 1996 at the age of sixty-nine.

FILMMAKING IN EXILE

Filmmaking also has been the concern of Cubans living in exile. Like Cubans on the island, many of exile films are political in nature, meant to reveal a reality that is not represented by island filmmakers. As a group they do not have the support of an organization like the ICAIC, and their films are not of the same quality. However, they have managed to produce some films worthy of reflection. Of the filmmakers who left early in the revolution, Orlando Jiménez-Leal, codirector of *P.M.*, has been active. In 1980 he and Almendos codirected *Conducta impropia* (Improper Conduct), the first exile film to receive wide recognition and distribution. *Conducta impropia* reveals and denounces the government's discriminatory policies toward homosexuals and dissidents, detained in UMAP concentration camps. It includes interviews with leading Cuban intellectuals like Cabrera Infante, Reinaldo Arenas, Heberto Padilla, and Franqui. León Ichaso and Jiménez-Leal's *El Super* (Superintendent, 1979) is about exiled Cubans living in New York. To make ends meet, the main character is forced to take on the job of a building superintendent and describes his life as a Cuban working in this capacity, until he and his family leave for Miami.

Of a more polemical nature is León Ichazo's *Azúcar amarga* (Bitter sugar, 1996), which attempts to reconstruct life under the Special Period. The narrative describes the conflict of a Cuban family portrayed by two brothers. The younger is a free-spirited rock musician who opposes the revolution. The older is an exemplary student and awaits his reward, to continue his studies abroad. By following their lives, the film uncovers the most sensitive problems facing Cubans today. The younger brother is arrested for his unconventional look, dress, and artistic expression. To dissent, he and his friends inject themselves with the AIDS virus, a decision some youth choose rather than confront the daily misery and declining standard of living. The revolution betrays the older brother. A model of the new man, he discovers that no one else upholds the values of the revolution. His girlfriend, who must make ends meet, becomes a *jinetera*, a prostitute, and accepts an Italian businessman as a client. Toward the end of the film, he realizes that his loyalty and sacrifice were in vain. He will not be sent abroad for his professional development, and his girlfriend leaves for the United States.

Sergio Giral's *The Broken Image* (1998) is another denunciation against the Castro government. It captures the exile filmmakers' personal experiences of island cinema without the fear of censorship. It includes interviews with Jiménez-Leal, Eduardo Palma, Almendros, Alberto Roldán, and Roberto Fandero, among others.

CONCLUSION

There is every indication that Cuba will continue to produce high-quality cinema, worthy of international recognition. The movies, both documentaries and full-featured films, provide an opportunity to see the unfolding of time in Cuba and its revolution. Since it is illegal for U.S. citizens to travel to the island and difficult for others, Cuban films provide the world with the opportunity to satisfy more than a passing curiosity.

Cinema in Cuba will continue to walk a fine line between government pressures to celebrate the triumphs of the revolution and artistic creation. Bureaucratic officials who demand that art and culture conform to a particular ideology will seize opportunities to curtail artistic expressions. But inevitably the revolution will move away from the ideological framework once represented by the Soviet bloc countries and embrace the ideas of democracy.

Filmmakers will be at a distinct advantage. They will be able to document this process as it unfolds and express themselves with more freedom.

REFERENCES

Almendros, Néstor. "Pasado Meridiano." *Bohemia*, May 21, 1961.

Álvarez, Santiago, et al. *Cine y revolución en Cuba*. Barcelona: Editorial Fontamara, 1975.

A'Ness, Francine. "A Lesson in Synthesis: Nation Building and Images of a 'New Cuba' in *Fresa y chocolate*."*Lucero: A Journal of Iberian and Latin American Studies*, 7 (1996): 86–98.

Aufderheide, Pat. "Cuba Vision: Three Decades of Cuban Film." In *The Cuba Reader: The Making of a Revolutionary Society*. Ed. Philip Brenner, William M. LeoGrande, Donna Rich, and Daniel Siegel. New York: Grove Press, 1989, 498–506.

Burton, Julianne. "Film and Revolution in Cuba: The First Twenty-Five Years." In *New Latin American Cinema*. Ed. Michael T. Martin. Detroit: Wayne State, 1997. Vol. 2, 123–142.

Cabrera Infante, Guillermo. *A Twentieth Century Job*. Trans. Kenneth Hall and Guillermo Cabrera Infante. London: Faber and Faber, 1991.

Chanan, Michael. *The Cuban Image*. Bloomington: Indiana University Press, 1985.

García Espinosa, Julio. "Por un cine imperfecto." In *Cine y revolución en Cuba*. Ed. Santiago Álvarez et al. Barcelona: Editorial Fontamara, 1975. 37–53.

Gutiérrez Alea, Tomás. *The Viewer's Dialectic*. Havana: José Martí Publishing House, 1988.

Luis, William. "Cinema and Culture in Cuba: Personal Interview with Néstor Almendros." Trans. Virginia Lawreck, *Review: Latin American Literature and Arts* 37 (January–June 1987): 14–21.

———. *Literary Bondage: Slavery in Cuban Narrative*. Austin: University of Texas Press, 1990.

———. "Cultura afrocubana en la Revolución: Entrevista a Elio Ruiz." *Afro-Hispanic Review* 13, no. 1 (1994): 37–45.

———. "*Lunes de Revolución*: Literature and Culture in the First Years of the Cuban Revolution." In *Guillermo Cabrera Infante: Assays, Essays, and Other Arts*. Ed. Ardis L. Nelson. New York: Twayne Publishers, 1999. 16–38

Martínez Torres, Augusto, and Manuel Pérez Estremera. *Nuevo cine latinoamericano*. Barcelona: Editorial Anagrama, 1973.

Moore, Carlos. *Castro, the Blacks, and Africa*. Los Angeles: Center for Afro-American Studies, University of California, Los Angeles, 1988.

Mota, Francisco. "12 aspectos económicos de la cinematografía cubana." "Lunes va al cine" (issue title). *Lunes de Revolución* (1961): 58–60.

Oroz, Silvia, *Tomás Gutiérrez Alea: los filmes que no filmé*. Havana: UNEAC, 1989.

Orticón, Luis. "Imagen y sonido." *Bohemia*, May 28, 1961, 96.

Paranaguá, Paulo Antonio. "Cuban Cinema's Political Changes." In *New Latin American Cinema*. Ed. Michael T. Martin. Detroit: Wayne State, 1997. Vol. 2, 167–190.

West, Dennis. " 'Strawberry and Chocolate,' Ice Cream and Tolerance: Interview with Tomás Gutiérrez Alea." *Cineaste* 21, 1–2 (1995): 16–19.

Museum of the Revolution, previously the Presidential Palace.

Mural of Che Guevara and Camilio Cienfuegos.

Castillo de la Fuerza in Old Havana.

Members of the Brigada Antonio Maceo working in construction on the outskirts of Havana.

On the road to El Cobre, in Oriente Province.

Church of the Merced in Old Havana.

Afro-Cuban religious performances in the Cathedral of Havana plaza.

Church of La Caridad del Cobre in Santiago de Cuba.

Church of St. Lazarus in Rincón.

Bodeguita del Medio, in Havana, a favorite bar/restaurant of writer Ernest Hemingway.

Buildings in Old Havana.

Typical street in the city of Trinidad.

Classroom at the Campamento de Pioneros Ismaelillo.

Apartment building in Alamar.

Woman on wrought-iron balcony in Central Havana.

Cuban man relaxing in chair.

Street in the City of Caibarién.

Balcony with laundry on Ánima Street in central Havana.

Street in Havana with Alemejeira Hospital
in the background.

Central Havana street.

Woman with groceries on Central Havana street.

William Luis (right) with writer Eloy Machado Pérez (El Ámbia). (Courtesy of Hossiri Godo-Solo)

William Luis (left) and writer Daisy Rubiera Castillo. (Courtesy of Hossiri Godo-Solo)

Vendor performance outside of Havana for the Brigada Antonio Maceo.

6

Literature

NINETEENTH-CENTURY LITERATURE

THE ORIGIN of Cuban literature in general and the novel in particular can be traced to Domingo del Monte (1804–1853) and his famed literary circle. A member of the influential sociedad Económica de Amigos del País (Friends of the Country's Economic Society), del Monte was in charge of the newly constituted literary commission, which he transformed into the Academia Cubana de Literatura. He wanted to promote a Cuban literature that reflected the island's culture. Del Monte's ideas were daring for the period, and he encountered resistance from the members of the society who supported slavery. Del Monte is better known for his literary salon, which he held in his home in Matanzas and later in Havana between 1834 and 1839, where he put into practice his ideas on literature and culture. There, he met with writer friends and exposed them to his vast library and the latest European literary currents. He also encouraged them to abandon romanticism and accept realism, which included writing about slavery and incorporating blacks and slaves into the emerging Cuban literature.

To promote his political and literary ideas, del Monte encouraged the slave Juan Francisco Manzano (1797–1854) to write and publish poetry at a time when the slavery laws did not accord slaves the same rights as whites. Manzano was one of Cuba's first national writers, and his works are at the center of the nascent culture. He published two collections of poems, *Poesías líricas* (Lyric Poetry, 1821) and *Flores pasajeras* (Passing Flowers, 1830), and his compositions appeared with some regularity in the major publications of the period. Equally important, del Monte requested that Manzano write his *Autobiografía* (1835, published in Spanish in 1937), arguably the first narrative to document life on the island. In the only slave autobiography written in the history of Spanish America, Manzano describes both the good and bad moments under slavery. For example, the Señora Beatriz de Justis y Manzano treated him like a privileged child, but after her death, the Marquesa de Prado Ameno punished him like a common slave. Manzano also tells us that he taught himself to read and write by copying the letters that his master, Don Nicolás, discarded. Understandably, he wrote phonetically and with many grammatical mistakes. To make his testimony legible, del Monte asked the writer Anselmo Suárez y Romero (1818–1878) to correct Manzano's writings. Suárez y Romero did what del Monte requested, but also altered the events in Manzano's narration. There are two Manzano manuscripts: an original written by the slave in 1835 and a second that Suárez y Romero copied and corrected in 1839. In this other manuscript, Suárez y Romero reorganized the slave's written life and made his autobiography a stronger denunciation of slavery. After Suárez y Romero revised Manzano's manuscript, the slave poet was invited to del Monte's literary circle, where he read his autobiographical poem "Treinta años" (Thirty Years). That same year del Monte and his friends purchased Manzano's freedom. Manzano wrote a second part to his autobiography, which may have been a stronger denunciation against slavery. This second part was entrusted to writer Ramón de Palma y Romay, and it was lost. Manzano also authored a play in verse, *Zafira* (1841). Manzano's literary career came to an abrupt ending after the mulatto poet, Gabriel de la Concepción Valdés (1809–1844), commonly known as Plácido, accused him and del Monte of participating in the Conspiración de la Escalera (Ladder Conspiracy) of 1844. Manzano was imprisoned for one year. After his release, he never wrote again.

From del Monte's salon surfaced Cuban antislavery works. They include Manzano's *Autobiografía*, Suárez y Romero's *Francisco* (1839, published 1880), and Félix Tanco y Bosmeniel's (1798–1871) collection of stories, *Escenas de la vida privada en la isla de Cuba* (Scenes of the Private Life on the Island of Cuba, 1838). Though mild by today's standards, these works questioned and therefore undermined the prevailing Spanish discourse of the period—one that supported slavery and Cuba's colonial status. The antislavery works were censored but circulated clandestinely among the members of del Monte's circle. They represented a new form of writing and were used to fight slavery and the slave trade. Del Monte prepared an antislavery portfolio that included Manzano's works and gave it to Richard Madden, the

British arbiter in mixed courts, to present before the Antislavery Convention in London in 1840. Madden translated Manzano's autobiography as "Life of a Negro Poet." With some of his and Manzano's poems and an interview with del Monte, he published it in *Poems by a Slave in the Island of Cuba, Recently Liberated; translated from the Spanish by R. R. Madden, M.D. with the History of the Early Life of the Negro Poet, written by Himself; To which are prefixed Two Pieces Descriptive of Cuban Slavery and the Slave-Traffic* (London, 1840).

Cecilia Valdés, Cuba's national novel, was also written under del Monte's tutelage. Cirilo Villaverde (1812–1894), one of the most prolific writers of the century, was also a member of del Monte's literary circle. He wrote an early short story entitled "Cecilia Valdés" and a first volume in 1839, but the definitive version of his novel was not completed until 1882. *Cecilia Valdés* was finally published in New York, where Villaverde lived after escaping from jail in 1848 for conspiring against the Spanish government. Although Villaverde included the short story in the definitive work, the first and last versions of the novel are different. The early one documents the triangular relationship among the characters Leocadio, Cecilia, and Isabel; the definitive one does the same, and describes the incestuous relationship between Leonardo and Cecilia, who are half-brother and half-sister, and frames it around General Vives's administration (1812–1832). This version records the suffering of slaves, sheds light on the historic debate between sugar and coffee, and is an antislavery novel. When writing about events in Cuba, his residence in the United States during the post–Civil War years influenced Villaverde.

Early Cuban literature was not written or published exclusively on the island. An important body of work was written and published abroad. The United States became an adopted country to many Cuban writers who declared themselves against Cuba's colonial status. José María Heredia (1803–1839) was one of the early writers to seek exile in the United States, where he wrote and published his *Poesías* (Poetry, 1825). Others traveled to Europe. Gertrudis Gómez de Avellaneda (1814–1873) wrote most of her works in Spain, including *Sab* (1841), about slavery and the sacrifices the slave protagonist makes to help his mistress marry. Gómez de Avellaneda was not a member of the del Monte group, but she did profit from romanticism and the liberal reforms associated with the Spanish Constitution of 1812, which called for the elimination of slavery. Like Gómez de Avellaneda, la Condesa de Merlín, María de las Mercedes Santa Cruz y Montalvo (1789–1852), left Cuba at an early age, lived in France, and contributed to both French and

Cuban literatures. She wrote *Mis doce primeros años* (My First Twelve Years, 1831), *Viaje a la Habana* (Trip to Havana, 1844), and *La Havana* (1844), in three volumes.

The antislavery narrative offered Cuban literature its first coherent theme, but other themes were developing during the same period. Also a member of del Monte's salon, Ramón de Palma y Romay (1812–1860) originated *indigenismo* (literature about Amerindians) or what later became *ciboneyismo* (literature about the Cuban Ciboney tribe), which sought inspiration in the life and customs of Cuba's Amerindians. He wrote *Matanza y el Yumurí* (1837), about the tragic love between Ornofay and the princess Guarina. In this tradition, Gómez de Avellaneda wrote *Guatimozín* (1846), and *El cacique de Turmeque* (The Chief of Turmeque, 1860), about the Amerindian past. But Palma was also interested in *costumbrismo*, or the literature of customs. He researched *El cólera en La Habana* (Cholera in Havana, 1838), pertaining to this infestation in the capital city in 1833, and *La pascua en San Marcos* (Easter in San Marcos, 1838), a controversial novel critical of gambling and the upper classes.

The early literature had a lasting effect on writers in Cuba, and the antislavery theme continued well into the twentieth century. In the second half of the nineteenth century, Antonio Zambrana (1846–1922) wrote *El negro Francisco* (The Black Francisco, 1873), a rewriting of *Francisco*, and it was published not in Cuba, where slavery continued to be a viable institution until 1886, but in the United States. The critic Francisco Calcagno (1827–1903) also wrote fiction and used it to focus on certain Spanish administrators and slavery, as made evident in *Los crímenes de Concha* (Concha's Crimes, written in 1863, published in 1887), *Romualdo, uno de tantos* (Romualdo, One Among Many, 1881), and *Aponte* (1885), which refers to the leader of the Aponte conspiracy of 1812, who wanted to liberate Cuba and emancipate slaves. The black journalist and politician Martín Morúa Delgado (1857–1910) did not consider Villaverde's novel to be credible, and his *Sofía* (1891) is a rewriting of *Cecilia Valdés*. His *La familia Unzúazu* (The Unzúazu Family, 1901) is about independence and slavery.

José Martí (1853–1895) is Cuba's best-known writer and patriot. Like Villaverde and other writers who left the island, Martí's life and works can be divided into two parts: those written in Cuba, and those written in the United States, where he lived from 1880 to 1895, after he was expelled from the island. In fact, Martí's most important works were written and published outside the island. In New York he published *Ismaelillo* (1882), which contains fifteen poems to his son, and with it he initiated *modernismo*, a literary movement later associated with the Nicaraguan poet Rubén Darío. In Cuba *modernismo* recalls Julián del Casal, whose publications include *Hojas al viento* (Pages to the Wind, 1890) and *Nieve* (Snow, 1892). Martí's poetry came into fruition with his *Versos sencillos* (Simple Lines, 1891), an emotional recollection of his homeland, nature, and mankind. His other works include the collections *Versos Libres* (Free Lines, 1913), *Versos de amor* (Love Poetry, 1933), and *Flores del destierro* (Exile Flowers, 1933), under the pseudonym Adelaida Ral the novel *Amistad funesta* (Fatal Friendship, 1885), the acclaimed essay "Nuestra América" (Our America) and numerous articles published in newspapers in Spanish America and the United States. Martí died in 1895, fighting for Cuba's liberation from Spain.

TWENTIETH-CENTURY LITERATURE

Twentieth-century Cuban literature can be divided into two stages: the first beginning with the founding of the Republic of Cuba in 1902 and the second with Fidel Castro's takeover in 1959. The genesis of the republic did not produce the change everyone expected; the evils of the past continued into the present. Authors writing after the birth of the Cuban republic were disillusioned with the outcome of events. They refer to the decay of Cuban society and reflect the mood of the time.

Of this period, two writers stand out. The first, Miguel del Carrión (1875–1929), used psychology and naturalism to criticize false religion in *El milagro* (The Miracle, 1903). In his other works—*Las honradas* (The Dignified, 1917), *Las impuras* (The Impure, 1919), and the unfinished *La esfinge* (The Sphinx, 1961)—del Carrión explored the feminine psyche and women's rights and issues. The second writer, Carlos Loveira (1881–1928), distinguished himself as a student of societal problems and attacked marital infidelity and the hypocrisy of critics who also engage in the same practice in *Los inmorales* (The Immorals, 1919) and corruption that accompanied independence, in *Generales y doctores* (Generals and Doctors, 1920). *Juan Criollo* (1927), his most ambitious work, narrates the negative influences of the period as society moved from colony to independence and the republic.

The start of the century also provided fertile ground for the development of the Cuban short story. Periodicals of the nineteenth century helped to promote short fiction, and this genre can also be traced to del Monte's literary circle. The modern Cuban short story began with Jesús Castellanos (1879–1912), who wrote about local themes, but it was Alfonso Hernández Catá (1885–1940) who gave it international recognition. These two men were the first important short story writers of their generation, and in their work they demonstrated a variety of interests. Castellanos's first work of fiction, *De tierra adentro* (From the Hinterland, 1906), contains stories about the Cuban countryside. His "En las montañas" (In the Mountains) describes the region of Vuelta Abajo and its people, thus recalling Villaverde's *Excursión a Vuelta Abajo* (Excursion to Vuelta Abajo, 1891), a nineteenth-century travel story first published in two magazines in 1838 and 1842. "En las montañas" deals with the lives of black people, a theme initiated by the antislavery narrative, written during the same period as *Excursión a Vuelta Abajo*. The countryside is a concern Castellanos takes up in *La manigua sentimental* (The Sentimental Thicket, 1910). "La agonía de la garza" (The Agony of the Heron) conveys a sense of oral tradition as the story of the terrible occurrences of a survivor is passed from him to a bartender and then to the narrator. "La agonía de la garza," a testimonial of sorts, takes place in the narrator's coastal village, where the victims of tragic events are black coal workers whom the narrator knew.

Castellanos's literary career, though important, was short. He wrote one collection of short stories and two novels, *La conjura* (The Plot, 1909) and *La manigua sentimental*, before dying at an early age. Like Castellanos, Hernández Catá also died prematurely (in an airplane accident), but he left behind a large body of plays, essays, and poetry. He was best known, however, for histories and short novels. His themes included animals, in *La casa de las fieras* (The House of Wild Animals, 1922); psychology, in *Manicomio* (Insane Asylum, 1931); and, most important, culture, in stories like "Los chinos" (The Chinese, 1923). "Los chinos" was the first story of the twentieth century to inscribe Asians into Cuban literature and thereby uncover their presence in and contribution to Cuban society and culture. The Chinese were brought to Cuba after 1847 to work in the sugarcane fields and were still employed in this capacity in the 1920s. The Chinese, as well as Haitians and Jamaicans, worked alongside Afro-Cubans and mulattos. As was the case with blacks and other slaves, the Chinese were a source of cheap labor and were often discriminated against and even massacred. Hernández Catá's "Don Cayetano el informal" (The Unmannerly Don Cayetano, 1929) is critical of the U.S. presence in Cuba and affirms pride in Cuban nationality.

Like Castellanos and Hernández Catá, Luis Felipe Rodríguez (1884–1947) also demonstrated a concern for culture and nationality and opposed the national state of affairs. In so doing, he provided another dissenting voice. His social and political themes influenced many writers in succeeding generations. Written during the Machado dictatorship, Rodríguez's *La pascua de la tierra natal* (Christmas Homeland, 1923), and especially his *Relatos de Marcos Antilla* (Tales of Marcos Antilla, 1932), describe life in the countryside and portray the suffering of the farmworkers, who were the victims of the nation's socioeconomic and political systems. His stories record the customs and speech of the *guajiro* (peasant), and they consider him a national symbol. According to Rodríguez, the *guajiro* and Cuban nationalism were both victims of large landowners and North American companies. "La guardarraya" (Borderline, 1932) takes place in a sugarcane field, and Marcos Antilla witnesses the exploitation of characters similar to those in Castellanos's and Hernández Catá's works. In depicting the sufferings of these characters, however, Rodríguez's intent was more political than that of the other two authors. In "La guardarraya," he criticizes Mr. Norton, a representative of the Cubanacán Sugar Company, for not allowing Cubans and Antillean workers to celebrate Christmas Eve. In "El despojo" (The Dispossession, 1925), Ramón Iznaga, a veteran of the two wars of independence, is on the verge of being forced to abandon the farm his family had worked for generations, when a conflict develops between workers and owners. Faced with the possibility of this loss, Iznaga suffers a fatal heart attack and is buried in a public cemetery, which, symbolically, becomes his only plot of land.

Despite the contributions of the early authors, a well-defined group of writers did not emerge until the mid-1920s and early 1930s, a period of increasing U.S. influence on the island, which included support for the dictator Gerardo Machado (1925–1933). The corrupt politics of this historical moment are depicted in the literature of the era, as is the people's frustration with the government. The intellectual and political fervor of the time was evident in the groups of writers who came together to support a common cause. This was most evident in the Protesta de los Trece and the Grupo Minorista, but also in the pages of the magazines *Social* and the *Revista de Avance*. In the Protesta de los Trece, a group of thirteen writers, artists, and lawyers boycotted the Academy of Science to protest the corrupt administration of President Zayas (1921–1925). The group included Rubén Martínez Villena (1899–1934), Jorge Mañach (1898–1961), Juan Marinello (1898–1977), Francisco Ichaso (1901–1962), Félix Lizaso (1891–1967), José Manuel Acosta, José Zacarías Tallet (1893–1985), José A. Fernández de Castro (1897–1951), Primitivo Cordero Leiva, Alberto Lamar Schweyer (1902–1942), Luis Gómez Wangüemert, Calixto Masó y Vázquez, and José R. García Pedrosa. The Grupo Minorista was a small group of well-to-do writers and artists interested in social, political, and cultural reform. Machado persecuted members of the Grupo Minorista.

Afro-Cuban Poetry

Afro-Cuban poetry developed during the Machado years in two stages. It began as an expression of Negrismo, in 1928, with Ramón Guirao's (1908–

1949) "Bailadora de rumba" (Rumba Dancer) and José Zacarías Tallet's "La rumba," which accented the rhythms of Afro-Cuban culture. These and other poems were influenced by a European rediscovery of blacks and Africa, essential elements of the European vanguard movements. Cubans looked to their culture for the meaningful and authentic expression that Afro-Cubans represented. The interest in blacks in Cuba continued a tradition that can be traced to aspects of Manzano's poetry and del Monte's support for black themes evident in the antislavery narrative. In the twentieth century, it can be seen in Fernando Ortiz's (1881–1969) study of black criminals in *Hampa afro-cubana: los negros brujos* (Afro-Cuban Underworld: Black Sorcerers, 1905), but more so with a different emphasis in *Los negros esclavos* (The Black Slaves, 1916), *Los cabildos afrocubanos* (The Afro-Cuban Organizations, 1923), and *La fiesta afrocubana del Día de Reyes* (Afro-Cuban Festival of the Three Kings, 1926). Works such as Tallet's "La rumba" and "Quintín Barahona," Guirao's *Bongó* (1934), and Emilio Ballagas's *Cuaderno de poesía negra* (Black Poetry Notebook, 1934) concentrated on form, reproducing the musicality of Afro-Cuban culture and the sensuous images of the *mulata*. A few important anthologies helped to define and promote Negrismo. Guirao edited the anthology *Órbita de la poesía afrocubana* (Field of Afro-Cuban Poetry, 1939), and Ballagas's *Antología de la poesía negra hispanoamericana* (Anthology of Black Spanish American Poetry, 1935) and *Mapa de la poesía negra americana* (Map of Black American Poetry, 1946).

The second movement corresponded to a more authentic expression of Afro-Cuban culture and social protest as conveyed by Afro-Cuban poets like Nicolás Guillén (1902–1989), Marcelino Arozarena (1912–1996), and Regino Pedroso (1896–1983). These writers drew on a culture familiar to them and referred to the social and religious life of Afro-Cubans. Guillén, the best representative of the second movement, captures Afro-Cuban religion in "Sensemayá," a poem about the ritual killing of a snake, expressed within the Palo Mayombe religion. Guillén and other Afro-Cuban poets also wrote about the condition of blacks and stressed racial pride, as seen in Guillén's "Negro bembón" (Big Lips), "Sabás," and "Balada de los dos abuelos" (Ballad of the Two Grandfathers). The Afro-Cuban stage of Guillén's poetry was present in his early work, *Motivos de son* (Son Motifs, 1930), *Sóngoro Cosongo* (1931), and *West Indies Ltd.* (1934). Guillén also developed social concerns present in his second and third books and others that transcended the Afro-Cuban experience and encompassed other aspects of Cuban life. *Cantos para soldados y sones para turistas* (Songs for Soldiers and Sones for Tourists, 1937) and *España, poema en cuatro angustias y una esperanza* (Spain, Poem in Four Anguishes and One Hope, 1937), inspired by the Spanish Civil War, belong to this other stage in Guillén's poetry. Works such as *El son entero* (The Whole Son, 1947) and *La paloma de vuelo popular* (The Dove of Popular Fight, 1959) contain poems with social and political referents, as well as other works composed in the Cuban revolution, such as *Tengo* (I Have, 1964), *El gran zoo* (The Great Zoo, 1967), and *El diario que a diario* (The Daily Diary, 1972).

Orígenes

The Afro-Cuban poetic movement did not represent a unified group of writers who met to discuss their ideas, as were those involved with the Grupo Minorista or even the *Revista de Avance*. They were writers who were reacting to literary and historical circumstances, which included the popularity of the *son*, a musical composition with Afro-Cuban influence. But there was another group of writers who would react to a different time. These writers were bought together by José Lezama Lima (1910–1976), the intellectual leader of his generation, around journals such as *Vérbum* (1937), *Espuela de Plata* (Silver Spur, 1939–1941), *Nadie Parecía* (Nobody Could Interfere, 1942–1944), and above all *Orígenes* (Origins, 1944–1956). Orígenes was a group and a periodical of the same name that appeared four times a year to coincide with each of the seasons, edited by Lezama and José Rodríguez Feo (b. 1920). *Orígenes* informed the reader of the most recent European trends and promoted both European and Cuban culture. Whereas the Grupo Minorista was involved in the politics of the time, the Orígenes group members detached themselves from the sociopolitical circumstances that surrounded them and concentrated on the aesthetics. Eliseo Diego (b. 1920), Fina García Marruz (b. 1923), Ángel Gaztelu (b. 1914), Julián Orbón (1925–1991), Octavio Smith (b. 1921), and Cintio Vitier (b. 1921), all important poets, belonged to Orígenes. Contributors to the journal also included Guillermo Cabrera Infante (b. 1929), Alejo Carpentier (1904–1980), Pablo Armando Fernández (b. 1930), and Roberto Fernández Retamar (b. 1930).

Nuestro Tiempo

If the members of the Orígenes were apathetic about politics in Cuban society, the Cultural Society Nuestro Tiempo looked to join intellectual activity and politics. Carlos Franqui (b. 1921) was one of the originators of the group, but he abandoned the society when it was taken over by members of the Partido Socialista Popular, the Cuban Communist party. Nuestro Tiempo, which also had a bimonthly publication of the same name, sponsored literary and artistic competitions, book exhibits, and music and cinematographic events. Harold Gramatges (1918) and Juan Blanco (1919) edited the magazine, which was published from 1954 to 1959.

Alejo Carpentier

Alejo Carpentier is one of the giants of Cuban literature. With the Argentine Jorge Luis Borges, he has contributed to the popularity that contemporary Spanish-American literature currently enjoys. Carpentier began his career during the turbulent 1920s and 1930s, during the Machado dictatorship. He was one of the founders of the *Revista de Avance*, wrote for *Social*, was on the editorial board of *Carteles*, joined the Grupo Minorista, and in 1927 was imprisoned by Machado's henchmen. *El acoso* (Manhunt, 1956) is a story in which Carpentier refers to the Machado years; this short novel narrates the type of betrayal that often occurs in a politically repressive society. However, the start of Carpentier's literary career coincided with Negrismo and Afro-Cuban poetry, and he explored blacks, their culture, and rituals in "El milagro de Anaquillé" (The Miracle of Anaquillé, 1927), "La rebambaramba" (The Commotion, 1928), *¡Ecue Yamba-Ó!* (Lord Be Praised, 1933), "Histoire de Lunes" (Tale of Moons, 1933), "Viaje a la semilla" (Journey Back to the Source, 1944), and "Los fugitivos" (The Fugitives, 1946). The collection *Guerra del tiempo* (War of Time, 1958) contains Carpentier's most widely read stories: "El camino de Santiago" (The Highroad of Saint James), "Viaje a la semilla," and "Semejante a la noche" (Like the Night).

"Viaje a la semilla" is Carpentier's best work of this period. In this story, Carpentier juxtaposes the black world to the white, African to European culture, and chronological to mythical time. For the author, the white world is destructive, and the black is constructive. At the beginning of the story, whites demolish the house that belongs to Marcial, the marqués de Capellanías. Later, an old black man, through some act of magic corresponding to Afro-Cuban religion, sets time marching backward and reconstructs the house and everything else that had been destroyed by time and by humankind. This journey to the source, to which the title refers, is an attempt to negate chronological time, to deny the present and start anew. The story privileges a beginning over an end, mythical time over chronological time, and African religion and culture over Western culture. To negate the validity of chronological time is to eradicate not only the forces that produced the economic downfall of the Marqués and his and the Marquesas's death, but also slavery and the colonization of the island. Thus, the journey to the source provides another cycle and a chance for history to redeem itself. Carpentier implies that the second time around, events will unfold differently and more justly: there will be harmony, for instance, between humankind and objects. He also implies, however, that within the context of Cuba and the Caribbean, the African and Western worlds and their religions will always be separate, though they are components of the same culture.

In "Viaje a la semilla" and in "Los fugitivos," a story published two years later, there are interactions between human characters and dogs. The relationships between the child Marcial and Canelo, his dog, in the first story and between Cimarrón and Perro in the second (in which Marcial is also present) are quite similar. This similarity reflects some overall connections between the two stories. Both of the human-animal pairs distance themselves from civilization and return to an origin; that is, to the natural world and thereby to a time before the presence of Western society. In "Viaje a la semilla," the origin is identified as a time before history and the presence of contemporary culture. According to the surrealists, this past was associated with Africa. The two stories also reveal an identification with children and animals, one already made by the surrealists. In the primitive world described in "Los fugitivos," Cimarrón regresses to an animal (doglike) state. In "Viaje a la semilla" Marcial returns to his childhood and also imitates and acts like his dog. Although these and other stories have historical themes, they also underscore Carpentier's interest in music, as he so aptly shows with his research on *La música en Cuba* (Music in Cuba, 1946). Carpentier's novel *El acoso* closely follows the structure of Beethoven's Symphony No. 3 (Eroica), the same one the protagonist listens to. Carpentier's short stories have similar musical undercurrents.

Carpentier is an exceptional novelist. His first novel continues the interests of his early stories. *¡Ecue Yamba-Ó!* describes Afro-Cuban rites, religions, and secret societies and may be the only novel associated with Negrismo; it also falls into the tradition of the Spanish American *novela de la tierra* (Novel of the Earth) of the 1920s and 1930s. His next novel, *El reino de este mundo* (The Kingdom of This World, 1949) is also about blacks, but in the neighboring country of Haiti. Carpentier's visit in 1943 helped him formulate his ideas about the "real maravilloso" (marvellous realism) in America, often confused with magical realism; the latter corresponds to the German expressionist movement; the former is a combination of the magic of African religions and the reality of Western culture. In this work, he records transitions in Haitian history, from slavery to emancipation and the creation of the first black nation, from Mackandal's slave rebellion to Henri Christophe's ruthless rule over the northern part of the island to Boyer's mulatto government.

However, Carpentier's two other novels of this first period had little to do with blacks. *El acoso* describes the end of the Machado dictatorship, when the protagonist is hunted for betraying his political allies. As with *El reino de este mundo*, *Los pasos perdidos* (The Lost Steps, 1953) reflects on the origin of America, a theme developed by other major writers of the period. The setting is the South American jungle, and the protagonist, alienated from contemporary society, travels to the past, to an origin before time and writing, which he visits but to which he cannot return.

Lino Novás Calvo

Like Carpentier, Lino Novás Calvo wrote about the Machado years; he stands next to Carpentier as one of the formidable short story writers of the century. "La noche de Ramón Yendía" (The Dark Night of Ramón Yendía, 1933), one of Novás Calvo's best works, captures the tension evident the day after Machado fled the country. The narrator, Yendía, who had once helped the revolutionaries, turns informer under police pressure. The narrative is set in the present, and the narrator's plight mirrors that of Machado's cronies, who were also hunted down. The story is ironic in that Yendía thinks himself guilty, but after his pursuit and death, he is identified as a revolutionary hero. Thus, in "La noche de Ramón Yendía," Novás Calvo demonstrates the extent to which political chaos has become part of Cuban nationality, and the closing moments of the story suggest both an end to and a continuation of the turmoil in that country. Subsequent events have proved this suggestion to be prophetic.

Novás Calvo had already dealt with political themes in a lesser-known story he published in *Revista de Occidente* in 1932, a Spanish journal that publicized European trends throughout Spanish America. "Aquella noche salieron los muertos" (That Night the Dead Rose from the Grave) is about Captain Amiana's control over a slave colony, his betrayal and death, and the freeing of slaves. The captain, his control over the island, and his death have been shown to allude to Cuba and the Machado dictatorship (Roses 1986, 67–70). The method used to kill Amiana recalls a failed plot to assassinate Machado that was put into effect the same year the story was written and published.

Novás Calvo's best stories were written before the Castro government came to power and the author's subsequent exile. These stories have been compiled in *La luna nona y otros cuentos* (The Ninth Moon and Other Stories, 1942), *No sé quien soy* (I Don't Know Who I Am, 1945), *Cayo canas* (Palm Key, 1946), and *En los traspatios* (Between Neighbors, 1946). Some of the narratives in these collections eschew the overtly political in order to explore the complexity of Cuban culture.

As Hernández Catá had done in "Los chinos," Novás Calvo celebrates Chinese traditions in "La luna nona" (The Ninth Moon). In this story he describes the Chinese festival of the ninth moon and reproduces the dialects of this sector of the Cuban population. Like other short story writers such as Carpentier, Lydia Cabrera, and Romulo Lachataneré, Novás Calvo had an interest in blacks and in Afro-Cuban culture and religion. In 1931 he published "La cabeza pensante" (A Thinking Man) in *Orbe*, a story about a mulatto woman who uses Afro-Cuban religion to control her husband. His interest in the Afro-Cuban theme is most visible and best developed in "La luna de los ñáñigos" (The Moon of the Ñáñigos, 1932), which describes aspects of Afro-Cuban religion, rituals, and powers. The story depicts the neo-African secret society of the Ñáñigos and shows how whites were attracted to it. The concept of race is transcended when Garrida, a white woman, joins the group and becomes indistinguishable from its members. (In a second version of this story, "En las afueras" [The Outskirts, 1943], the Afro-Cuban element is deemphasized.) The moon in the title is a female symbol and therefore refers to Garrida. The author contrasts the white moon to the dark night, but he also implies that just as the moon belongs to the night, Garrida belongs to the Ñáñigos. He also draws a contrast between a black woman who kills herself for a white man and the white woman who wants to live her life as an Afro-Cuban. The theme of blacks and slavery in the nineteenth century continues with Novás Calvo, who earned his reputation as a short story writer. He also wrote *El negrero: vida novelada de Pedro Blanco Fernández de Trava* (The Slave Trader, 1933), which has not received the attention it merits. It documents slavery and the slave trade off the West African coast of Gallinas and in Cuba, and the life of Pedro Blanco, one of the most notorious yet successful slave traders of the nineteenth century. Novás Calvo models Blanco's life after another slaver, Theodore Canot, as told in Brantz Mayer's *Adventures of an African Slaver*.

Lydia Cabrera

Among the many other Cuban short story writers who merit attention, Lydia Cabrera (1899–1999) is of particular importance. Cabrera was a student of Fernando Ortiz and lived in Paris during the period when texts dealing with black themes were becoming prevalent. With the help of informants, she was able to penetrate Afro-Cuban culture and society and write about many of their myths. Her works include *Cuentos negros de Cuba* (Afro-

Cuban Stories, 1940), twenty-two stories she recollected from her childhood, three of which she published in French translation in 1934, and *Por qué* (Why? 1948), twenty-eight stories that attempt to answer the question, Why? *El monte* (The Wilderness, 1954) is her third and most important work. The *monte* is the sacred space where the living and the dead, animals and humans, nature and people come together. Based on extensive research, the book gathers Afro-Cuban legends and folk remedies. The Yoruba legends and traditions inscribed in her stories reveal detailed knowledge of Afro-Cuban culture and religion. Cabrera also records the Yoruba language in *Anagó. Vocabulario lucumí (El youruba que se habla en Cuba)* (Yoruba Vocabulary, 1957), and stories told to her by members of the Abakuá secret society in *La sociedad secreta Abakuá, narrada por viejos adeptos* (The Abakuá Secret Society, 1959). Cabrera produced her most important work before she left the island in 1959.

Other Short Story Writers

Three novelists of the republican period also distinguished themselves as short story writers: Enrique Serpa (1900–1968), Carlos Montenegro (1900–1981), and Enrique Labrador Ruiz (1902–1990). Serpa's works emphasize the social and the psychological and include *Felisa y yo* (Felisa and I, 1937) and *Noche de fiesta* (Party Night, 1951), but he is also known for his novels, *Contrabando* (Contraband, 1938) and *La trampa* (The Trap, 1956), which describe the political climate of the times. Montenegro's works focus on freedom and prison, anti-imperialism, and the war of independence. They include *El renuevo y otros cuentos* (The Renewal and Other Stories, 1929), *Dos barcos* (Two Ships, 1934), and *Los héroes* (Heroes, 1941) and the novel *Hombres sin mujeres* (Men Without Women, 1938). The work of Enrique Labrador Ruiz, the most experimental of the three, highlights aspects of culture and includes *El gallo en el espejo* (The Rooster in the Mirror, 1953). Labrador Ruiz also wrote novels, which include the thematically challenging trilogy *El laberinto de sí mismo* (The Labyrinth of Himself, 1933), *Cresival* (1936), and *Anteo* (1940).

Other members of this generation include Onelio Jorge Cardoso's *Taita, diga usted como* (Grandfather, Tell Us How, 1945) and *El cuentero* (The Storyteller, 1958); Félix Pita Rodríguez (1909), who wrote *Cárcel de fuego* (Jail of Fire, 1948) and *Tobías* (1955); and Virgilio Piñera's (1912–1979) *Cuentos fríos* (Cold Stories) in 1956. Piñera was better known as a poet and playwright. He collaborated with José Lezama Lima and published collections of poems: *Las furias* (The Furies, 1941), *La isla en peso* (The Weighted Island,

1943), and *Poesía y prosa* (Poetry and Prose, 1944); the plays *Electra Garrigó* (1943), *Jesús* (1948), and *Falsa alarma* (False Alarm, 1948); and the novel *La carne de René* (René's Meat, 1953). He was the secretary of the literary magazine *Ciclón* and also contributed to *Carteles*. Piñera was interested in the literature of the absurd, made popular in narratives by Franz Kafka and in plays by Eugene Ionesco and Samuel Beckett. Piñera's works have been summarized as follows: "His major theme is that life is a succession of terrible blows. Our journey on this earth, Piñera implies, is one in which the human being never ascends toward a superior form of existence but rather descends to a more obscure recess of poverty and pain. . . . The individual, even when given a choice regarding his social or economic condition, consistently chooses the lower form of life" (González-Cruz, 1990 363).

REVOLUTIONARY TIMES

Carpentier's work, and that of other writers of the pre-revolutionary period, had limited interest and circulation. The Cuban reading public preferred European and North American work, made available in translation. All this would change with Castro and his revolution, which transformed Cuban society, culture, and literature. Next to the creation of the republic, Castro's revolution is Cuba's most important event of this century. Shortly after Batista fled the country, intellectuals associated with the 26th of July Movement, which brought Castro to power, seized the existing mechanisms for publication and created new ones to publicize a different type of literature—one more closely tied to a new historical reality. Cuba's literary boom coincided with the Campaign for Literacy in the 1960s and with the Latin American novel of the boom period in the same decade, a literary explosion that bought contemporary Latin American literature and culture to the attention of a world audience. In fact, one is related to the other, as events in Cuba helped create the conditions for the popularity of the Latin American novel. Certainly Castro's policies and the Cuban missile crisis made Cuba and Latin America the preferred areas of study in academic and political circles.

The early stages of the revolution were associated with enthusiasm and overwhelming support for the newly created rebel government, represented by Castro and his 26th of July Movement. However, Castro's support came from other quarters too, and as the revolution matured, Castro shifted his allegiance to that of the Partido Socialista Popular, the Cuban Communist party. Carlos Franqui's newspaper *Revolución* and Guillermo Cabrera Infante's literary supplement *Lunes de Revolución* became vehicles for publicizing a certain interpretation of culture—one that supported a liberal position within the government—and they opened their pages to established and young writers alike. The Consejo Nacional de Cultura (National Council of Culture) and the Instituto de Arte e Industria Cinematográficas (Institute of Cinematic Arts and Industry) offered a different orientation, as embodied by the philosophy of the Communist party.

These two factions clashed after the release of the short documentary *P.M.*, filmed and directed by Sabá Cabrera and Orlando Jiménez-Leal, and it received the support of *Lunes*. Although it appeared to be an innocuous sixteen-minute film about Afro-Cuban nightlife, members of the Communist party, whose power was increasing, made an issue of the film. They exaggerated its importance and considered it antirevolutionary. If anything, *P.M.*, filmed in the style of the innovative Free Cinema, represented a departure from that of neorealism of the World War II era supported by the ICAIC and whose members had invited Cesare Zavattini to teach film seminars in Cuba. It was widely known that Cabrera Infante was an avid fan of Hollywood movies. The debate was captured in an issue of *Lunes de Revolución* entitled "Lunes va al cine" (Lunes Goes to the Movies), which contained pictures of Rita Hayworth, Sophia Loren, Greta Garbo, and Jean Harlow, among other sexy women of the times. The action to censor *P.M.* was, in effect, Alfredo Guevara and the ICAIC's way of challenging the power of *Lunes de Revolución*. Franqui and Cabrera did not see eye to eye with Guevara, Carlos Rafael Rodríguez, and other members of the Communist party, and their differences about politics and art had already been tested during the prerevolutionary period with the society Nuestro Tiempo. However, this time real power was at stake, providing the opportunity to influence culture in the new Cuba. Franqui was the editor of *Revolución*, the official newspaper of the 26th of July Movement and enjoyed Castro's support. The Communist party was the best-organized group on the island, and it offered Castro national and international connections to stay in and increase his power.

When Castro proclaimed a socialist revolution in April 1961, the political pendulum had swung away from his support of the 26th of July Movement and toward the direction of the Communist party. *P.M.* and *Lunes* became the first targets and, therefore, casualties. The three June (16, 23, 30) meetings held at the National Library were convened to make an example out of the directors of *P.M.* and their *Lunes* friends. While some writers expressed an opinion, which included the frightened Virgilio Piñera, everyone soon realized that criticism and dissension would not be tolerated. During the third and final meeting, Castro proclaimed his now-famous "Palabras a los intelectuales" (Words to the Intellectuals), which states: "dentro de la Revolución, todo; contra la Revolución, nada. Contra la Revolución nada, porque la Revolución tiene sus derechos y el primer derecho de la Revolución es el derecho a existir y frente al derecho de la Revolución de ser y de existir, nadie" (Within the revolution everything, outside the revolution nothing, because the revolution has a right to exist) (Castro 1977, 17). This proclamation, though somewhat ambiguous, would be interpreted in many different ways and used as a guiding force in setting policy for culture in the new society.

To combat *Lunes*'s influence, other government-sponsored literary organizations, restrictive in their interpretation of literary production, emerged. The Union of Writers and Artists of Cuba (UNEAC) and Casa de las Américas were the two most important organizations to surface. Each held literary contests and published journals and books. Casa de las Américas was created to break the U.S. literary and cultural blockade. Culture and literature became weapons to combat the cultural influences of U.S. imperialism.

Castro's words and their impact on culture in the revolution precipitated an effort to control nongovernmental and independent groups and organizations. The group and private publishing house El Puente also fell prey to the orthodox ideas of the members of the Communist party. The El Puente gathered many young writers who preferred to accentuate the aesthetics to the political, and government officials accused them of being homosexuals. The group's leaders, Ana María Simó and José Mario, and others were detained in camps known as the Unidad de Ayuda a la Producción (Production Help Unit). These work camps were set up to indoctrinate writers into abandoning what government officials considered to be a bourgeois sexual orientation, which according to their beliefs, could be altered. The ultimate aim was to make these writers heterosexuals and productive members in the new society. Those who were not subjected to the camps were prevented from continuing their literary careers for many years.

Regardless of the conflict between writers and government, the revolution, whether in its early stages, with the help of *Lunes de Revolución*, or later, with government-supported organizations like the UNEAC, created an infrastructure that allowed authors to write and publish their work. Many now-established writers, like César Leante (b. 1928) and Miguel Barnet (b. 1940), claim that without the revolution, they would not have had the opportunity to develop their literary skills. Many others also have welcomed the opportunity to express themselves on the written page. In his *Prose Fiction of the Cuban Revolution*, Seymour Menton surveys practically all of the writers and works of fiction published from the revolution up to the time of publication. He divides Cuban narrative into four stages and periods: The Struggle against

Tyranny (1959–1960), Exorcism and Existentialism (1961–1965), Epos, Experimentation, and Escapism (1966–1970), and The Ideological Novel (1971–1973). Although there are some works that do not fit into these periods, Menton's study continues to be the most exhaustive on the subject. Menton's book is also the first to give scholarly attention to works written outside the island that denounce the Castro government.

By the time Castro and his rebel army entered Havana, Carpentier was living in Venezuela. Shortly after his return to the island, Carpentier published *El siglo de las luces* (Explosion in a Cathedral, 1962), which has been celebrated as the novel of the revolution and refers to tyranny and change. The French guillotine enforced broken promises. The cycles of liberation and oppression were already present in *El reino de este mundo*, but in *El siglo de las luces* he applies them to a different historical context. The novel's ending describes another change, the uprising against the Napoleonic forces.

El recurso del método (Reasons of State, 1974) presents a composite picture of many ruthless leaders of the region and describes the similarities and differences between the dictator and a rebel student. *Concierto barroco* (Baroque Concert, 1974) inverts the conquest of America as a Mexican and his servant travel to Europe. The novel underscores America's contribution to Western music. *La consagración de la primavera* (Rite of Spring, 1978) is Carpentier's only novel to describe events in the revolution, and here he does so only at the end, as he narrates events related to the Spanish Civil War and the Batista dictatorship. Spring, in the title, implying change and rebirth, also refers to composer Igor Stravinsky's ballet score, thus mixing literature and music, which he had done in earlier works. Carpentier's last novel, *El arpa y la sombra* (The Harp and the Shadow, 1979), alludes to music and to Christopher Columbus's proposed canonization and his less saintly attributes.

Novás Calvo has not received the attention he deserved in the postrevolutionary period. He had declared himself an enemy of the Castro government at a time when the Cuban revolution enjoyed wide support. After his exile to the United States, Novás Calvo published one collection of stories, *Maneras de contar* (Ways of Storytelling, 1970), but he was never to receive the kind of attention he received prior to leaving the island.

The Padilla Affair

The most publicized conflict between writers and government officials occurred during the Padilla affair. Heberto Padilla, who collaborated in *Lunes de Revolución*, had become dissatisfied with the established order. He was already a recognized poet and had published *El justo tiempo humano* (The

Just Human Time, 1962), which had won honorable mention from Casa de las Américas the year before. At the outset of the revolution, he and others had attacked the consecrated writers of *Orígenes* (1944–1956), and after the closing of *Lunes* he was critical of Castro's policies.

In 1968 Padilla was awarded the UNEAC poetry prize for his controversial *Fuera del juego* (Out of the Game), which contained poems that referred to the Stalinist tendencies of the revolution. *Fuera del juego* was published, but not without a declaration from the UNEAC denouncing its content. Meanwhile, events continued to change rapidly in Cuba. In 1970 Castro announced his 10-million-ton harvest, a goal previously unattained that was to show the government's resolve. In order to meet this goal, Castro had to mobilize all able workers to cut and harvest sugarcane. Castro did not attain his goal. Although a record 8.5 tons was harvested, the government lost the ideological battle. Officials found themselves on the defensive and overreacted to criticism. The following year, the government made an example of Padilla and accused him of conspiring against the revolution. Padilla was detained for one month. The day of his release he was escorted to a meeting of the UNEAC, where he delivered a staged confession. He admitted to the charges of counterrevolutionary activities and accused his wife, Belkis Cuza Malé (b. 1942), and close friends Pablo Armando Fernández, César López (b. 1933), and Lezama Lima of being enemies of the revolution.

Padilla's arrest concerned many Western intellectuals. His detainment was followed by an open letter to Castro that was published in the Paris newspaper *Le Monde* and signed by European and Latin American writers who supported the revolution, including Mario Vargas Llosa, Julio Cortázar, Gabriel García Márquez, Simone de Beauvoir, and Jean Paul Sartre. The signatories intervened on Padilla's behalf and asked Castro to respect freedom of expression. A second *Le Monde* letter followed Padilla's confession, this time signed by many of the same writers who had signed the first one, but excluded others who felt the need to stand by the revolution at any cost. García Márquez and Julio Cortázar's names were visibly absent from the second one. Padilla provides an interpretation of this period in *La mala memoria* (Self-portrait of the Other, 1989). He has authored a book of poems, *El hombre junto al mar* (Man by the Sea, 1981), and the novel *En mi jardín pastan los heroes* (Heroes Are Grazing in My Garden, 1982), about discontent with the revolution.

The issues surrounding the Padilla affair were carried over to the Primer Congreso Nacional de Educación y Cultura (First National Congress of Education and Culture). In his closing speech, Castro, who reacted as if he were trapped in a corner, attacked bourgeois writers who lived in the major capitals of the Western world and from the comfort of their homes dared to criticize the revolution. He emphasized that the revolution did not need those kinds of friends, and they would no longer be welcomed in Cuba.

Castro became less tolerant of dissenters on the island. Essentially the Padilla affair had forced writers into two groups: those who supported unconditionally Castro's revolution and those who denounced the lack of free expression. The poet Roberto Fernández Retamar, who had also published in *Lunes de Revolución* but had become editor of *Casa de las Américas* and emerged as the revolution's most esteemed literary critic, echoed Castro's position. Prior to the revolution, he had published *Elegía como un himno* (Elegy Like a Hymn, 1950), *Patrias 1949–1951* (Countries, 1952), and *Alabanzas, Conversaciones* (Praises, Conversations, 1955). In the revolution he published *Con las mismas manos* (With the Same Hands, 1962), *Poesía reunida* (Gathered Poetry, 1948–1965 [1966]), *Buena suerte viviendo* (Good Luck Living, 1967), *Que veremos arder* (We Will See It Burn, 1970), *A quien pueda interesar* (Poesía 1958–1970) (To Whom It May Concern), *Cuaderno paralelo* (Parallel Notebook, 1973), *Circunstancia de poesía* (Circunstance of Poetry, 1975), *Revolución nuestra, amor nuestro* (Our Revolution, Our Love, 1976), *Palabra de mi pueblo* (Word of My People, 1980), *Circunstancia y Juana* (Juana and Circunstance, 1980), and *Poeta en La Habana* (Poet in Havana, 1982), works that support the ideals of the revolution.

Retamar will be remembered especially for his essay in defense of the revolution. In *Calibán*, Retamar relies on Shakespeare's *The Tempest* to study the relationship between Prospero and Caliban; that is, the United States and Cuba, the oppressor and oppressed. In a revolutionary reading of Shakespeare's play, Retamar associates Cuba and the revolution with Caliban, and writers like Jorge Luis Borges and Carlos Fuentes with Prospero or U.S. imperialism. Since then, Retamar has reconsidered his earlier essay. He recants his previous position in "Caliban Revisited" (1986) and attributes it to juvenile passion. These and other events were in the background as writers produced their works and inevitably influenced what they wrote and how they wrote.

José Lezama Lima

José Lezama Lima, another giant of Spanish American literature, was celebrated in Cuba as the poet of *Muerte de Narciso* (Narcissus's Death, 1937), *Enemigo rumor* (Hostile Murmur, 1941), *Aventuras sigilosas* (Secret Adventures, 1945), and *Analecta del reloj* (Analects of the Clock, 1953), works that celebrated images and metaphors and mixed the real with the imaginary. He is also known for the collection of essays *La expresión americana* (American Countenance, 1957) and *Tratados en La Habana* (Treaties in Havana, 1958), and as editor of the famed *Orígenes* (1944–1956), which promoted the aesthetic value of art. He was the intellectual leader of his generation.

In the revolution, Lezama continued his literary career with works such as *La cantidad hechizada* (The Magic Quantity, 1970), *Las eras imaginarias* (Imaginary Eras, 1971), and *Fragmentos a su imán* (Fragments of His Magnet, 1977). But it was *Paradiso* (1966) that bought him international recognition and earned him a reputation as one of the most creative and complex authors of the twentieth century—as the Marcel Proust of Latin America. A few chapters of the novel had appeared in *Orígenes*, but *Paradiso* met with resistance from government officials because of its explicit homosexual descriptions. Rumor has it that Castro himself read the novel and ordered it distributed. Lezama's masterwork *Paradiso* is a bildungsroman that narrates the life of the character José Cemí, who is guided by his classmates Ricardo Fronesis and Eugenio Foción, and later by Oppiano Licario. The novel is rich in symbolism from various cultures, including Christian, Oriental, Greek, and Nordic mythologies. The novel can be divided into the following parts: "1) The familiar, which includes the most distinctive events pertaining to the main character, José Cemí, and which is distinguished by its autobiographical flavor and by the experiences entwined around the image of the genealogical tree; 2) one that introduces a world alien to the familiar one, containing phallic allusions and descriptions, and references to man's sexual origins, as well as to their multiple manifestations; 3) one for events that occur without apparent causality, thereby destroying the temporal dimension; 4) one that contains the final encounter between Cemí and Oppiano Licario, his poetic and intellectual mentor" (Ulloa and Ulloa 1994, 193). Lezama published posthumously *Oppiano Licario* (1977), named after a character who appears in *Paradiso*, but this novel did not have the same impact as the earlier one.

Virgillo Piñera

Virgilio Piñera continued to be active in the postrevolutionary period. He wrote for *Revolución* and was an intellectual mentor to the younger writers of *Lunes de Revolución*. He published short stories, *Cuentos* (Stories, 1964) and *El que vino a salvarme* (The One Who Came to Save Me, 1970); novels, *Pequeñas maniobras* (Small Maneuvers, 1963) and *Presiones y diamantes* (Pressures and Diamonds, 1967); and plays, *Dos viejos pánicos* (Two Old Panics, 1968) and *Estudio en blanco y negro* (A Black and White Study, 1970). The short stories in *Un fogonazo* (A Flash, 1987) and the play *Una caja de zapatos vacía* (An Empty Shoe Box, 1986) were released posthumously. Piñera had problems with the revolution and from the early years was persecuted for his sexual orientation. He died of a heart attack in 1979.

Guillermo Cabrera Infante

Guillermo Cabrera Infante is one of the few writers to equal Carpentier in literary stature. Prior to 1959 he was editor of the movie section of *Carteles*; however, he is better known as the editor of the controversial literary supplement *Lunes de Revolución*. Cabrera Infante became dissatisfied with the revolution and has lived in London since 1966. He is the author of a collection of stories and vignettes, *Así en la paz como en la guerra* (Writes of Passage, 1960) and of movie reviews, *Un oficio del siglo veinte* (A Twentieth Century Job, 1963). But his *Tres tristes tigres* (Three Trapped Tigers, 1967) placed him alongside Julio Cortázar, Carlos Fuentes, Mario Vargas Llosa, and Gabriel García Márquez as writers of the Latin American boom. Perhaps inspired by *P.M., Tres tristes tigres* showcases Havana's nightlife on the eve of the revolution. The chapters in the novel are presented as acts of the famed Tropicana nightclub. The novel is a conglomeration of voices, and one of the chapters even parodies the stars of Cuban literature like Carpentier, Lezama Lima, Piñera, Novás Calvo, and Lydia Cabrera. Havana appears as a protagonist, and so does Cuban speech, as the character Bustrófedon becomes the originator of word plays with allusions that permeate the novel. Havana is the space in which Silvestre and Arsenio and a host of other characters intermingle. Havana is also the space of Villaverde's *Cecilia Valdés*, as the reader follows the main characters throughout parts of the city.

The autobiographical *La Habana para un Infante difunto* (Infante's Inferno, 1979) narrates the protagonist's sexual exploits, from his early encounters with Julieta to his conquest of Margarita, while still married to his wife. Cabrera Infante was particularly fond of *Tres tristes tigres* and *La Habana para un Infante difunto*, and he gathered the chapters on La Estrella, of the first, and those on Margarita, of the second, and with "Metafinal," a story about Estrella's death omitted from the first novel, published them under the title *Ella cantaba boleros* (She Sang Songs of Love, 1996). Cabrera Infante's other works include *Holy Smoke* (1985), written in English, about the history of cigar and popular culture; *Mea Cuba* (1992), a collection of politically oriented biographical sketches of many of Cuba's contemporary writers; *Delito por bailar el chachachá* (Penalty For Dancing the Chachachá, 1995), three stories that take place in the same restaurant in Havana of the

1950s; and *Cine or sardina* (Movie or Meals, 1997), which mixes a history of film with autobiography.

Severo Sarduy

Severo Sarduy (1936–1993), whose first work appeared in *Ciclón* and *Carteles* in the 1950s, was an admirer of Lezama, and his fiction shows the same linguistic complexities evident in the master. However, unlike Lezama, Sarduy wrote all of his important work abroad. He obtained a scholarship to study art criticism in Europe and stayed in Paris, where he joined the French literary group Tel Quel, becoming the Latin American series editor of Editions du Seul. He incorporated techniques associated with the *nouveau roman* into his works. His first novel, *Gestos* (Gestures, 1963), describes life during the Batista dictatorship and captures with imaginative flare the activities of a black woman who by day washes clothing and by night is a terrorist. In *De donde son los cantantes* (From Cuba with a Song, 1967) Sarduy is in search of the origin of Cuban culture, represented by his Spanish, African, and Chinese characters, and whose gender identity shifts. Christ makes an appearance toward the end of the novel, and it even snows in Havana. With *Cobra* (1972) Sarduy transcends Cuban culture; his protagonist, a transvestite, searches for meaning and identity in other parts of the world. *Maitreya* (1978) takes the search to Asia, and seeks it in Buddhism, but returns to Cuba and the United States. *Colibrí* (Hummingbird, 1984) takes place in a homosexual brothel in the Latin American jungle, where the protagonist works as a dancer and wrestler. He escapes persecution, only to return and impose on others the same condition that he suffered. Sarduy's last work was *Cocuyo* (Cocoon, 1990), published before his untimely death in 1992.

Edmundo Desnoes

Many of the writers who remained in Cuba and wrote about contemporary events in the new society did so from an ideological perspective, which considered the revolutionaries good and the counterrevolutionaries and U.S. officials bad. There are a few novelists who were successful in describing the complexities of the revolution. Edmundo Desnoes best captures a period of transition and conflict. He was welcomed by Lezama into the Orígenes group, but for personal reasons broke with its leader. He worked in New York as an editor of *Visión* and after the change in government returned to the island. Desnoes had written about events in the revolution with *No hay problema* (There's No Problem, 1961) and *El cataclismo* (The Cataclysm,

1965), but he was most successful with *Memorias del subdesarrollo* (Inconsolable Memories, 1965). Desnoes describes effectively the experience of a well-to-do businessman who, unlike the rest of his family, decides to stay in Cuba. The novel narrates how the revolutionary process affects him directly and leads him to question his upbringing; he finally recognizes the reasons for the change. Desnoes added to the novel political essays that had become part of the film script of the movie of the same name, directed by Tomás Gutiérrez Alea, the revolution's most accomplished filmmaker. Most evident is the insertion of the Bay of Pigs invasion.

Desnoes received permission from the Ministry of Culture to travel to the United States in 1979 and has not returned to Cuba. During this period, other established writers who felt betrayed by the revolution also abandoned the island. They include Heberto Padilla, his wife, Belkis Cuza Malé, and Reinaldo Arenas (1943–1990), who were known to have problems in Cuba, but also Antonio Benítez Rojo (1931) and César Leante, who held important administrative positions in the government. Jesús Díaz (b. 1941), the editor of *El Caimán Barbudo* during the Padilla years, is another famous exile. He was also the director of the film *55 hermanos* (55 Brothers and Sisters, 1978), about the return to Cuba of sons and daughters of the exiles. The exile of these writers set the groundwork for others to follow in their footsteps.

The New Generation

The Cuban revolution produced a generation of outstanding writers who began to write for the first time after 1959; they include Benítez Rojo, Arenas, Nancy Morejón (b. 1944), Manuel Cofiño (1936–1986), Jesús Díaz (b. 1941), and Miguel Barnet (b. 1940). Of this new generation of Cuban writers, Manuel Cofiño was one of the more successful authors to narrate the impact of the revolution on society, with direct language and unambiguous plot. In *La última mujer y el próximo combate* (The Last Woman and the Next Combat), winner of the 1971 Casa de las Américas Prize, the protagonist sacrifices his marriage for the revolution and succeeds in helping peasants.

The Testimonial Narrative

Writers of the revolution are also responsible for developing the testimonial narrative, and its popularity has fueled the Spanish American testimonial literature. The early works were written to document the accomplishments of the revolution, events that were taking place at the time they were unfolding. Leante's *Con las milicias* (With the Militias), the first work published by the UNEAC in 1962, is a journalistic account of men who were defending Cuba from internal and external aggression. Leante compiled his information during the first years of the revolutionary society, when he was a field correspondent in the militia. The importance of this work is not only the sacrifices the militia made during a critical moment in Cuban history, but as an early literature that records a revolutionary process. And as a testimonial work, *Con las milicias*, along with Lisandro Otero's *Cuba: Z.D.A.* (1960), about agricultural development in the revolution, became precursors of what came to be called the testimonial novel.

The testimonial novel is based on interviews with an informant, usually someone marginal to society and whose story has not been recorded or for which there is little information. The writer edits the interviews and writes the book. However, it is difficult to remain totally objective, and the editing process coincides with the writer's interpretation of events. Miguel Barnet's *Biografía de un cimarrón* (The Autobiography of a Runway Slave, 1966) was the first testimonial novel to receive international attention. He interviews Esteban Montejo, a 106-year-old Afro-Cuban who lived during slavery. The novel narrates his life throughout different periods in Cuban history: slavery, emancipation, and the republic. Although the interviews also dealt with events in the revolution, these have been edited from the novel. Barnet's other works include *Canción de Rachel* (Rachel's Song, 1969), about the Cuban vendette; *Gallegos* (1981), about people who migrated to Cuba from Galicia, Spain; and *La vida real* (The Real Life, 1986), about Cuban exiles in the United States. Barnet is also a poet who has published *La piedra fina y el pavo real* (The Smooth Stone and the Peacock, 1963), *Isla de Güijes* (Island of Güijes, 1964), *La sagrada familia* (The Holy Family, 1967), which was awarded a Casa de las América prize, *Orikis y otros poemas* (Orikis and Other Poems, 1980), and *Carta de noche* (Night Letter, 1982), which received the UNEAC prize.

Nancy Morejón

Another significant change to emerge from the literature of the revolution is the slow but steady increase in the number of women writers. Nancy Morejón is one of the first women and Afro-Cubans to achieve national and international acclaim. *Mutismos* (Silence, 1962) and *Amor, ciudad atribuida* (Love, Attributed to the City, 1964), collections that are in unison with the political mood associated with the early stage of the Cuban revolution, conveyed a desire to understand and embrace the revolution's significance. Morejón's early poems are marked by an intimate and personal voice, full of heightened emotions and a sense of her Afro-Cuban heritage. Whereas *Mutismos* depicts pessimism, solitude, and despair, *Amor, cuidad atribuidad* celebrates a life full of love and excitement. *Richard trajo su flauta* (Richard Brought His Flute, 1967) marks a change in Morejón's poetry, away from the abstract metaphors of her earlier works and toward a more conversational style known in the works of other revolutionary poets and more accessible to readers. *Richard trajo su flauta* embraces political and historical themes, which complement those being articulated by government officials. The intimacy seen in *Mutismos* is transferred to poems about Morejón's family, where she also continues to explore the topics of race and Afro-Cuban religions.

Barnet and Morejón were members of El Puente, and this may help to explain Morejón's concern for the abstract, which Lezama represented for the younger writers. It also clarifies why twelve years passed between *Richard trajo su flauta* and *Parajes de una epoca* (Places of an Era, 1979), which reflects a stronger commitment to a revolutionary voice and ideology. This new-found political voice is also heard in *Octubre imprescindible* (Indispensable October, 1982) and *Cuaderno de Granada* (Granada Notebook, 1984). These collections were written after the government became less tolerant with dissension, as represented by Padilla's arrest in 1971, and became forever associated with the Padilla affair. During this period the government disbanded Afro-Cuban study groups, composed of black intellectuals who wanted to study their traditions, and looked to Black Panther party members traveling to Cuba for inspiration and guidance. However, in *Cuadernos de Granada* there is another change in Morejón's poetry: away from conversational poetry and toward concern for structure and form. These poems follow a rigid line and rhyme scheme. Morejón's revolutionary voice is visibly absent from her most recent publications, *Piedra pulida* (Polished Stone, 1986) and *Paisaje célebre* (Famous Scenery, 1993), which perhaps point to a continual distancing from the revolutionary language of earlier poems.

Eloy Machado Pérez

Like Morejón, Eloy Machado Pérez (El Ámbia) is an Afro-Cuban poet. But unlike other members of his generation, he comes from humble origins and only received a sixth grade education; in essence he is a self-educated person. A plumber by profession, his poetry is based on the life and experiences of the marginalized person.

Poems such as "Chacho Sandunga," "Maferefún Che," "Ecue" (Lord), and "Tautaya, remember, compota no va" (Tautaya, Remember, Compote Is Not Acceptable) are consumed by Afro-Cuban metaphors, images, and rhythms—

faces, names, words, thoughts, stories, events, African countries, and voices of Afro-Cuban gods. Others like "Flaco" (Skinny) and "Ecue" also convey a unity between the revolution and Afro-Cubans, according to and as a result of the current policy that allows the practice of Afro-Cuban religions. Certainly, the presence of Cuban troops in African countries like Angola and Ethiopia justifies the synthesis between blacks and the revolution. Still others like "Brindo" speak to his past, as he celebrates his mother, as origin and the guardian of culture.

Machado Pérez's poetic vision offers an understanding of life based on the customs of oral tradition with an insistence unknown in previous Cuban works. Herein lies the strength of his poetry. His writing is not contaminated by a series of values associated with a profound understanding of the act of writing. His poetry, therefore, is not written for a Western elite (which would also include Marxists), but for an Afro-Cuban audience, who understands his work's linguistic nuances and religious contexts. His tropes are uncomplicated and are taken from ordinary speech and life, but they penetrate the very soul of Afro-Cuban culture and religion.

Reinaldo Arenas

Of those writers who became novelists after 1959, Reinaldo Arenas was the most active and best known. He wrote about events in the revolution and was critical of the Castro government. His first novel, *Celestino antes del alba* (Celestino Before Dawn, 1967), received a first mention in a national competition, yet this was the only work he published in Cuba. *El mundo alucinante* (Hallucinations, 1968) and *El palacio de las blanquísimas mofestas* (Palace of the White Skunks, 1980) were smuggled out of the country and published first in French. Arenas became dissatisfied with the Cuban government, which persecuted him for his sexual preference. He escaped detention and went into hiding, fleeing the island during the Mariel boatlift in 1980. In the United States he continued to write and denounce the Castro government until he died from AIDS in December 1990.

Arenas's international standing can be attributed to *El mundo alucinante*, awarded *Le Monde*'s first prize for foreign novels. The novel narrates the life of the seventeenth-century Fray Servando Teresa de Mier and uses his memoirs as a subtext. It describes his travels and experiences, including his polemical sermon about the origins of the Virgin of Guadalupe that caused his downfall, and struggles for Mexican independence both at home and abroad. He writes not to reconstruct history but to subvert it and uncover its multiple facets.

Arenas wrote and published most of his works in the United States. They include the novels *Otra vez el mar* (Farewell to the Sea, 1982), which he had begun in Cuba; *Arturo, la estrella más brillánte* (Arturo, the Brightest Star, 1984), about a homosexual in a rehabilitation camp; *La loma del ángel* (Graveyard of the Angels, 1987), another rewriting of *Cecilia Valdés*; and *El portero* (The Doorman, 1989), about life in New York. He also published the poems *El central* (The Sugar Mill, 1981), *Voluntad de vivir manifestándose* (The Will to Live Demonstrating, 1989), and *Leprosorio* (Leproos, 1990); an experimental play, *Persecución* (Persecution, 1985); and a collection of essays, *Necesidad de libertad* (Necessity for Freedom, 1986). All of these works denounce the political, moral, social, and sexual oppression of Cuban society by the Castro government.

The most important work of his exile period is his autobiography *Antes que anochezca* (Before Night Falls, 1992), a scathing denunciation of the Castro government that he wrote on his deathbed. Arenas provides the reader with his version of events about his life. He uses homosexuality as a weapon against Castro's supporters as he accuses police and government officials of being homosexuals and engaging in similar acts. Before he died, Arenas also completed the novels *El asalto* (The Assault, 1991) and *El color del verano* (The Color of Summer, 1991) and a collection of short stories, *Adios a mamá* (Goodbye Mom, 1995).

Arenas was a gifted writer with an extraordinary imagination. He was one of the few internationally renowned writers whose work is barely known in his own country. Given the nature of his work and his stature in the world community, Arenas's reputation will outlast the Castro administration, and eventually he will receive his overdue recognition in Cuba.

Post-1980 Literature

Since Arenas and other important writers left Cuba in the 1980s, there has been little of interest written on the island, in spite of the loosening of restrictions of previous decades.

Perhaps of importance is Senel Paz (b. 1950), who published the short stories *El niño aquel* (That Boy, 1980) and the novel *Un rey en el jardín* (A King in the Garden, 1983). But it was *El lobo, el bosque y el hombre nuevo* (The Wolf, the Woods, and the New Man, 1991), winner of the Juan Rulfo Prize, that made Paz an instant success in Cuba. The title story was made into Gutiérrez Alea's featured film *Fresa y chocolate* (Strawberry and Chocolate). The story touches on the taboo subject of homosexuality in the new society. The lives of David and Diego, who represent opposites, become intertwined as sexual preferences and commitment to the revolution are explored. Although the story and the film version by Gutiérrez Alea are far from Arena's depictions, the mere mention of the subject in literature is enough to signal even a modest and measured change.

Of interest is Daisy Rubiera Castillo's *Reyita, sencillamente* (Simply Reyita, 1997), a testimonial narrative of the experiences of the author's mother, from her birth when the Republic of Cuba was founded in 1902 to the present time of writing. *Reyita* is of historical importance: It is the first narration to provide a personal and collective history from the perspective of an Afro-Cuban woman, who often demystifies history and provides her own interpretation of events. As a young woman Reyita's aim was to marry a white man, not because she wanted to "improve her race," but because she did not want to expose her children to the racial hatred she endured, including that of her own mother. However, toward the end of the narration the reader discovers that her white husband had tricked her and, much to her surprise, they were never married.

Reyita also talks about events for which there are little research, such as the Guerrita del Doce, also mentioned by Esteban Montejo in *Biografía de un cimarrón*, and Marcus Garvey's ideas and presence in Cuba. The text concludes with Rubiera Castillo's chapter "Nuevas verdades" (New Truths) in which the author sets out to corroborate information provided by her mother and father. After consulting the Achieves in Cárdenas and talking with her long-lost cousin Justa Julia, Rubiera Castillo learns that her mother erred.

The revolutionary discourse is reduced to a minimum and the narration highlights Reyita's strong spiritualist beliefs, which she still holds. As a young girl she was able to predict the start of the Guerrita del Doce. In fact, any time she prays, whether it is to San Lázaro (Babalu-Ayé) or to La Virgen de la Caridad del Cobre (Oshún), the saints always answer her prayers. The interviews were concluded after the fall of the Soviet block but before Pope John Paul II's visit to Cuba, when religion ceased to be the "opiate of the masses."

Though Reyita belongs to the testimonial narrative tradition, its content conforms to the one expressed in Cuban fiction, thus blurring the line between the two genres. It refers to the mixing of the races and the questioning of origins as a fixed and identifiable entity. Reyita's grandmother, Isabel, and her granddaughter's own life respond to the whitening process already outlined in *Cecilia Valdés*, which underscores the generational exploitation of black or mulatta women by white men. The blending of testimonial narrative and Cuban fiction style is mirrored in the blending of the voices of Reyita and Daisy Rubiera Castillo in *Reyita, sencillamente.*

Literature Written Abroad

Cuban literature written outside Cuba continues to be fueled by established writers. Certainly Leante's *Muelle de Caballería* (Caballería Peer, 1973), *Los guerrilleros negros* (The Black Guerrillas, 1976); *Calembour* (Word Game, 1988), and *El bello ojo de la tuerta* (The One-eyed's Beautiful Eye, 1999); Antonio Benítez Rojo's *Tute de reyes* (King's Game, 1967), *El mar de las lentejas* (Sea of Lentiles, 1979), and *Paso de los vientos* (Wind's Passage, 1999); and Jesús Díaz's *Los años duros* (The Difficult Years, 1966), *Las iniciales de la tierra* (The Earth's Initials, 1987), and *Dime algo sobre Cuba* (Tell Me Something about Cuba, 1998) should be mentioned. But there is a more exciting trend created by women who have found strength from the women's movement to question the macho, male-dominated culture, and express themselves as sexual beings, which is still not possible in today's Cuba.

In narrative, Mayra Montero and Zoé Valdés have been most explicit about women and their sexual needs. In Montero's *La última noche que pasé contigo* (The Last Night I Spent with You, 1994), whose title is based on the well-known bolero, outlines the triangular relations among the characters, which includes betrayal, and lesbian sex. She has also incorporated Afro-Cuban religion into *Como un mensajero tuyo* (The Messenger, 1997), about Caruso's 1920 performance of *Aida* in Havana, and *En la oscuridad* (In the Palm of Darkness, 1995), about an American herpetologist searching for a significant amphibian in Haiti.

Like Arenas, Valdés had the manuscript of her first novel smuggled out of Cuba before she left the island in 1995. *La nada cotidiana* (Yocandra in the Paradise of Nada, 1996) certainly would not have been published in Cuba. The novel's protagonist, Patria (the Spanish word for fatherland) significantly born two minutes after 1 May 1959, is disillusioned with the revolution, which is described as a hell of sorts. The younger generation, raised to be revolutionaries, have been promised a paradise, but must suffer during the Special Period, where sacrifice and austerity are more important than ever before. She tries to find meaning or escape through writing and passionate sex. Valdés has also published *La hija del embajador* (The Ambassador's Daughter, 1995), about a young women in Paris who gets involved with a thief; *Café nostalgia* (1997), about friends who keep in touch through the telephone, Internet, and fax; and *Te di la vida entera* (I Gave You All I Had,

1988), which re-creates life in Havana before and during the Castro government, and in which Cuca Martínez's love for Juan Pérez is constant and unwavering.

Cuban Americans

Another literary phenomenon associated with the Cuban revolution has to do with literature published and written in the United States. This literature is written for the most part in English by the sons and daughters of Cuban exiles. This growing and exciting trend complements the literature written by Latinos and Chicanos. These Cuban-American writers bring the two languages and cultures together, and their works are at the forefront of a literary movement that is both U.S. and Spanish American.

In narrative Oscar Hijuelos, who won the Pulitzer Prize for *The Mambo Kings Play Songs of Love* (1989), merits recognition. The novel describes the musical and sexual exploits of the Castillo brothers, who left Cuba in the 1940s as the mambo became popular in both Cuba and the United States. The brothers represent two different migrants. Nestor looks to the past with nostalgia. He wants to remain in Cuba with his girlfriend María, who inspired him to write twelve versions of the hit, "Beautiful Maria of My Soul." Cesar wants to achieve the American dream, which the blond Vana Vane represents. Ultimately Nestor commits suicide. After his brother's death, Cesar takes on the characteristics of his brother; he looks to the past and commits a slow suicide by drinking himself to death. The novel was made into a full-length motion picture featuring Antonio Banderas and singer Celia Cruz and the percussionist Tito Puente. Hijuelos has also written *Our Home in the Last World* (1983), *The Fourteen Daughters of Emilio Montez O'Brien* (1993), and *Empress of the Splendid Season* (1999) but these have not been as successful as *The Mambo Kings*.

Cristina García has also emerged as a significant writer, and has published *Dreaming in Cuban* (1992) and *The Aguero Sisters* (1997). Both novels take place in Cuba and the United States, and suggest that the present course of events refers to the political circumstances of the time, but can be traced to an earlier time.

In poetry there is also a group that should not be overlooked. These can be divided by gender. The women write about their new-found sexual liberation and explore topics that were not possible on the island. They include Lourdes Gil, Iralda Ituralde, and Maya Islas. The men write about political events on the island and therefore are closer to their exiled counterparts who write in English. They attempt to come to terms with their past and view the island from a nostalgic point of view. These and other writers are also aware of the inevitable mixing of the two cultures. The male writers include Ricardo Pau-Llosa, and Julio Martínez, and Gustavo Pérez Firmat. Pau-Llosa has been successful in placing his poems in mainstream journals, suggesting that U.S. readers have accepted his work.

Conclusion

Regardless of the time and historical circumstances, Cuba has produced more than its share of internationally known writers. This was the case in both the nineteenth and twentieth centuries. Cuban writers have also contributed to Latino literature written in English in the United States, and they are arguably among the best writers of U.S. literature. Writers like Hijuelos and García already have a significant following among mainstream readers in the United States.

References

Barnet, Miguel. "La novela testimonio: socio-literatura." In *La canción de Rachel.* Barcelona: Editorial Estela, 1970. 125–50.

Benítez Rojo, Antonio. " 'Viaje a la semilla,' o el texto como espectáculo." *Discurso Literario* 3, 1 (1985): 53–74.

Casal, Lourdes, ed. *El caso Padilla.* Miami: Ediciones Universal, 1971.

Castro, Fidel. "Palabras a los intelectuales." In *Política cultural de la Revolución Cubana: Documentos.* Havana: Editorial de Ciencias Sociales, 1977. 5–47.

De Céspedes, Carlos Manuel. "Prólogo a un exilio prolongado." *Encuentro de la Cultura Cubana* 15 (1999–2000): 27–33.

Giacoman, Helmy F. "The Use of Music in Literature: 'El Ocoso' [*sic*], by A. C., and Symphony No. 3 (Eroica), by Beethoven." *Studies in Short Fiction* 8, 1 (1971): 103–11.

González-Cruz, Luis F. "Virgilio Piñera Llera." In *Dictionary of Twentieth-Century Cuban Literature.* Ed. Julio A. Martínez. Westport, Conn.: Greenwood Press, 1990. 361–370.

González, Echevarría, Roberto. *Alejo Carpentier: The Pilgrim at Home.* Ithaca, N.Y.: Cornell University Press, 1977.

Howe, Linda. "Afro-Cuban Intellectuals: Revolutionary Politics and Cultural Production." *Revista de Estudios Hispánicos* 33, 3 (1999): 407–439.

Jrade, Cathy L. *Modernismo, Modernity, and the Development of Spanish American Literature.* Austin: University of Texas Press, 1998.

Luis, William. "America Revisited: An Interview with Edmundo Desnoes." *Latin American Literary Review* 11, no. 21 (1982): 7–20.

———. "Autobiografía del esclavo Juan Francisco Manzano: versión de Suárez y Romero." In *La historia en la literatura iberoamericana*. Ed. Raquel Chang-Rodríguez and Gabriella de Beer. Hanover, N.H.: Ediciones del Norte, 1989. 259–268.

———. *Literary Bondage: Slavery in Cuban Narrative*. Austin: University of Texas Press, 1990.

———. "Culture as Text: The Cuban/Caribbean Connection." In *Translating Latin America: Culture As Text*. Ed. William Luis and Julio Rodríguez-Luis. Binghamton, N.Y.: Center for Research in Translation, 1991. 7–22.

———. "Historia, naturaleza y memoria en 'Viaje a la semilla.' " *Revista Iberoamericana*, no. 154 (1991): 151–160.

———. "How to Read *Sab*." *Revista de Estudios Hispánicos* 32 (1998): 175–186.

———. *Dance Between Two Cultures: Latino Caribbean Literature Written in the United States*. Nashville, Tenn.: Vanderbilt University Press, 1997.

———. "*Lunes de Revolución*: Literature and Culture in the First Years of the Cuban Revolution." In *Guillermo Cabrera Infante: Assays, Essays, and Other Arts*. Ed. Ardis Nelson. New York: Twayne Publishers, 1999. 16–38.

———. "El Lugar de la Escritura." *Encuentra de la Cultura Cubana* 15 (1999–2000): 50–60.

Madden, Richard. *The Life and Poems of a Cuban Slave: Juan Francisco Manzano*. Ed. Edward Mullen. Hamden, Conn.: Archon Books, 1991.

Méndez Rodenas, Adriana. *Gender and Nationalism in Colonial Cuba: The Travels of Santa Cruz y Montalvo, Condesa de Merlin*. Nashville, Tenn.: Vanderbilt University Press, 1998.

Menton, Seymour. *Prose Fiction of the Cuban Revolution*. Austin: University of Texas Press, 1975.

Moore, Carlos. *Cuba, the Blacks, and Africa*. Los Angeles: Center for Afro-American Studies, University of California, Los Angeles, 1988.

Rojas, Rafael. "Martí en las entrañas del monstruo." *Encuentro de la Cultura Cubana*, 15 (1999–2000): 34–49.

Roses, Lorraine. *Voices of the Storyteller*. Westport, Conn.: Greenwood Press, 1986.

Ulloa, J. C., and L. A. de Ulloa. "José Lezama Lima." In *Modern Latin American Fiction Writers, First Series*. Ed. William Luis. Detroit: Gale Publishers, 1992. 183–196.

7

Performing Arts

MUSIC

CUBAN MUSIC is lively, energetic, and invigorating, but also soft, sensual, and emotional. The music makes listeners want to dance and touches the deepest parts of the soul. Indeed, Cubans carry music in their blood. The uniqueness of Cuban music lies in the varying degrees in which African and European traditions have come together, offering a distinct blend of the two.

Cuban music is characterized by the *cinquillo cubano*, a group of syncopated notes that form a regular beat that alternate with another one that is not syncopated; the first is considered strong, and the latter weak. The *cinquillo* is apparently of African origins and resembles the rhythms of sacred rituals.

EARLY FORMS

The first Cuban composition has been attributed to Teodora Ginés who, with her sister Micaela Ginés, migrated from the Dominican Republic to Santiago de Cuba toward the end of the sixteenth century. There she was part of a musical group made up of her sister, the Spaniards Pascual de Ochoa and Pedro Almanza, and the Portuguese Jácome Viceira. Teodora Ginés was famous for her songs. In 1562 she composed "Son de la Ma' Teodora" (The Ma' Teodora Son), a question-and-answer song and a single-line refrain, that combined Spanish lyrics and African rhythm. The tres, a Cuban guitar with three pairs of strings, dates to this period. It has been suggested that the sisters' mandolin lost two pairs of strings and became similar to the tres. It is also believed that in 1892 a rustic instrument with three double cords was played in Santiago de Cuba. Other Cuban instruments are the Arabic laúd, the Spanish bandurria, with twelve strings, and the Spanish tiple, with five double chords.

The Contradanza

In the nineteenth century the contradanza achieved popular recognition throughout the island. It is derived from the European counterdance, bought to Cuba by the French fleeing from the nearby island of Santo Domingo, toward the end of the eighteenth century. In Cuba it came into contact with African music. As it was molded by local influences, the counterdance lost its collective aspect and was danced in pairs. Two distinct contradanzas developed—one in Oriente and the other in Havana, the latter becoming elegant in character. "San Pascual Bailón," the earliest contradanza dates to 1803.

The Danzón

The danzón, popular during the second half of the nineteenth century, had its origin in the contradanza. Miguel Filde's "Las Alturas de Simpson" (The Heights of Simpson, 1879) is considered the first danzón. This and other danzones are made up of thirty-two beats. This composition begins with an introduction of eight beats, which is repeated and accompanied by a clarinet. José Urfe incorporated aspects of the son from the province of Oriente into his "El bombín de Barreto" (Barreto's Bowler, 1910), which gave the danzón its present-day character.

The Habanera

The habanera, another musical composition associated with Cuba throughout the world, dates to the second half of the nineteenth century. It had its origin in the criollo danza, itself a modification of the European danza. The habanera influenced the work of world-renowned composers like Isaac Albéniz, Maurice Ravel, Georges Bizet, Claude Achille Debussy, Gabriel Urbain Faure, and Charles Camille Saint-Saëns. It also shaped the development of Latin American music, most evident in the Argentine tango. The habanera is written in a two-four beat. It has an introduction that is followed by two parts of eight to sixteen beats.

The Bolero

The Cuban bolero, which spread rapidly throughout Latin America and the Caribbean, had its birth in the mid-nineteenth century in Santiago de Cuba. This sentimental composition has song and dance components. The Cuban bolero is different from the Spanish bolero. The Spanish bolero is based on a three-four beat and the Cuban on a two-four beat. The first examples of the bolero were based on the cinquillo rhythm, and the first such composition can be traced to José Pepe's "Tristezas" (Sadness, 1883)

The bolero was taken to Havana by troubadours from the eastern part of the island, including Sindo Garay, Alberto Villalón, and Rosendo Ruiz.

Toward the 1920s, the bolero combined with the son, to become the bolero-son. Many Cuban composers would honor the bolero by writing in this genre. Gonzálo Roig's "Nunca te lo diré" (I Will Never Tell You, 1949), Ernesto Lecuona's "Noche azul" (Blue Night, 1928), Eliseo Grenet's "Las perlas de tu bocal" (The Pearls of Your Mouth, 1935–1939), and Julio Brito's "Mira que eres linda" (You Are So Pretty, 1935) are but a few examples. The bolero continued its popularity in the 1940s and 1950s, and was sung by musicians of other nationalities, each giving it its own style.

During this period, the "feeling movement" emerged, known for its expressive and conversational style. In the 1950s, new combinations developed, such as the bolero-mambo, bolero-cha, and the bolero-moruno.

La Guajira

Singers of la Guajira focus on themes that pertain to life in the rural areas of the island. By employing a ten-syllable line, practitioners of this genre alternate between a three-four and a six-eight tempo.

NINETEENTH-CENTURY MUSICIANS

Cuba had many exceptional nineteenth-century musicians. A considerable number of them were of African descent, since this was one of the few professional jobs that blacks could hold. Some, like Tomás Buelta y Flores (1798–1851), had orchestras and played popular music. Buelta y Flores was a successful musician who accumulated a small fortune. Claudio Brindis de Salas (1800–1872), a violinist and contrabassist, directed the Concha de Oro, the most popular orchestra of his times. He composed danzas with a Creole flavor, popular among the aristocracy. However, successful black professionals like Buelta y Flores and Brindis de Salas were punished for allegedly participating in the ladder conspiracy of 1844, in which blacks were accused of inciting to rebel. Captain General O'Donnell expelled Brindis de Salas; he was not allowed to return to Cuba until 1848 and was then imprisoned for two years.

Claudio José Domingo Brindis de Salas (1852–1911), son of Claudio Brindis de Salas, became a legend in his time of classical music. He studied with his father and the Belgian Vandertgucht, and completed his studies in Paris. Known as the "black Paganini," Claudio José received numerous international awards. He was bestowed with the title of baron, made a citizen of Germany, and became Emperor William II's chamber musician. He even married a German noble. Claudio José also toured Latin America. But his fame declined toward the end of his life, and he died poor in Argentina in 1911.

REPUBLICAN TRENDS

When the republic of Cuba was proclaimed in 1902, two musical compositions were popular: the danzón and the son. Both of these compositions represent two extremes. The danzón is played indoors, requires a full orchestra, and caters to the upper classes. Three or four musicians play the son outdoors, and to the popular classes. The first groups of son music were composed of guitars, bongos, a base, claves (two wooden sticks), and maracas. According to composer Emilio Grenet (1908–1941), the son "is made up of a fixed refrain of no more than four beats originally called montunos, sung in chorus, and a contrasting motif for voice that does not surpass eight beats" (*Diccionario de la música cuban* 1981, 392). Today the *son* is rich and has unlimited variants. Some of these include the son montuno, the changui, the sucu-sucu, the nongo, the regina, the son de los permanentes, the bachata oriental, the son habanero, the guajira son, the guaracha son, the bolero son, the pregón son, the afro son, the son guaguancó, the mambo, and the cha-cha-chá.

In his song "Son de la loma" (They Are from the Mountain, 1922, recorded in 1929) Miguel Matamoros (1894–1971) plays with the words son (from the verb to be) and son (the musical composition) and sings about the *son*'s origins. The lyrics explain that the singers "son de la loma y cantan en llano" (are from the mountains, and sing in the city).

The son originated in the province of Oriente, in small cities such as Guantánamo, Baracoa, Manzanillo, and Santiago de Cuba, and was taken to the capital by the Soldados del Ejército Permanente (army soldiers), around 1909. At first the son was prohibited because of a perceived immoral character, but its popularity could not be curtailed. Among the many groups that contributed to the success of the son were the Sexteto Habanero, the Septeto Nacional, and the Sexteto Ignacio Piñeiro. Piñeiro is known for compositions such as "Cuatro palomas" (Four Pigeons, 1927), "Esas no son cubanas" (They Are Not Cuban Women, 1927), "No jueges con los santos" (Don't Play with the Saints, 1928), "Suavecito" (Softly, 1930), and "Échale salsita" (Add Sauce to It, 1933), which may have given title to the modern salsa. In 1933 George Gershwin visited Havana, befriended Piñeiro, and relied on some of his music for his "Obertura cubana."

The son is the first modern expression of Cuban culture, for it mixes well the Spanish and African cultures. It would also influence all aspects of Cuban life and in particular literature. This is most evident in Nicolás Guillén's *Motivos de son* (Son Motifs, 1930) and *Sóngoro cosongo* (1931), whose titles contained this popular musical composition and whose contents recontextualized the Afro-Cuban experience and expression. The son, in fact, would extend to other parts of the world, including the United States.

If the son had its start in the rural areas, the rumba began in urban centers and semirural areas with close proximity to sugarcane mills, heavily populated by Afro-Cubans of humble origins. It combines both Spanish and African traditions, but the latter is stronger and clearly present in the rhythm. In fact, the rumba borrows from Afro-Cuban religions, though it does not contain any sacred rituals. Every rumba features a soloist and chorus, who alternate, and a single dancer or a pair. The musical instruments include the clave, the drum, the *quinto* (a higher-pitched drum), and spoons. The percussion could also be made of a codfish or candle wooden box.

There are different types of rumbas. The yambú, perhaps the earliest, is danced slowly, as older people do; the columbia can be performed by a man or a couple, in which pelvic movements are accentuated; and the guaguancó is characterized by a singer who recants a story, usually with a double meaning. As the couple dances, the man is engaged in a sexual conquest from which the woman must protect herself. Some of the earlier rumbas are "Lala no sabe hacer na" (Lala Doesn't Know How to Do Anything); "Tus condiciones" (Your conditions); "Mamá' buela" (Ma Granma), in which the grandmother criticizes the grandson for not going to school; "La mañunga," danced around a bottle; and "El gavilán" (Hawk), in which the participant hunts its prey. Some of the best-known professional dancers of the 1940s, when the rhumba flourished, were Blanquita Amaro, María Antonieta Pons, Amelia Vargas, and Ninón Sevilla.

Other typical Cuban rhythms related to the rumba are congas, comparsas, and chambelonas, which had their origin in the colonial period but were popular in the republic. They can be spontaneous or organized by groups or neighborhoods, and are danced in a line or by a group of people, during carnival or other festivities. The conga, possibly of Bantu origin, refers to the musical instrument of the same name or other drums. It has led to what is popularly known as conga music, which is unrehearsed and danced to the beat of the rhythm. Musicians and participants dance a line, improvising steps. The comparsa is danced by a collectivity and in a more systematic way, with richly decorated costumes, befitting a particular theme. In Havana comparsas fall into three categories: typical (El Alacrán, Las Bolleras, La Gangá), artistic (Las Jardineras, Príncipes de Rajá, Las Fruteras), and extra (Los Dandys de Belén, Las Marqueses, Los Marqueses de Atarés) (Galán 1983, 327). The chambelona is known for its drums and horns and may find its origin in the descendants of Calabar. The chambelona has political connotations. For example, the military rebellion against President Mario García Menocal in February 1917 was known as the chambelona.

The mambo was influenced by the rumba, but also by the *ritmo nuevo* (new rhythm) of the charanga musicians, which dates to the beginning of the twentieth century. The new rhythm is made up of violin, flute, piano, contrabass, timbale, and güiro. Later it acquired a drum, two violins, and three singers and is best represented by the orchestra Arcaño y sus Maravillas. But the origin of the mambo is attributed to Orestes López (1908–1972), a composer and musician in Arcaño's orchestra, who in 1938 composed the mambo danzón. A conga drum was added for the first time to the "mambo" section of the danzón "charanga" orchestration. Arsenio Rodríguez (1911–1972) also added the conga drum to his configuration of bongo, guitar, clave, maracas, bass, trumpet, piano, and timbales. Dámaso Pérez Prado (1916–1989) developed the mambo and became its greatest promoter. Although he began his career playing in cabaret orchestras, by 1944 Pérez Prado was incorporating North American jazz into his rhythms. In 1947 he went to work in Mexico and by 1950 founded his own orchestra. The following year he created his own version of the mambo. He was known for his rhythmic grunts and compositions such as "Rico mambo," "Mambo no. 5," "Mambo no. 8," and "Mambo en sax." Pérez Prado has left a lasting mark in films such as *México nunca duerme* (Mexico Never Sleeps, 1959), *Mi mujer necesita marido* (My Wife Needs a Husband, 1959), *Kika* (1993), *Bambalinas* (1957), *Cha-Cha-Cha-Boom* (1956), *Underwater!* (1955), *Serenata en Acapulco* (1951), *Al son del mambo* (Mambo Son, 1950), and *Al fuego lento* (Slow Fire, 1978).

The mambo, danced to a fast beat, gave way to the slower and rhythmic cha-cha-chá. Influenced by Orestes and Israel López, musicians in the Arcaño y sus Maravillas orchestra, the cha-cha-chá was created by Enrique Jorrin (b. 1926) in the late 1940s, who also modified the *nuevo ritmo* (new rhythm) of the danzón he played and incorporated a faster and well-known montunos (of the wilderness—fast tempo son). Jorrín explained the cha-cha-chá's origin:

> I wrote a few danzones in which the orchestra musicians inserted brief choruses. The public liked this and I continued in that direction. In the "Constancia Danzón" I added a few known montunos and the public's participation in the chorus inspired me to write more of these types of danzones. I asked the orchestra to sing in unison. And this allowed us to accomplish three things: You can hear the lyrics with more clarity, with more force, and you could mask the quality of the musicians' voices, who in reality were not singers. In 1948 I changed the style of a Mexican song, Guty de Cárdenas' "Nunca." I did the first part in its original style, and the second one I gave it a different melodic rhythm. It was so well received that I separated the last parts from the danzón, that is, the last trio or montuno. Songs like "La engañadora" (1951) emerged, with an introduction, a repeated part A, B, and A, ending with a coda in the style of a rumba. Toward the beginning of the composition I watched the moves of the danzón-mambo dancers. I observed the difficulty the majority of them were having with the syncopated rhythms; the dancer's steps were produced off beat, that is, in the second and fourth quaver of the beat (2/4). The off beat dancers and the syncopated melody make it difficult to mark the steps according to the music. I started to write melodies you could dance to without accompaniment, procuring to limit the syncopated. This displaced the accent produced in the fourth quaver (2/4)—in the mambo—toward the first beat—in the cha-cha-chá—. The cha-cha-chá is born with melodies that can be danced to, and the balance that emerges on beat and off beat. (*Diccionario de la música cubana* 1981, 111–113)

COMPOSERS AND MUSICIANS

Cuba has been blessed with many exceptional composers and musicians. The first two of considerable merit are Guillermo Tomás (1868–1933) and Eduardo Sánchez de Fuentes (1874–1944), who carried the nineteenth-century traditions into the twentieth—in particular those represented in Europe by Debussy, Wagner, Berlioz, and Ravel. Sánchez composed a *habanera*, "Tu" (You), and the operas "Yumurí," and "La dolorosa" (The Painful One).

Gonzalo Roig (1890–1970) studied piano and violin, and began his professional career in 1907 as a pianist for the movie theater Monte Carlo. That same year he wrote his first *son*, "La voz del infortunio" (The unfortunate's voice). With Ernesto Lecuona, César Pérez Sentenat, and others, in 1927 he founded the Orquesta Sinfónica de La Habana. He was also director of the Escuela and of the Banda Municipal de Música de La Habana (the municipal band), publicizing Cuban music, and he added his own particular style to musical arrangements. He founded the Orquesta Ignacio Cervantes in 1929, and that same year toured and directed bands in the United States. In 1938 he inaugurated the National Opera, which he directed, and wrote the score for the film *Sucedió en La Habana* (It Happened in Havana). Roig was an activist and brought into existence many unions which include Sociedad de Autores Cubanos (Society for Cuban Authors), Federación Nacional de Autores de Cuba (National Federation of Cuban Authors), and Sociedad Nacional de Autores de Cuba (National Society of Cuban Authors). Although Roig wrote in every conceivable category of music, he is especially remembered for his "El Clarín" (The Bugle), "La hija del sol" (The Sun's Daughter) and, in particular, "Cecilia Valdés," a zarzuela based on Cirilo Villaverde's *Cecilia Valdés*.

Ernesto Lecuona (1896–1963), one of the most important musicians of the republican period, started his musical career as a pianist and graduated from the National Conservatory at the age of seventeen. He studied in New York and in 1916 made his first public appearance outside Cuba. Lecuona was a pianist, composer, and theater composer, and wrote *zarzuelas*, operettas, theater reviews, ballets, and an opera. As a piano composer Lecuona wrote 176 pieces. Some of these are a tribute to Spain and include "Córdoba," "Andaluza," "Alhambra," "Gitanerías," "Guadalquivir," and "Malagueña," which comprise the Andalucia Suite; and "Ante el Escorial" (In Front of the Escorial), "Zambra" (named for a Moorish festival), "Gitana" (Gypsy), "Aragonesa," "Granada," "San Francisco," and "La Habanera." As a composer he wrote 406 songs, some of which are "Siboney," "Damisela encantadora" (Enchanting Damsel), "Recordar" (Remember), "Arrullo de palma" (The Cooling of the Palm Tree), "Siempre en mi corazón" (Always in my Heart), "Dame de tus rosas" (Give Me Your Flowers), and "Noche azul" (Blue Night). He also composed seventy danzas like "Ahí viene el chino" (Here Comes the Chinaman), "Danza negra" (Black Danza), "La comparsa" (Festive Procession), "La malagueña" (The Malagueña [a woman from Málaga, Spain]), and "Danza lucumí" (Lucumi Danza). Finally, as a theater composer he is remembered for *zarzuelas* such as "Maria la O," "El cafetal" (The Coffee Plantation), and "Rosa la china" (Rosa the Chinese Woman).

During the 1930s and 1940s Lecuona wrote music for films, including those for Hollywood studios. For MGM he wrote music for *Under Cuban Skies* (1931), *Free Soul* (1931), *Susana Lenox* (1931), and *The Cross and the Sword* (1934); for Warner Brothers, *Always in My Heart* (1942) and *One More Tomorrow* (1946); for United Artists, *All This and Glamour Too* (1937); for Universal Pictures, *Cuban Pete* (1946); for Inspiration Picture, *Hell Harbor* (1930); for Fox Film Corporation, *Las fronteras del amor* (Love's Frontiers, 1934); for 20th Century Fox, *Carnival in Costa Rica* (1947); and for Columbia Pictures, *When You're in Love* (1937). He also wrote music for films produced in Spanish America: the Mexican *María la O* (1936), the Argentine *Buenos Aires* (1958), and the Spanish *La última* (The Last One, 1937). In 1942 he was nominated for an Academy Award.

Amadeo Roldán (1901–1939) and Alejandro García Caturla (1906–1940) are credited with giving Cuban music its "Cubanness," or Cuban Character. With the rediscovery of Afro-Cubanism, they used the drum as a new orchestra section and combined it with European traditions. Roldán was born in Paris and studied at the Real Conservatorio de Música y Declamación of Madrid. At the age of fifteen, he was an accomplished violinist and won the Sarasate prize for violin. He studied harmony and composition with the Spaniards Conrado del Campo and, later, Benito García Parra, and in Cuba with Pedro Sanjuán. In 1919 Roldán traveled to Cuba to work as a professor in a Havana conservatory. In 1922 he played the violin for the Havana Symphonic Orchestra, under the direction of Gonzalo Roig, and in 1924 for the Havana Philharmonic Orchestra, under the direction of Pedro Sanjuán. One year later Roldán wrote "Obertura sobre temas cubanos" (Overture about Cuban Themes) in which he incorporated elements from Cuban folklore. In 1927 Roldán joined Carpentier in organizing the Música Nueva concert series, which exposed Cubans to contemporary universal music. That same year he founded the Cuarteto de La Habana (Havana Quartet). He also directed the Philharmonic Orchestra in 1934. He composed "La Rebambaramba" (The Commotion, 1928) and "El milagro de Anaquillé" (The Miracle of Anaquillé, 1929), with text by Carpentier; "Tres pequeños poemas" (Three Brief Poems, 1926); and "Tres toques" (Three Drumbeats)—all for orchestras. Roldán wrote music for Nicolás Guillén's poems *Motivos de son* (Son Motifs) and "Mulato" (Mulatto). He was a member of the vanguard Grupo Minorista and joined Fernando Ortiz in promoting the values of the Cuban folklore.

García Caturla was born in Remedios. A lawyer by profession, he was also an accomplished violinist, composer, and orchestra director. A gifted musician, he played the piano, saxophone, clarinet, and percussion. In Cuba he studied with Fernando Estrems, María Montalván, and Pedro Sanjuán and in 1928 in Paris with Nadie Boulanger. The following year his "Bembé (Mouvement Afro-Cubain)" premiered, a work that François Gaillard had requested. In 1938 his "Obertura cubana" won the Concurso Nacional de Música. After 1930 his biggest influences were Stravinsky, Milhaud, and Falla; he considered Stravinsky's *The Rite of Spring* (1913) the most important composition of the century.

As a violinist García Caturla played for the Orquesta Sinfónica de La Habana, under the direction of Gonzalo Roig, and the Philarmonic, under Pedro Sanjuán. Though he played many musical instruments, he was also known for his baritone voice.

He wrote a variety of music that includes the *son*, minuet, bolero, *rumba*, *guajira*, and vals. He is famous for "La rumba," "Tres danzas cubanas," "Yamba-O," and "Obertura cubana," for orchestra. García Caturla never abandoned the law, which led to a premature death: he was assassinated by a felon whom he was going to sentence.

José Ardévol (1911–1981), composer, director, and professor, was born in Spain but became a naturalized citizen of Cuba. He studied with his father, Fernando Ardévol, and with Hermann Scherchen. In 1930 he went to Havana and worked with Roldán and García Caturla. By 1934 he founded the Orquesta de Cámara de La Habana (Chamber Orchestra), which he directed until 1952, and played international as well as national chamber music.

Between 1932 and 1945 Ardévol was mentor to the Renovation Group, made up of his young composer students interested in classical and neoclassical compositions. He mentored these students, who went on to influence Cuban music. They include Harold Gramatges, Edgardo Martín, Julián Orbón, Argeliers León, Hilario González, and Margot and Virginia Fleites. Ardévol wrote over one hundred classical compositions, like "Concierto No. 2 para 6 instrumentos de arco" (Concerto No. 2 for 6 Arch Instruments), "Música de cámara para seis instrumentos" (Chamber Music for Six Instruments), "Música para pequeña orquesta" (Music for a Small Orchestra), and, in the revolutionary period, "La Victoria de Playa Girón" (Bay of Pigs Victory, cantata) and "Che Comandante" (Commander Che, cantata).

During the 1940s and 1950s, the music of Caturla and Roldán was played at the most important music festivals in Europe and America. This was also the case with compositions written by Ardévol, Gramatges, Orbón, and Martín. For example, Ardévol, who wrote more than one hundred compositions, received second prize for his "Cuarteto No. 2" at the International Chamber Music Contest held in Washington, D.C., in 1944, first prize with "Sinfonía No. 3" at the Symphonic International Contest in Ricordi in 1949, and, with Revueltas' "Sensemayá," the Tríptico de Santiago, the best composition in the last decades (most likely the 1940s and 1950s), at the International Festival of Colombia in 1953. Gramatges won first prize for his symphony at the International Symphony of the Americas Contest in 1958, and Orbón was awarded the Landaeta Prize for his Tres Versiones Sinfónicas at the First Festival of the Latin American Contest held in Caracas in 1954.

Leo Brouwer (b. 1939) is a representative musician of the younger generation who reached maturity in the revolution. A composer, guitarist, percussionist, and orchestra director, he graduated from the Juilliard School of Music and University of Hartford. He taught at the Conservatorio Amadeo Roldán and is the director of the Departamento Experimental of the Instituto Cubano de Arte e Industria Cinematográficos (the movie industry). As a guitarist, he traveled extensively. In 1972 he played the guitar for Hans Werner Henze's opera, *El cimarrón* (The Maroon).

Benny Moré (1919–1963) is one of the legendary personalities of Cuban music and the well-established orchestra scene. Born in Santa Isabel de las Lajas, he moved to Havana in 1940, where he sang in local establishments and in the streets. In 1945 he traveled to Mexico with Miguel Matamoros and later joined Pérez Prado, whom many consider to be the mambo king. He returned to Cuba in 1953 to stay, and founded his own orchestra, Banda Gigante de Benny Moré. He sang in all musical genres and in all vocal registers. He was known for his voice but also his peculiar manner of dress, namely large suits.

Before Castro assumed power, Havana was known for its nightlife, which included many well-known cabarets. The most famous is Tropicana, an outdoor cabaret with spectacular song and dance shows, which continues into the present period. Others were Montmatre, San Souci, La Campana, Casino Parisién, Cabaret Nacional, and the Salón Elegante of the Riviera Hotel. Singers such as Celia Cruz, Olga Guillot, Pedro Vargas, Zoraida Marrero, Rolando La Serie, La Freddy, Bobby Collazo, and Beny Moré were regular attractions at these popular nightspots. This aspect of Cuban life is reproduced in Guillermo Cabrera Infante's *Tres tristes tigres* (Three Trapped Tigers, 1967) and in Zoé Valdés' *Te di la vida entera* (I Gave You All I Had, 1998).

NUEVA TROBA

While many of the compositions developed in the republic continued in the revolutionary period, there were new elements introduced that would be associated with the current political government. Movimiento de la Nueva

Troba (The Nueva Troba Movement), made up of groups and soloists, attempts to convey a message to listeners about the accomplishments of the revolution. Pablo Milanés and Silvio Rodríguez are the two most important exponents of the Nueva Troba, and their music became popular throughout Latin America. Since the fall of the Berlin Wall, which initiated the Special Period, younger singers like Carlos Valera have initiated protest music critical of government policies and decisions.

CUBAN EXPORTS AND THE CONTEMPORARY SCENE

Cuban music has been popular in the United States. RCA Victor and Columbia Records launched their record companies by featuring the music of El Sexteto Habanero and the Septeto Ignacio Piñeiro, respectively. Cuban musicians traveled to the neighboring country to satisfy a North American appetite for Cuban music. Cuban sounds were promoted by such well-known figures as Don Aspiazu, who made popular Moisés Simóns's "El manicero" (The Peanut Vendor), and Xavier Cugat, who composed the music for and appeared in many Hollywood movies of the period. Other musicians, such as Machito, Miguel Valdés, and Chano Pozo, a gifted conga musician who played with jazz trumpeter Dizzy Gillespie, spread Cuban rhythms outside the island. In fact, these and other musicians also benefited from their immediate environment. They incorporated a North American music style into their own and achieved the distinct mambo and salsa music played on the East Coast, known throughout the world. Other popular Cuban musicians include Desi Arnaz, who was married to the comedian Lucille Ball and featured on the *I Love Lucy* show, who popularized the conga line in the United States.

Traditional Cuban music has experienced a resurgence in Cuba and the United States. Musicians of the Buena Vista Social Club, made up of singer, guitarist, and composer Compay Segundo, pianist Rubén González, laoud Barbarito Torres, bass Orlando "Cachaito" López, maracas Albert Valdés, trumpet Manuel "Guajiro" Mirabal, and singers Ibrahim Ferrer, Eliades Ochoa, and Omara Portuondo won a Grammy in 1997 with their album *Buena Vista Social Club*, and it became an international success. In 1996 blues guitarist Ry Cooder, who went to Cuba looking for a bolero singer for his Cuban music project, rediscovered the group. Those who wanted to distance themselves from the past had forgotten these musicians, who were popular before the revolution. Ferrer made a living shining shoes, and González claimed that he had arthritis. The album includes memorable sons and boleros like "Chan chan," "Del camino a la vereda," "Dos gardenias," "El carretero," and "La bayamesa." The success of the group led to German-born director Wim Wenders' *Buena Vista Social Club* (1999), a documentary that chronicles the project, the difficulties the musicians had to overcome living in Cuba, and their performance at Carnegie Hall in 1998. The Hollywood Foreign Press Association awarded the film a Golden Globe in 2000.

Since the revolution, and like many other Cubans, musicians have also sought exile in the United States. Well-established singers like Olga Guillot, La Lupe, and Celia Cruz continue to sing for a Spanish-speaking audience. Of these Cruz has been most active and has achieved international stardom. Other Cuban sensations living in the United States include Paquito D'Rivera, who felt the government did not support his jazz orientation.

There is a new generation of Cuban musicians who were born or raised in the United States and are creatively combining Cuban and North American music and lyrics. Gloria Estefan and groups like Alma, Willie Chirino, Clouds, Conjunto Impacto, Hansel y Raúl, Carlos Oliva y Los Sobrinos del Juez, Orquesta Inmensidad, and Miguel Oscar y La Fontasía are a few examples of this new generation. Estefan left Cuba at an early age and with fellow musicians became the Miami Sound Machine, which incorporated Cuban and North American traditions into her unique style. The Miami Sound Machine recorded "Renacer," its first hit, in 1979, and "Conga" its first crossover hit. The group slowly fell apart, and Gloria has become its only representative. Only her husband, Emilio Estefan, remains. In the original group, he played the *tumbadora*, but became Gloria's manager. Since then she has gone on to record popular tunes such as "Rhythm Is Going to Get You" (1987) and "Oye Mi Canto" (1989).

THE SYMPHONY

The Havana Symphony was established in September 1922 through the efforts of Ernesto Lecuona and Gonzalo Roig, and debuted one month later at the National Theater, and its first program included Weber's "Oberon," Massenet's "Escenas pintorescas," Saint-Saëns' "Concert no. 2 in sol minor op. 22 for piano and orchestra," featuring soloist Ernesto Lecuona, Rhienberg's Vision, Hach's Aria de la Suite en re, and Wagner's "Tannhäser." The Havana Symphony was disbanded shortly before Batista abandoned the country.

Two years later, Pedro Sanjuán founded the Philharmonic Orchestra of

Havana, with the purpose of exposing Cubans to symphonic music. Roldán was its director from 1932 to 1939, Massimo Freccia until 1944, as well as Erich Kleiber, Juan José Castro, Alberto Bolet, Igor Markévich, and others.

Classical music has been supported in revolutionary Cuba. The National Symphony and the National Chamber were founded after the Castro take-over. Enrique Gonzalez Mántici directed the National Symphony, and Manuel Duchesne Cuzán was his assistant director. Roberto Sánchez Ferrer conducted the National Chamber. The symphony exists to publicize national and international music throughout the island. Shortly after its creation, the international community considered it to be the best orchestra in Latin America. For economic reasons, the National Chamber Orchestra was dissolved in 1965.

DANCE

Ballet

Cuba's classical ballet is synonymous with its leading world-class ballerina, Alicia Alonso. Alonso, and fellow dancers Alberto and Fernando Alonso, began their careers in the newly formed Escuela de Ballet de Pro-Arte Musical in 1931. In 1936 Alicia Alonso studied at the School of American Ballet. Two years later she performed in two Broadway musicals, *Great Lady* and *Stars in Your Eyes*, and one year later, at the insistence of Lincoln Kirstein, she joined the American Ballet Caravan. She also had the distinction of dancing in Eduardo Sánchez de Fuente's *Dioné*, the first Cuban ballet, performed in the Auditorium Theater choreographed by Milenoff, and music by Havana Symphonic Orchestra, under the direction of Gonzalo Roig.

Alonso formed the Academia Nacional de Ballet (National Ballet Academy) in 1948 and in 1959 the National Ballet, which has taken this art form throughout the country and has represented Cuba throughout the world.

The Cuban National Ballet is best exemplified by its activities during 1977 when it performed in theaters throughout the island and reached more than 20,000 spectators. Ten works made their world premiere that year, including Alberto Méndez's *Juventud* (Youth) and *Canción para la extraña flor, pas de deux* (Song for the Strange Flower); Gustavo Herrera's *Concierto en Mi menor* (Concert in Mi Minor); Gladys González's *Nace un Comité* (A Committee is Born) and *Leningrado* (Leningrad); and Iván Tenorio's *Ñancahuazú*. These and other works were interpreted by Alonso and ballerinas like Aurora Bosch, María Elena Llorente, Josefina Méndez, Jorge Esquivel, and Orlando Salgado.

In addition, that same year Alicia Alonso and Jorge Esquivel performed in the United States and Latin America, where spectators were treated to *Giselle*, which has become synonymous with Alonso's majestic performance.

Two of the young leading figures of the National Ballet are the sisters Lorena and Lorna Feijoo. In 1991 Lorena left the island and danced for the Joffrey Ballet of Chicago. (Other dancers who left the island include Rosario Suárez, José Manuel Carreño, and Carlos Acosta.) Lorna, almost four years younger than her sister, remained in Cuba. Critics have praised both sisters for their talent. Lorna is particularly fond of dancing *Swan Lake* and *Giselle*. Other promising stars of Cuba's National Ballet include Nelson Madrigal and José Manuel Carreño. In 1998, the National Ballet was allowed to perform in the United States.

The Cuban National Ballet is not the only one that exists in the island. There are others like the Ballet de Camagüey, which dates to 1967, which Vicentina de la Torre founded and directed. Other directors include Joaquín Banegas, Silvia Marichal, and Fernando Alonso.

Popular Dance

A different expression of dance comes from the Conjunto Folklórico Nacional de Cuba, founded by folklorist Rogelio Martínez Furé and Mexican choreographer Rodolfo Reyes, which brings popular musical and dance expressions of Cubans to the stage. Martínez Furé envisioned more than a mere representation of popular traditions of music and dance—one that responded to an expression present in the local communities from which they emerged. Among their many tasks, researchers of the Conjunto incorporate old and little-known materials, as well as contemporary expressions, relying on informants for authentication. They have demystified many superficial aspects associated with Cuba's folklore and added the dynamic element inherent in any popular expression. The Conjunto began auditioning in April 1962 and on 25 July 1963, it performed "Yorubá, Congo, Rumbas y Comparsas." Other dances were soon added, like "Abuduá, Música popular," "Yorubá-iyesá" (1965); "Alafin de Oyó" (1971); "Baile de palo," "Makuta," "Zapateo," "Baile de chancletas," and "Mi Comité" (1977); "Arará," "Guateque," "Tríptico oriental" (1979), "Odebí," "El cazador," "Trinitarias" (1982), and "Palenque" (1985). These dances have been arranged and performed by closely following their African traditions. In twenty-three years, the Conjunto has been on tour twenty-five times, visiting thirty-one countries, and has amassed a long list of awards and prizes.

The Danza Nacional de Cuba (national dance) was established the year Castro took power, though modern dance had its origin in the 1930s. The

Danza Nacional has included in its repertoire elements of Cuban culture that underscore its African heritage, as represented by Afro-Cuban traditions. And like the Conjunto, it has been successful in international festivals. Its repertoire has included Arnaldo Paterson's *Elaboración técnica* (Technical Elaboration); Eduardo Rivero's *Sulkary y Okantomi*; Víctor Cuéllar's *Panorama de la danza y la música cubanas* (Panorama of Cuban Music and Dance); and Gerardo Lastra's *Negra Fuló* (Black Fuló) and *Suite afrocubana* (Afro-Cuban Suite).

THEATER

Havana's Coliseo, built in 1775, was Cuba's first theater. It was built through the initiative of Captain General Marqués de la Torre and directed by Antonio Fernández Trevejo. The Coliseo was renovated in 1803 and reopened under a new name, the Príncipe Theatre.

In 1834 the Tacón Theater, named after the infamous Captain General Miguel Tacón, was constructed with slave labor, a tax levied on slaves entering the island, and resources provided by Francisco Marty y Torrens, who held the fish monopoly. In 1838 the Tacón Theater opened its doors with carnival dances. Francisco Covarrubias (1774–1850), who began as an actor, became the most important playwright of the period, staging many of his dramas in the theater, which were based on Spanish models, including those of Ramón de la Cruz. He wrote a number of popular *sainetes*, including "La valla de los gallos" (The Rooster's Cockpit, 1814), "Las tertulias de La Habana" (The Havana Literary Circle, 1814), and "Los velorios de La Habana" (The Havana Wakes, 1818). In 1846 the theater featured Italian and French operas and Spanish *zarzuelas*.

The famed Alhambra Theatre, founded in 1890, staged *zarzuelas, juguetes, revistas*, and *comedias*. Actresses like Blanca Becerra, Luz Gis, Blanca Vázquez, Hortesia López, and actors like Arquímedes Pous and Ramón Espigul debuted there. Regino López was director, Federico Villoch, writer, Miguel Arias, stage director, and Jorge Anckermann, musical arranger. Miguel Barnet's *Canción de Rachel* (Rachel's Song, 1969) is about the Cuban *vedette* who performed at the Alhambra Theater. The theater developed its own vernacular genre known as "Alambresco" (Alhambra-like), which was based on the *bufo* Theatre of the previous century. However, the theater was demolished a few years after Machado's downfall, in 1935. The genre that became synonymous with the Alhambra was continued at the Martí Theater (1931–1936), which staged well-known *zarzuelas* such as "Cecilia Valdés," "La perla del Caribe," and "María Belén Chacón."

The Sociedad de Fomento del Teatro (1912) and the Teatro Cubano (1914) were products of the republican period, founded for the purpose of creating a more traditional theater environment on the island and promoting plays by José Antonio Ramos.

Theater in Cuba evolved during the 1920s, a period that coincided with widespread receptivity to Cuban popuplar music. This was also a time in which the record, movie, and radio industries developed, and there was an increase in the number of Cuban songs, orchestras, and singers.

During this period, the Teatro Operático hosted international figures visiting Cuba. French and Spanish *zarzuelas* and comedy companies performed there, as did Italian tenor Enrico Caruso, Amelita Galli Cursi, and María Barrientos, among many others. The Tacón Theater later became the National Theater. In fact, in June 1920 a bomb exploded while Caruso sang at the National Theater; luckily nothing happened. (This is the subject of Mayra Montero's *Como un mensajero tuyo* [The Messenger, 1998].) During the 1920s, the National Theater staged operas like Guiseppe Verdi's *Rigoletto* and *Aida*, Gaetano Donizetti's *La Favorita*, and Gioacchino Rossini's *The Barber of Seville*. (In 1962 it became the García Lorca Theatre, and the seat of operas and ballets.)

Similar activities were taking place in theaters around the country. In Havana events were staged in Payret, Teatro Nacional, Teatro Martí (previously Irojoa), Teatro Comedia, and Teatro Actualidades; in Pinar del Río, Teatro Riesgo, in Matanzas Sauto, Velasco, and Niza; in Santa Clara Teatro Caridad; in Cienfuegos Terry; in Camagüey Principal; and in Santiago de Cuba Casa Blanca.

In 1936 the theater group Cueva was born, made up of students, professors, and writers. More professional groups emerged, with help from exiles fleeing conditions in Europe, including the Spanish Civil War, around the Teatro Universitario, la Academia de Arte Dramático, el Patronato del Teatro, Farseros, Prometeo, among others. These better-trained companies permitted the staging of works like Carlos Felipe's *El chino* (The Chinaman, 1959), Virgilio Piñera's *Electra Garrigó* (1943), and Romando Ferrer's *Lila, la mariposa* (Lila, the Butterfly, 1954).

Of the dramatists whose works were staged during the early republican period, José Antonio Ramos (1885–1946) should be noted. His *Tembladera* (Shaker, 1918) had a social and political context and reflected U.S. influence on the island. In the 1950s Virgilio Piñera and Carlos Felipe were particularly successful. Piñera is credited with introducing the theater of the absurd with his play *Electra Garrigó*.

The Teatro Popular was founded between 1942 and 1943, but was forced to close two years later. This theater was associated with the Feración de Trabajadores de La Habana and other labor unions. Made up of professionals and amateurs, its mission was to serve the masses by providing theater-going opportunities to those who did not possess the means to do so. The works staged pertained to social problems. The Teatro Popular was known for its portable stages, which allowed members to transport their stages to different areas and regions of the country.

Theater received support in Cuba with the creation of the Teatro Nacional. Soon after the revolution, an increasing number of playwrights emerged; some of them included Abelardo Estorino, José R. Brene, Nicolás Dorr, José Triana, Manuel Reguera Saumell, Héctor Quintero, and Antón Arrufat. These and other playwrights would bring much deserved attention to Cuban theater.

The official policy declared at the Primer Seminario Nacional de Danza y Teatro in 1967 was that theater responds to reality and seeks the individual's responsibility within society.

Theater has not been without certain problems and consequences. For example, performances of Eugenio Hernández Espinosa's *María Antonia* (1967), which presents strong black characters and undermines the traditional images of Afro-Cubans, were cancelled. A similar situation occurred with Antón Arrufat's *Siete contra Tebas* (Seven against Thebes, 1968), the UNEAC prize in 1968, which was also censored. Government officials interpreted it as criticizing the lack of freedom on the island. The play, which circulated clandestinely on the island, was not performed until 1970, and then not in Cuba, but in Mexico, and directed by Salvador Flores with students from the Marta Verduzco group. Hernández and Arrufat are two playwrights who encountered problems for daring to express their ideas, which challenged the government's control over the arts.

The Escambray Theater was created in 1971, after the Primer Congreso Nacional de Educación y Cultura, for the purpose of considering culture as an arm of the revolution and transforming reality. The theater created its own repertory and was known for its unique style, and stagecraft. By the time of the Special Period, Cuban theater had taken a different direction, bringing it closer to the theater of the absurd and unmasking Cuba's political reality. Most recently, the Escambray Theater does not reproduce history as it occurred but as fragmented and revealed by the characters. Abelardo Estorino's *Morir del cuento* (To Die from the Story, 1983) represents an important moment in the new trend. He does not reproduce history as it occurred; rather he dismantles it to show the complexities of history. Rafael González Rodríguez's *Molinos de viento* (Windmills, 1983) is an example of recent Escambray Theater. The playwright is critical of mistakes in Cuba's educational system. Rafael González Rodríguez's *Calle Cuba 80 bajo la lluvia* (80 Cuba Street in the Rain, 1988) is about the younger and older generations, the present and the past, and the ethical issues each represents. Reinaldo Montero's *Fabriles* (Manufacturing, 1992) is about a factory worker, Emilio, who has conversations with God about Cuba's technological problems, and Enrique, who in Italy forgets about his job and chases women. Of particular interest are Alberto Pedro's *Weekend en Bahía* (1986), about Cuban exiles and islanders, and *Manteca* (Lard, 1993), about the collapse of socialism and three brothers' need to make ends meet.

Cuban resourcefulness is also evident in the theater. In 1988 Víctor Varela performed his play *La cuarta pared* (The Fourth Wall) in an apartment as an alternative theater, to an audience of eight. This led to the formation of Teatro del Obstáculo, which uses scarcity as part of their production. Some of the Cuban actors who developed after the revolution include Albio Paz, Raúl Pomares, Flora Lauten, Arturo Estévez, René Ariza, Freddy Artiles, Eduardo Roberño, Jesús Díaz, José Carril, and Rogelio Martínez Furé. Some no longer live in Cuba.

Dolores Prida, who dramatizes the exile Cuban experience, as Cuban and North American cultures meet, has continued the tradition of Cuban theater in the United States. At the Repertorio Español in New York City, she has staged *Beautiful Señoritas*, *Coser y Cantar* (To Sew and Sing, 1991), and *Casa Propia* (A House of Her Own, 1999), the last about a Cuban family wanting to buy a house in an ethnically diverse community. It addresses others that have to do with machismo, feminism, bilingualism, and others pertinent to both Cuban and U.S. cultures.

REFERENCES

Ardévol, José. *Introducción a Cuba: La música*. Havana: Instituto del Libro, 1969.

Benítez Rojo, Antonio. "The Role of Music in the Emergence of Afro-Cuban Culture." *Research in African Literatures* 29, 1 (Spring 1998): 179–184.

Blutstein, Howard I., et al. *Area Handbook for Cuba*. Washington, D.C.: U.S. Government Printing Office, 1971.

Boudet, Rosa Ileana. "New Playwrights, New Challenges: Current Cuban Theatre." In *Bridging Enigma: Cubans on Cuba*, ed. Ambrosio Fornet. *The South Atlantic Quarterly* 96, 1 (1997): 31–51.

Brower, Leo. *La música, lo cubano y la innovación*. Havana: Editorial Letras Cubanas, 1992.

Carpentier, Alejo. *La música en Cuba*. Mexico: Fondo de Cultura Económica, 1946.

Collazo, Bobby. *La última noche que pasé contigo: 40 años de farándula cubana*. San Juan: Editorial Cubanacán, 1987.

Díaz Ayala, Cristóbal. *Cuando salí de la Habana:* 1898–1997 *cien años de música cubana por el mundo.* San Juan, P.R.: Fundación Musicalia, 1998.

————. "Intercambios, diásporas, fusiones." *Encuentro de la Cultura Cubana* 15 (1999–2000): 86–95.

Diccionario de la literatura cubana. Havana: Editorial Letras Cubanas, 1980.

Galán, Natalio. *Cuba y sus sones.* Valencia: Pre-Texto/Música, 1983.

González Freire, Natividad. *Teatro cubano (1927–1961).* Havana: Ministerio de Relaciones Exteriores, 1961.

Hidalgo, Narciso J. Blacks. "The Son and AfroCuban Discourse." Ph.D. dissertation, Indiana University, 1999.

"Homenaje a Virgilio Piñera." *Encuentro de la Cultura Cubana* 14 (1999): 3–44.

Luis, Carlos M. *El oficio de la mirada.* Miami: Ediciones Universal, 1998.

Martínez Furé, Rogelio. *Diálogos imaginarios.* Havana: Editorial Letras Cubanas, 1997.

Mosquera, Gerardo. "De regreso." *Encuentro de la Cultura Cubana* 15 (1999–2000): 147–153.

Orovio, Helio. *El bolero cubano.* Santiago de Cuba: Editorial Oriente, 1994.

————. *La conga, la rumba: columbia, yambú y guaguancó.* Santiago de Cuba: Editorial Oriente, 1994.

————. *El danzón, el mambo y el chachachá.* Santiago de Cuba: Editorial Oriente, 1994.

————. *Diccionario de la música cubana.* Havana: Editorial Letras Cubanas, 1981.

————. *El son, la guaracha y la salsa.* Santiago de Cuba: Editorial Oriente, 1994.

Pérez Firmat, Gustavo. *Life on the Hyphen: The Cuban-American Way.* Austin: University of Texas Press, 1994.

Perfiles culturales: Cuba 1977. Havana: Editorial Orbe, 1978.

Prida, Dolores. "El teatro Cubano en Estudos Unidos." *Encuentro de la Cultura Cubana* 15 (1999–2000): 137–141.

8

Art

Nineteenth-Century Painting

BISHOP Juan José Díaz de Espada y Landa (1756–1832), of the diocese of Havana, was the first important promoter of art in the nineteenth century. A friend of Spanish painter Francisco José de Goya y Lucientes (Goya), he was aware of the role art played for the Catholic church, a tradition that continued into the nineteenth century. It has been said that when the bishop was named to the diocese in 1802, he carried with him a valuable collection of paintings.

Cuba's first art school, the Academia de San Alejandro, was founded by the Intendente (Quartermaster general) Alejandro Ramírez in 1818 at the request of the French painter Juan Bautista Vermay (1786–1833), who also became its first director. Vermay, who had arrived in Cuba with recommendations from Goya, was known for his frescoes in the Havana Cathedral and some canvases in the Edificio del Templete (Small Temple). His portrait of the Manrique de Lara family, painted in a simple setting, is a departure from the more elegant style of the period. Under Vermay, for lack of resources the school emphasized drawing. At the Academia de San Alejandro, Vermay continued the teachings of his mentor, French painter Jacques-Louis David (1748–1825), and promoted neoclassicism. Unlike him, Vermay's successors were not interested in themes that pertained to the island or in developing a Cuban art, preferring to concentrate on European artistic traditions.

In the nineteenth century, two artistic directions developed. One was influenced by the tobacco and sugar economies, and developed into a realistic current that included the theme of the nation and its people. The other was more formal. It was represented by Vermay and his disciples Colson and J. Leclerc and was associated with the San Alejandro Academy. This other current celebrated beauty and embraced the French-Italian academic style.

The Frenchman Edward Laplante made the first efforts to reproduce local Cuban customs with illustrations of *ingenios* (sugar mills) and life on the plantation. Some illustrations were included in J.G. Cantero and Laplante's *Los ingenios de Cuba* (The Cuban Sugar Mills, 1857). The presence of blacks, which became a constant in Cuban art, was popularized by etchers like Laplante and his countrymen Hipólito Garneray (1787–1858) and Federico Mialhe (1810–1881), the Basque Víctor Patricio de Landaluze (1828–1877), and in the lithographs of cigar boxes. Garneray's *Vie d'une habitation pres de La Havane* (View from a Room Near Havana) illustrates slaves working in a sugarcane field under the watchful eye of the overseer. Mialhe is known for his lithographs of colonial life entitled *Isla de Cuba pintoresca* (The Picturesque Island of Cuba, 1839–1842) and *Viaje pintoresco alrededor de la isla de Cuba* (Picturesque Journey Around the Island of Cuba, 1848). He was also famous for the costumed figures of *Zapateado* (Tap-dance, 1848) but also *El quitrín* (Coach), *El panadero y el malojero* (The Baker and the Corn Vendor), and above all his *Día de Reyes* (Three Kings), which depicts blacks in their African costumes celebrating the Epiphany. Landaluze, who arrived in Cuba during the 1850s, concentrated on reproducing the colorful attire of the different local groups on the island, which appeared in the book *Tipos y costumbres* (Types and Habits, 1881), which included "La mulatta de rumbo" (The Wandering Mulatta), "Los negros curros" (The Evil Blacks), and "El cimarrón" (The Maroon).

In the second half of the century, the academic style and a romantic landscape school developed. Antonio Rodríguez Morey (1850– 1898) represents the academic, realistic style of landscape, as seen in his *Sinfonía en verde* (Symphony in Green). The romantic school can be traced to Miguel Arias and paintings like his *Paisaje cubano* (Cuban Landscape). Esteban Chartrand (1840–1883) is one of the main representatives of the romantic school of Fountainebleau. He is noted for *Choza de la bruja* (The Witch's Hut), a tropical landscape filtered through dark colors then in vogue in French painting (Barbizon school–style).

REPUBLICAN-ERA ART

With the establishment of the republic, little changed in Cuban art. This period is characterized by romanticism and the traditional styles taught at the Academia de San Alejandro, which, with the Ateneo de la Habana sponsored exhibits on French paintings.

During this early period, two artists stand out: Armando Menocal (1861–1942) and Leopoldo Romañach (1862–1951). Menocal began his career by painting in the colorful Spanish style. In 1917 he painted portraits for the presidential palace. His *Niño campesino* (Peasant Child, 1932) was influenced by impressionist Claude Monet and the impressionist school, which became a characteristic of Cuban academic art. Romañach had studied in Spain, Italy, and France and taught at the Academia de San Alejandro, but preferred a more traditional approach of academic art, as seen, for example, in *Campesino italiano* (Italian Peasant). Romañach taught almost all of the modernists who would revolutionize art in the late 1920s and 1930s. Even though he was not a modernist, he was not an obstacle to their developing style.

Cuba, like many of the artistic/culture centers of the West, appeared to lag behind the contemporary currents developing in Paris. In 1908 French painter Blanche Z. de Baralt became one of the first to introduce the new ideas on the island, with a talk on the interpretation of light in the paintings of the impressionists and Sorolla's influence. However, most Cuban painters were content to follow a Spanish tradition, which in Cuba highlighted a realism manifested in the tropical landscape.

The first exhibitions of modern art were held during the Machado dictatorship, in 1927. A group of artists and caricaturists opposed the influence of nineteenth-century academicism of the San Alejandro School and became independent of it. The Cuban modernist movement became a part of a national reaffirmation against Machado and U.S. political influence. The leaders were Víctor Manuel García (1897–1969) and the painter and caricaturist Rafael Blanco (1885–1955), who provided an alternative to the Academia de San Alejandro. Both were associated with *Social* (1916–1933), a magazine that played a crucial role in introducing modernism to Cuba and was the voice of the Grupo Minorista. These and other artists looked to the Cuban landscape and countryside for inspiration. Artists like Víctor Manuel, Carlos Enríquez (1900–1957), Amelia Peláez del Casal (1896–1968), Fidelio Ponce de León (1895–1949), and Eduardo Abela (1888–1963) belonged to the Asociación de Pintores y Escultores (Painters and Sculptors Association, 1915), and their position was represented by the vanguard *Revista de Avance*.

The magazine brought together the political and artistic vanguard and looked to improve the human condition.

Some artists left the island during Machado's dictatorship and traveled to Europe, where they were exposed to cubism, surrealism, and other contemporary movements. Víctor Manuel went to France in 1925 and was influenced by Gauguin's works. He became a precursor to painters who concentrated on cubism (Peláez), surrealism (Enríquez), and his own primitivism and constructivism. Víctor Manuel was the first to introduce European currents into Cuban art and had an impact on its direction and those who followed him. He made Cuba's landscape, flora and fauna, and traditions a constant in Cuban painting. One scholar summarizes the development of Cuban painters during this important stage:

> Their avant-garde activity, although also formally derived from diverse European movements, was driven by an enthusiasm for discovering and expressing qualities uniquely their own: a preoccupation with social issues, an interest in the workings of culture and a will to incorporate the popular into learned discourse. This new consciousness shattered the colonial vision and give rise to a truly Cuban mode of expression. Among the prominent features of this movement are the expressive use of colour, the importance of the role of light, a quality for sensuality, a baroque style, a deeper exploration of the environment and an imaginative vision of popular origin. (Mosquera 1996, "Painting, Graphic Arts and Sculpture," 8: 233)

In 1927 the *Revista de Avance* sponsored the Exposición de Arte Nuevo (Exposition of New Art), which effectively combined European modernism with a sense of Cubanness. The magazine also reviewed exhibits in Cuba and abroad. Painters such as Víctor Manuel and Abela were illustrators for the *Revista de Avance*. These and other artists gathered around the Asociación de Pintores y Escultores and the Asociación del Club Cubano de Bellas Artes, for whom the essayist Jorge Mañach delivered talks on the history of Cuban painting.

Of this group of painters, Eduardo Abela, Fidelio Ponce, Carlos Enríquez, Amelia Peláez, and Wifredo Lam are but four examples of this rich stage in Cuban art. The 1920s and 1930s brought these different painters together. Abela and Peláez graduated from San Alejandro, Lam and Ponce attended the Academia briefly, and Enríquez was self-taught, and all but Ponce lived in Europe. But by the mid-1920s they opposed everything that San Alejandro stood for.

Enríquez traveled throughout United States, Latin America, and Europe, where he lived between 1930 and 1934. His paintings were influenced by surrealism, in particular by the works of Salvador Dalí and Francis Picabia. After his stay in Europe, he returned to his native Cuba and worked on a variety of themes, two of which stand out: eroticism and nationalism. The nude representations, which suggest lesbianism, caused his Havana exhibit to be closed on the first day. Enríquez was also interested in the countryside and in the figure of the *guajiro* (peasant). His works include the collage *Nuevo ripalda* (New Ripalda, 1934), *Virgen del Cobre* (Our Lady of El Cobre, 1933), *Rey de los campos de Cuba* (King of the Cuban Fields, 1934), *Desnudos* (Nudes, 1934), and *Eva* (1940), *El rapto de las mulatas* (The Abduction of the Mulatto Women, 1938), and *Trópico* (Tropics, 1947).

Unlike his contemporaries, Ponce had minimal artistic training and exposure, but was able to develop a unique style, which was shaped by the works of El Greco, Rembrandt, Amadeo Modigliani, and fellow Cuban Romañach. He painted landscapes as well as elongated figures of women, children, and saints, all of which were lacking in details. His paintings include *La familia* (The Family, 1934), *Cabeza de Cristo* (Head of Christ, 1934), *Niños* (Children, 1938), and *San Ignacio Loyola* (St. Ignatius of Loyola, 1940).

Abela lived in Paris, where he was exposed to the French modern style. This early period is characterized for his treatment of the *guajiro*, as seen in *Jinetes del pueblo* (Riders from Town, 1928) and, with an element of exoticism, *Los novios* (The Lovers, 1938). After a second trip to Europe, between 1934 and 1937, Abela was drawn to the Mexican mularists, and painted Amerindian-like figures. He later returned to themes of the Cuban countryside.

Abela also worked for the newly created General Administration for Culture. He founded the Escuela Libre de Artes Plásticas (Free School of Plastic Arts), later known as the Estudio Libre, which followed its Mexican model and represented an alternative to the academic style. Students learned to express themselves openly, which they later carried into their paintings. The Estudio Libre, which was free of charge, emphasized avant-garde ideas and promoted national art. The Academia de San Alejandro felt threatened and prohibited its faculty from teaching at the Estudio Libre, which motivated Abela to hire younger artists like René Portocarrero (1912–1985), Mariano Rodríguez (1912–1990), and Lorenzo Romero Arciaga (b. 1905), among others. Many students attended the Academia during regular hours and then took classes at the Estudio Libre. The school was successful but closed in December 1938, five months after it began, once its subsidy from the Directory of Culture ceased.

Amelia Peláez was arguably the most important Cuban artist who used the colonial period as a sign of identity. A student of Romañach, Peláez was known for her still lifes and paintings of women, and at times she combined the two. She was also influenced by the works of Henri Matisse, Georges Braque, Picasso, and Alexandra Exter. Peláez used geometric figures and subjected them to strong dark lines as seen in *Mujer* (Woman, 1928) and *La costurera* (The Seamstress, 1936). She also worked with the *vitral*, panes of colored glass, which often functioned as a window. Peláez brought together the flat panes and cubism to produce an original Latin American art.

Wifredo Lam (1902–1982) is the painter with the most international exposure. He lived in Paris a good part of his life, where he was influenced by Picasso's cubism and African images. He was also a friend of André Breton and joined the surrealist group. When he returned to Cuba at the start of World War II, Lam found in Afro-Cuban traditions what Europeans were looking for in African imagery. Best known for *La presencia enterna* (The Eternal Presence, 1944), *La jungla* (The Jungle, 1943), and *Ritual yoruba* (Yoruba Ritual, 1946) Lam combined the African with surrealism, in search of the primitive, and the sexual.

For example, Peláez concentrated on color and geometric patterns while Lam, Carlos Enríquez, and Fidelio Ponce were fascinated by the spontaneity of the unconscious and its abstract representations. The latter painters uncover another way of approaching the concept of time, which does not rely on metaphors or juxtapositions evident in Peláez's work. Although Lam does bring together the tribal and the modern, he is not oriented toward an academic understanding of representation, but to the magic and the ritual associated with dreams and the subconscious (Pau-Llosa, 1989).

The post–World War II period featured a second generation of Cuban painters influenced by Pablo Picasso and Mexican painters who concentrated on indigenism. These painters looked at form and color, but not as a means toward propaganda, as evident in the case of the Mexicans. Rather, they focused on the Afro-Cuban traditions. This generation includes painters from the previous generation and others like Cundo Bermúdez (b. 1914), René Portocarrero, Mariano Rodríguez, Mario Carreño (1913–1999), and Lam. These and others founded the Agrupación de Pintores y Escultores Cubanos (Group of Cuban Painters and Sculptors, 1947–1950) and elaborated on national themes. Mariano, Portocarrero, and Bermúdez also participated in the literary magazines *Nadie parecía* (1939–1941) and *Espuela de plata* (1942–1944), under the influence of the poet José Lezama Lima. Peláez, Portocarrero, Mariano, and Roberto Diago also provided illustrations for Lezama's *Orígenes* (1944–1956). In fact, Peláez and Portocarrero formed the regionalist School of Havana, created in opposition to the Cuban School of Mexico, influenced by the Mexican muralists.

There were other activities taking place to promote Cuban art. In 1940 the First National Congress of Art was celebrated in Santiago de Cuba, and in that same year the cultural section of the Ministry of Education created the National Institute of Plastic Arts. Cuban art gained wide exposure when exhibited in the United States, first at the Latin American Art Exposition in New York's Riverside Museum (1939) and later at the Exhibition of Modern Cuban Painters in New York's Museum of Modern Art and Washington, D.C.'s National Museum (1944).

Two main currents preoccupied artists: abstractionism and an unconscious, dream-like art. If Peláez represented the first, Bermúdez combined the two. He used Peláez's flat color space with images in colorful dress. A search for national elements and a fixation on details are evident in the depiction of home interiors and furnishings. This is the period in which Mariano, Víctor Manuel, Antonio Gattorno, Marcelo Pogolotti, and Abela provided a new national reality to Cuban painting, as they looked to rural landscapes, towns, plants, and fruits for inspiration. With Peláez and Portocarrero, Mariano used vibrant colors to paint tropical fruits.

Mariano Rodríguez is best known for his depiction of farmers, fruits, and roosters. Although these themes were expressed in the colonial period, they found new meaning in Mariano's works. Often he brought together in his canvases women, fruits, and the interior of houses. His early sketches highlighted women, faces, hands, and other parts of the body, without emphasizing color. As the years passed, he added shadow and color, a technique he carried over to his oil paintings. *Unidad* (Unity, 1936) was awarded a prize at the 1938 II Salón Nacional de Pintura y Escultura.

Gallos (1941), *Mujer de la sombrilla* (Woman with a Parasol, 1942), and *Maternidad* (Motherhood, 1943) take his previous experiences to a new level. The pineapples, mangos, and other fruits are reproduced with certain realism, but without abandoning his love for total abstraction. But unlike his earlier work, and as is the case with *La mujer con pajarera* (Woman with Birdcage, 1940), the painter appears to be in total control of colors, which he mixes with mastery. The human figures at the beach, in the countryside, and in park settings are surrounded by nature and domestic animals.

René Portocarrero uses vibrant colors and encircled lines that appear to move. He paints imaginary mythological figures, mixing colors and lines, as well as flowers, women, and butterflies, which intertwine and flow with ease. *Mujer con mariposa* (Woman with Butterfly, 1942), *Mujer en gris* (Woman in Gray, 1960), and *Figura ornamentada* (Ornamental Figure, 1963) in the murals of Havana's Plaza of the Revolution are but three examples. His portraits were used to illustrate the Bibioteca Era's Mexico edition of Lezama Lima's baroque novel *Paradiso* (1966).

The next generation of Cuban artists can be characterized by a rebellious attitude. In April 1953, one year after Batista's coup, the Havana exposition of the Grupo de los Once (Group of Eleven) marked the presence of painters and sculptors who showed an interest in exploring abstract art. This was done not as individuals, as had occurred with artists of previous generations, but as a group. They looked for freedom of expression in visual language devoid of politics. Members also paid close attention to what was taking place in the artistic world in the United States and France with regard to art school, but also to scholarships and the commercialization of art. Founded in 1950, the group was made up of René Aila, Francisco Antigua, José I. Bermúdez, Agustín Cárdenas, Hugo Consuegra, Fayad Jamís, José Antonio, Guido Llinás, Antonio Vidal, and Tomás Oliva y Viredo, and later to be supported by Víctor Manuel, Portocarrero, Mariano, and Raúl Martínez, who preferred to paint in black and white instead of in the colors his predecessors used.

In 1953, to commemorate the centennial of Martí's birth, government officials organized the international Bienal Hispanoamericana de Arte at the Museo Nacional. Three generations of Cuban artists boycotted the event and the Museo Nacional. Instead, to express their opposition to the event and dictatorship, the following year they held an anti-biennial in Havana, Santiago de Cuba, and Camagüey. These activities culminated in the Primer Festival Universitario (First University Festival) of contemporary Cuban art, sponsored by the University of Havana's student organization. The artists also boycotted exhibitions in Venezuela and the Pan-American Union in protest against Batista. The dictatorship reacted with the power of censorship, and for this reason the rest of the decade was noted for a lack of expositions, and an absence of political caricatures. Artists also stayed away from the Salón Nacional exposition, presented by the cultural section at the National Museum in 1957. Instead, dissenting artists held a counterexposition in front of the National Museum. This group wanted to go beyond the folkloric representations of the previous two generations by experimenting with form.

The Grupo de los Diez Artistas Concretos (Group of Ten Concret Artists) made their presence felt in the 1950s. They were Sandú Darié (b. 1908), Luis Martínez Pedro (b. 1910), Loló Soldevilla, José A. Mijares (b. 1922), Arcay Corratgé (b. 1928), Alberto Menocal, Pedro de Orá (b. 1931), Pedro Álvarez, Rafael Soriano (b. 1920), and Antonio J. Molina (b. 1928). These artists concentrated on geometric figures familiar in the work of the French artist Victor Vasarély and the Dutch Piet Mondrian. Although this group had less of an impact than the Grupo de los Once, abstract art continued to develop on the island. Painters such as Ángel Acosta León (1930–1964) and Jorge Camacho (b. 1934) and sculptors like Agustín Cárdenas followed in the footsteps of surrealist painters like Lam. Of these painters Rafael Soriano is a major figure in Latin American art, and his style of painting brings together a Cuban and Latin American tradition. He is influenced by Enríquez, whose styles he fuses to gain access to the subconscious.

POST-REVOLUTION ART

As with literature and other communicative forms of expression after 1959, art in Cuba experienced its own boom. The idea of an open and plural society created an impetus to both continue the traditions of the past and to explore new ones. There were more artists, more people who appreciated art, more museums, and more galleries to exhibit artists. The Palacio de Bellas Arts, inaugurated in 1954, was renamed Museo Nacional de Bellas Artes (Nacional Museum of Fine Arts). It was later reorganized to house collections confiscated from exiles. The Museo Nacional holds works from Europe and Latin America and the best collection of Cuban art in the world.

Some artists hailed the new heroes and historical events with their works. *Lunes de Revolución* provided a gathering place for writers and artists who were committed to the revolution but preferred to express themselves as intellectuals. The covers of *Lunes de Revolución* expressed the creative and experimental avenues some wished to pursue, as seen in those designed by Tony Évora and Pedro Lucci. With the closing of *Lunes de Revolución* in 1961 and Castro's words to the intellectuals—"Within the revolution, everything; against the revolution nothing"—there was pressure from government officials to produce a more politically and socially committed form of art.

In 1962 the Escuela Nacional de Arte was created in Havana to bring formal instruction to art with Marxist-Leninist content. Raúl Martínez (b. 1927), Servando Cabrera Moreno (1923–1981), Luis Martínez Pedro (b. 1910), and Antonia Eiriz (b. 1929) were among its Cuban professors. Students participated in and contributed to the art scene. When Lam brought the Salon de Mai to Havana in 1968, which showcased the most avant-garde art in the world and included paintings by Picasso and Miró, among others, students from the school participated in its organization and success. This event left a lasting impression and set the groundwork for the 1970 Salón Nacional, the last opened artistic exhibition.

Under the Castro government, established painters like Eiriz and Mariano began to reflect historical events in their paintings. Eiriz painted *Mi compañera* (My Comrade, 1962), *La anunciación* (The Annunciation, 1963–1964), and *La muerte en pelotas* (Naked Death, 1966). She also assembled *Homenaje a Lezama* (Homage to Lezama, 1965) and *El vendedor de periódicos* (The Newspaper Boy, 1964). But reviewers were critical of the apparent political satire in her work, and she was kept from painting and teaching in 1969. Through the Comités de Defensa de la Revolución (Committees in Defense of the Revolution), she worked with children and adults.

In the 1960s Mariano returned to reflect the immediate reality. *Los hombres y las plantas vigilan* (Men and Plants Watch), *Asamblea popular* (People's Assembly), and *De la sierra al llano* (From the Mountains to the Plains), all from 1962–1965, reflect contemporary Cuban life in the revolution, though with a certain level of abstraction. Mariano revisited the theme of "Fruta y realidad," with a series of paintings but to the pineapple, the banana, mango, and papaya and the woman, he added the armed man. A lifelong Communist, Mariano is the only major artist to enjoy the official support of the Castro government.

Raúl Martínez began his career in 1947 with figures in Cuban landscape, but his representative work started in 1956, when he began his abstract work, and he thus belongs to this generational group of painters. By 1963 he had incorporated revolutionary themes into his paintings, as evident in his *26 de julio* (1964), in which the date is scribbled over a canvas with a photo of Castro. Martínez was more successful than Mariano or Eiriz in adjusting to the demands of the revolution, and created an art for the people. In 1965 Martínez moved away from abstraction and produced an art that was more accessible. He painted recognizable images and accompanied them by popular sayings, which included those of Martí, Castro, and Che. From this period is *Martí y la estrella* (Martí and the Star, 1966), a painting of Martí's face reproduced sixteen times, or *Fénix* (Phoenix, 1968) in which Che's face appears nine times, with his name and the letters of America placed throughout seven of the nine faces. This type of art placed Martínez at the forefront of a Cuban pop aesthetics, ironically based on U.S. pop art.

Posters

The Cuban revolution found a new art form in silk-screened posters, particularly in the 1965–1970 period. The posters were a spontaneous creation, independent of ideology or political policy, but served the purpose of advertisement. Influenced by Polish artists, Cuban posters combine poetry, politics, and aesthetics. Casa de las Américas produced the first cultural posters of any significance shortly after it was founded in 1960. But it was the Instituto Cubano de Arte e Industria Cinematográficas (Cuban Institute of Cinematic Art and Industry) that set the standard for this art form. There were other organizations that used the poster, such as the Unión Nacional de Escritores y Artistas de Cuba (Cuba's National Union of Writers and Artists) and the Organization of Solidarity with the People of Asia, Africa, and Latin America, created in 1966 to address the political tension resulting from the split between China and the Soviet Union.

The posters were intended to complement films rather than to advertise them:

> The atmosphere of poster creation was closer to the one in a good university design class than to a commercial advertising corporation. Artists spurred each other's creativity in search of elegant visual solutions, rather than concerning themselves with the translation of an image into future sales. Instead of following the descriptive rules of pamphletary information or using abstraction for idealization, the artists used symbolic integration and visual punning to create a new reality dedicated to the space provided by the poster. The lack of capitalist pressure was particularly beneficial for the film poster. There was no profit to be derived by drawing large crowds since people would go to see the film anyway. The posters therefore functioned as announcements and not as publicity. . . . In a synthetic manner, the poster satisfied some of the same needs as a good catalogue does for an exhibit. (Camnitzer 1994, 110)

The poster was an art form that could be appreciated by the masses, thereby reducing the distance between art and the public. An example of this art is Raúl Martínez's *Lucía* (1968), which features the faces of the film's three women accompanied by the following inscription: "A Cuban film by Humberto Solás with Raquel Revuelta, Eslinda Nuñez, Adela Legra."

THE CONTEMPORARY SCENE

Through education and the development and the spread of a certain understanding of culture, Cubans began to appreciate intellectual activities, addressing the new Cuban reality of which the public was an integral part. The number of those attending exhibits grew. The First Biennial of Havana, in 1984, drew more than 44,000 visitors in the first week, and a total of 200,000. The Second Biennial attracted more than 300,000 visitors.

The new art in Cuba can be said to have begun with the "Volumen I" exhibit of 14 January 1981, held at the Centro de Arte Internacional of Havana, which provided a new understanding of art in Cuba and Cuba's image within the international arena. Indicating that it would be the first of a series, "Volumen I" moved away from dogmatism and toward freedom of expression. Though it was well attended, the exhibit proved to be controversial. Ángel Tomás, the art critic for *El Caimán Barbudo* (The Bearded Caiman), attacked the exhibit because the artists appeared not to recognize a Cuban tradition and had abandoned a sense of national identity. He believed that the painters focused on formalism and aesthetics, which Tomás considered to be a danger that favored the enemy of the revolution. However, the artists were not doing anything different from what others had done before them. The generation of "Volumen I" was defined further as follows:

> The generation was defined more by a shared interest in experimentation than by age, level of studies, or aesthetic program. What gave importance to "Volume I," much more than the work exhibited, was the fact that the exhibition became the starting point for a series of group shows, which brought together several combinations of the individuals in the group, and it began a process of increasingly radical ruptures with Cuban art traditions. It also fueled the break with an epic past, opened the way for self-referential issues about art that were absent during the 1970s, and dealt with the international art scene without a guilt complex. (Camnitzer 1994, 5)

"Volumen I," which followed the creation of the Ministry of Culture in 1976, created the impetus for another boom in fine arts. Established and young artists began to explore and test the limits of artistic expression.

Flavio Garciandía (b. 1954) had an initial interest in exploring photorealism. He became aware of Frank Stella's work, which offered him the possibility of bringing together high culture and kitsch. He draws on the strength of both the popular and the traditional to produce a synthesis of the two, contaminating both styles to create different levels of interpretation. He has produced *Vereda tropical* (Tropical Path, 1982), *Los pies de plomo* (Leaden Feet, 1984), and *Tropicalia*, (Tropicality, 1990). In *El lago de los cisnes* (Swan Lake, 1983), which displays the elegance of swan figures over painted squares of masonite, he mixes the baroque with political images; in *El síndrome de Marco Polo* (The Syndrome of Marco Polo, 1986), he uses Chinese restaurant decorations with the popular Cuban comics character,

Elpidio Valdés, who is on a voyage through a series of unanswerable questions.

José Bedia (b. 1959), who emerged during the "Volumen I" exhibit in Havana, has become one of the most recognized and influential artists since Castro came to power, successfully fusing the African and the Amerindian with the contemporary in a manner that has brought him international acclaim. Although he is a descendant of Spaniards, Bedia is a practitioner of Palo Monte, one of the Afro-Cuban religions. A graduate of the ISA, he uses his extensive knowledge and research skills and his artistic imagination in reproducing symbolic representations of artifacts. His *Palero Arrangement* (1986), *¿Qué te han hecho Mamá Kalunga?* (Mama Kalunga, What Have They Done to You?, 1989), and *Sarabanda contra Siete Rayos* (Sarabanda Against Seven Rays, 1985) are of Afro-Cuban interest; *Crónicas americanas* (American Chronicles, 1982), of Ameridian concern; and *La comisión india y la comisión africana contra el mundo material* (The Indian Commission and the African Commission Against the Material World, 1987) combine the two. While Bedia does not concentrate on Western images, he is interested in uncovering the essence of images that appear to respond to marginal and Third World cultures. Bedia abandoned the island in the early 1990s and currently lives in Miami.

Cuenca, though not a part of "Volumen I," helped to shape Cuban art. A conceptualist who expresses himself with paintings and photographs, he is also interested in kitsch, which he relates to perception—how art and reality are seen. His *El futuro como espacio* (The Future as Space, 1979) is a visual collage that blends different views together. Another painting is *Ciencia e ideología* (Science and Ideology, 1989). His photographs include *Conocimiento* (Knowledge, 1983) and *Conocimiento: objeto, análisis, síntesis* (Knowledge: Object, Analysis, Synthesis, 1983). An understanding of theory is important for interpretation of Cuenca's works, so he accompanies his visual exhibits with a written text. In 1989 Cuenca left the island to reside in Mexico, where he painted a series of canvases titled *Naturaleza moderbunda* (Modernbunda Nature), a contraction of modern and moribund, calling for an end to modernism and postmodernism.

The younger generation of Cuban artists does not want to break with European aesthetic values but to broaden them with a vernacular understanding of Cuban reality. Five years after "Volumen I," these and other painters created specific and well-defined groups. Grupo Provisional (Provisional Group) is made up of Glexis Novoa (b. 1964), Carlos Rodríguez Cárdenas (b. 1962), and Segundo Planes (b. 1965); the last two studied at the Instituto

Superior de Arte, under Consuelo Castañeda and Garciandía. The Instituto was founded in 1976 and offered a five-year art degree. The group name refers to their fear of becoming institutionalized. These artists create while participating in happenings and have no permanent existence. Although they are aware of international influences, they prefer to concentrate on the national scene.

Arte Calle, led by Aldito Menéndez (b. 1970), opposed the art establishment and the idea of biennials. The group was more concerned with making art than with art itself. For example, at the UNEAC conference on art in 1987, members walked in with gas masks to avoid contamination. The following year, they staged a fake art exhibit in which the unsuspecting public became the focus of the event. Due to a government crackdown, the Arte Calle has ceased to exist.

Grupo Puré (Puree) opposed the individualism of previous generations and sought to provide collective productions. The group was integrated by Adriano Buergo, Ana Albertina Delgado, Ermy Taño Carrillo, Ciro Quintana, and Lázaro Saavedra. The members incorporated international influences to produce something truly unique. Like the Arte Calle, Grupo Puré disbanded.

Grupo 1.2.3 . . . 12 originated in 1987, when one of its members was asked to exhibit in a gallery and invited eleven of his friends to share the space. At times the group coincided with themes and relied on slogans, graffiti, and disconnected images and texts for their expression.

Another group included Tanya Angulo (b. 1968), Juan Pablo Ballester (b. 1966), José Ángel Toirac (b. 1966), and Ileana Villazón (1969). As a whole the group appropriated the works of others to make statements about culture and society. They came onto the art scene with constructions of penises painted in the style of artist of the new generation. The group ceased to exist in 1989.

Flora Fong (b. 1949) is a young artist of international fame who has won many prizes. Her work is influenced by Lam, as she combines Afro-Cuban motifs with abstraction. This is evident with *Costa adentro* (Interior Coast, 1995). Other younger artists whose works must be recognized include Consuelo Castañeda (b. 1958), Tomás Esson (b. 1963), Glexis Novoa (b. 1964), Ciro Quintana (b. 1964), and Abdel Hernández (b. 1968).

Cuban art is used mainly to decorate government and public spaces rather than to sell to collectors. With the changes produced by the Special Period, there is a return to galleries for the purpose of exhibiting and selling art to tourists for hard currency. The biennials also provide an opportunity for artistic exposure and international attention, as well as commercial outlets.

SCULPTURE

The first two decades of the republic were marked by an academic orientation that imitated the Italian, French, and Spanish Renaissance, the baroque, neoclassicism, realism, and impressionism, as well as the influence of Michelangelo and Auguste Rodín. The first sculptures were by Aurelio Melero, Ramiro Ortiz, Esteban Betancourt, Rodolfo Hernández Giro (1881–1970), Carlos Era, José Oliva Michelena (b. 1897), and Lucía Victoria Bacardí. Others worked in an eclectic style; among them were the Afro-Cubans Florencio Gelabert (1904–1995) and Caridad Ramírez (b. 1912).

Modern sculpture, which looks to abstraction, began to develop toward the first quarter of the twentieth century, as artists concentrated on the aesthetic value of form and its relation to the context in which the sculpture was located. These artists looked to express their own reality.

Cuba's sculptors include Juan José Sicre (1898–1974), who studied at San Alejandro but was one of the first to rebel against the school, placing him in the role of mentor to younger generations. Sicre, who had studied with Miguel Blay and J. de Creft, was a rationalist and had a particular concern for light. His signature sculpture is the monument to José Martí in Havana's Plaza de la Revolución.

Teodoro Ramos Blanco (1902–1972) is another graduate of San Alejandro and a student of Isabel Chapottin y Trigueros. Ramos specialized in Afro-Cuban themes and used local materials, such as the many varieties of wood found on the island.

Mario Santí (1910–1988) also graduated from the Academia de San Alejandro. He taught at the Escuela Provincial de Artes Plásticas in Oriente from 1935 to 1943 and at the Escuela Elemental de Artes Plásticas Aplicadas. He is best known as the sculptor of the bust of José María Heredia in Santiago de Cuba, the Monument to the Mothers in Cárdenas, and the José Martí necropolis of Santa Ifigenia in Santiago de Cuba. Santí left the island after the revolution and has taught at the University of Miami. He also designed the monument to Martí in Hialeah, Florida.

Ernesto Navarro (1904–1975) too studied at the Academia de San Alejandro with Chapottín. And like him, he preferred to work with wood, appreciating the different textures, without abandoning copper and wire. But unlike his compatriot, Navarro preferred abstract compositions, which allowed him to express his own sense of reality as sculpted statues.

Rita Longa (1913–2000) was another student of San Alejandro and of Chapottín. Her field of interest was highly decorative figures, emphasizing stylized and elegant ornaments. Among her ornamental monuments in Havana are the magestic "Virgen del Camino" (Lady of the Road), "Los Venados" (The Deer) in the Havana Zoo, and the facade of the Palacio de Bellas Artes.

PHOTOGRAPHY

Photography in Cuba dates to the first half of the nineteenth century, when Pedro Téllez de Girón brought the first photographic apparatus to the island in March of 1840. He is credited with taking the first picture, which he shot from the Palacio de los Capitanes Generales (Palace of the General Captains) and was later lost. The next picture is attributed to José Gómez de la Carrera, who at the beginning of the War of Independence set the standard for modern photojournalism. During the period of the republic, photographers like Generoso Funcasta, López Ortiz, Martínez Hilla, Ernesto Ocaña, Joaquín Blez, Constantino Arias, and Moisés Hernández played an important part in portraying the many aspects of Cuban society.

The photograph has become an indispensable tool for capturing the developments of the revolution and creating lasting images. However, the photography is also an artistic form.

Alberto Díaz Gutiérrez, "Korda" (b. 1928), and Raúl Corralvarela, "Corrales" (b. 1925), are the two most important photographers of the revolutionary period. Guillermo Cabrera Infante captures Korda's image, whom the author refers to as Codac, in his *Tres tristes tigres* and represents his sections as descriptions of photographic images. Korda's image of Che from 5 March 1960 is considered to be the most famous and most frequently reproduced photograph of this hero in the world. It is a close-up taken during a funeral, depicting a serious and somber individual, whose face is framed by his black beret and beard.

Korda and Corrales's revolutionary work is contained in Korda's *Che: el álbum* (Che: The Album, 1997), a collection of black and white photographs that have caused worldwide exposure of Che's image and elevated him to a mythical figure among revolutionaries. The album chronicles Che's life, from his childhood in Argentina to his involvement in armed insurrection in the Sierra Maestra and leadership in the revolution. The book reveals different sides of the Cuban hero: the fighter, the reader, the golf and baseball player, the worker (in construction and sugarcane fields), the ambassador, and the father figure with children. The book also chronicles the lives of others who participated in the armed overthrow of Batista, such as commander Camilo Cienfuegos, and Castro himself.

Casa de las Américas sponsored the first photographic exhibit, "First Sample of Cuban Culture," in 1966. Others were held in Mexico, like the "First Sample of Cuban Photography," in 1976 and "History of Cuban Photography," one year later. Photographers of the early part of the revolution include Marucha, Mayito, Ernesto Hernández, and Roberto Salas. Those of the later years include Marta María Pérez, René Peña, Abigail González, Julio Larramendi, and Cirenaica Moreira.

CUBAN ARTISTS ABROAD

Some Cuban artists living abroad after 1959 were based in Europe, but most went to the United States, where they continued the national traditions represented by the works of Lam, Peláez, and Portocarrero.

Severo Sarduy (1937–1993) is primarily known as the author of novels, but he was also a painter and this was the reason he left Cuba on a scholarship to study art in Paris, where he lived until his death. There was no division between Sarduy's writings and paintings; both address his passion for the baroque and are covered with images and metaphors. His ideas on painting are eloquently expressed in *Barroco* (1974) and *La simulación* (1982). His art represents different stages and interests, which include abstract art, the influence of Luis Feito, and his affinity for Asian religion and culture, in particular Buddhism. From the latter stage Sarduy painted with white borders, and colorful backgrounds, hundreds of closed strokes, which appeared at times as stains, to create animation. Some of these include *Canela* (Cinnamon, 1990), *Jardin japonais* (Japanese Garden, 1990), *Paysage* (Scenery, 1990–1991), and *Ville* (Village, 1991).

After the change in government, many established and recognized Cuban artists left the island. Their paintings are marked by the images of the country they left behind, as seen, for example, in the works of Cundo Bermúdez, Mario Carreño, and the sculptor Alfredo Lozano (1913). Of those with distinguished careers who left Cuba, Mijares and Soriano belonged to the Grupo de los Diez Artistas Concretos. Other artists in exile have been Félix Ramos (b. 1919), Emilio Sánchez (1921–1999), Gumersindo Barea (1901–1961), Edgardo Runken (1904–1968), Rafael Arazoza (b. 1919), Wilfredo Alcover (b. 1919), Baruj Salinas (b. 1935), and Zilia Sánchez (b. 1934). To this list should be added Jesse Fernández (1925–1986) who was a painter but was better known for his photographs, certainly among the best by a Cuban photographer.

Sculptors in exile include Enrique Gay García (b. 1928), whose works in bronze consist of "Icarus" and "Head"; Manuel Carbonell (b. 1918) known for his twenty-six-foot bronze Madonna of Fatima in New Jersey, seven-foot marble statue of José Martí in Key West, and Tequesta family at Brickell Bridge in Miami; Tony López (b. 1918) for his Carlos J. Finlay sculpture at the Jefferson Medical College in Philadelphia, the Antonio Maceo sculpture at Cuban Memorial Boulevard in Miami, and the Ernesto Lecuona relief sculpture at the Dade County Auditorium; and Rafael Consuegra (b. 1941), a teacher who works in ceramic abstract forms and in welded steel formations.

The younger generation of artists were either born or raised and educated in the United States. Unlike their exiled counterparts, these artists attempt to mediate between the North American environment and their parents' home country, often combining the two in their works. These artists belong to both cultures but are also marginal to them. Of these artists, Ana Mendieta (1948–1985) should be recognized. She left the island at the age of thirteen and did graduate work at the University of Iowa. Her work can be classified as feminist and Hispanic in nature. She has won many awards, including three National Endowment for the Arts grants and a Guggenheim fellowship. Her early work is characterized by images of blood, suffering, destruction, and death, where her body is presented as mutilated or as a corpse. Her later work includes her integration with nature, where her body becomes barely perceptible. She returned to Cuba in 1980 and traveled to the area of Jaruco, known for its limestone caves, where she worked with silhouettes, which could only be recorded in photographs. This stage of her work also includes more explicit sexual symbols. Mendieta met with a tragic death in 1985, the same year she married minimalist sculptor Carl Andre.

Other Cuban-American artists of Mendieta's generation include Ramón Alejandro (b. 1943), who lived in Paris and profited from the strong artistic tradition of the city. Currently, Alejandro resides in Miami. His work recalls aspects of Lam's work, but whereas Lam fused images, Alejandro juxtaposed them, which alludes to the transference between them. Paul Sierra (b. 1944) works with light and interiors and also paints lush tropical vegetation. Emilio Falero (b. 1947) creatively uses the work of other artists to produce his own; Juan González (1945–1986) used pencil to draw surrealist figures; the art of Luis Cruz Azaceta (b. 1942) is marked by the violent human condition; Juan Boza (b. 1941) is drawn to Afro-Cuban themes; and Tony Mendoza (b. 1941) photographs images in his immediate environment.

There is another generation of Cuban American sculptors. Some have reached national prominence, like Marc Andries Smit (b. 1954), whose public artworks include the Padre Félix Valera Monument in Miami, Diaspora bas-relief at San Carlos Institute in Key West, and the José Martí Monument in Orlando, Flordia; Ramón Lago (b. 1947), a friend of Andy Warhol, who is known for his relief sculptural depiction of Cuban political prisoners, "Silent Cry," at Florida International University; and María Brito-Avellana (b. 1947), a conceptualist who works with mixed media sculptures like "The Next Room" and "She Never Liked Dolls." While in the United States, the painter José Bedia has also moved into the "Installation venue."

The youngest generation of Cuban-American artists has already produced important works. Carlos Alfonzo (1950–1991) created symbols of his exiled experience. Photographer Mario Algaze (b. 1947) considers his work to be Cuban and Latin American. María Brito-Avellana (b. 1947) is a sculptor who relies on her unconscious; Gilberto López-Espina (b. 1949) photographs the human condition; María Martínez Cañas (b. 1960) combines art and photography creatively; Jorge Pardo (b. 1951) brings cultural and religious topics to his paintings and tile works; and Aramís O'Reilly (b. 1958) relies on surrealist images.

REFERENCES

Amelia Peláez, exposición retrospectiva 1924–1967. Havana: Museo Nacional, 1992.

Anreus, Alejandro. "Nostalgia de ida y vuelta." *Encuentro de la Cultura Cubana* 15 (1999–2000): 133–136.

Blocker, Jane. *Where Is Ana Mendieta?* Durham, N.C.: Duke University Press, 1999.

Camnitzer, Luis. *New Art of Cuba*. Austin: University of Texas Press, 1994.

Castellanos, Lázara. *Víctor Patricio Landaluze*. Havana: Letras Cubanas, 1991.

Cincuenta artistas plásticos cubanos. Havana: Ediciones Unión, 1996.

De Castro, Martha. *El arte en Cuba*. Miami: Ediciones Universal, 1970.

De Juan, Adelaida. *Pintura cubana: temas y variaciones*. Mexico: Universidad Nacional Autónoma de México, 1980.

Fuentes-Pérez, Ileana, Graciella Cruz-Taura, and Ricardo Pau-Llosa, eds. *Outside Cuba/Fuera de Cuba: Contemporary Cuban Visual Arts*. Office of Hispanic Arts Mason Gross School of the Arts, Rutgers, the State University of New Jersey, and the Research Institute for Cuban Studies, Graduate School of International Studies, University of Miami, 1989.

Korda. *Che; el álbum*. Buenos Aires: Editorial Perfil, 1997.

Martínez, Juan A. *Cuban Art and National Identity: The Vanguardia Painters, 1927–1950*. Gainesville: University of Florida Press, 1994.

Mosquera, Gerardo. *Contracandela. Ensayos sobre kitsch, identidad, arte abstracto y otros temas calientes*. Caracas: Monte Ávila Latinoamericana, 1993.

———. "Cultures" and "Painting, Graphic Arts and Sculpture." *The Dictionary of Art*, vol. 8. Ed. Jane Turner. London: Macmillan Publishers, 1996, 228–231, 233–234.

Ortiz, Fernando. *Wifredo Lam*. Havana: Ministerio de Educación, 1950.

Pau-Llosa, Ricardo. "Latin American Artists of the United States." *The Dictionary of Art*, vol. 18. Ed. Jane Turner. London: Macmilliam Publishers, 1996, 834–835.

Pintores cubanos. Havana: Gente Nueva, 1974.

René Portocarrero: Exposición antológica. Madrid: Ministerio de Cultura, 1984.

Severo Sarduy. Madrid: Museo Nacional Centro de Arte Reina Sofía, 1998.

Two Centuries of Cuban Art: 1759–1959. Daytona Beach, Fla.: Cuban Foundation Collection of the Museum of Arts and Sciences, 1980.

Wilfredo Lam. Paris: MAM/Musée D'Art moderne de la Ville de Paris, 1983.

Wifredo Lam: A Retrospective of Works on Paper. New York: American Society, 1992.

Glossary

Abakuá. Afro-Cuban secret society whose members were known as Ñáñi-gos.

Aché. Blessing of the Yoruba gods.

Ahijado. Initiate into Afro-Cuban religion.

Ajiaco. A dish made principally with root vegetables.

Azabache. Jet black stone.

Babalawo. Yoruba or Lucumí priest who is the guardian of secrets.

Babalú-Ayé. Saint Lazarus.

Balsa (balsero). Makeshift rafts used to escape from Cuba to the United States.

Bufo. Comic, buffoon.

Changó. Saint Barbara.

Cigarritos. Small cigars.

Coletilla. Statements appended to news stories disapproving of a position or content.

Comedia. A theatrical work without a tragic ending.

Comité de Defensa de la Revolución. Committee for the Defense of the Revolution.

Comparsa. Street dancing to the beat of conga drummers.

Congrí. Rice with red beans mixed together; popular in Santiago de Cuba.

Costumbrismo. Literature of customs.

Criollos. White Spaniards born in the colony.

Cuba Libre. A drink made with rum and Coca-Cola.

Diablitos. Íreme, Ñañas, or Ñáñigos (devil-like figures).

Eleguá. Saint Anthony.

Escuela en el campo. Schools in the countryside.

Guajiro. A Cuban peasant.

Guayabera. A long shirt meant to be worn over pants.

Isué. The main spiritual leader of the Abakuás or Ñáñigos; similar to a Catholic bishop.

Jinetera (Jinetero). Prostitute.

Juguete. Skit.

Lechón asado. Roast suckling pig.

Lucumí. Afro-Cubans originally from Nigeria's Yoruba tribe.

Macutos. Medicinal pouches that harness spiritual forces.

Madrina (Padrino). Godparent, teacher, and mentor of a Santería initiate.

Microbrigadas. Group of workers, usually from the same work center, who help each other build homes.

Mojito. A drink made with rum, freshly squeezed lime juice, sugar, sprigs of fresh mint, seltzer or club soda, and finely crushed ice.

Monte. The sacrificial space where the living and the dead, animals and humans, nature and men come together.

Moros y cristianos. Rice mixed with black beans.

Mulata. A mulatto woman.

Mutualista. Health maintenance program.

Ñáñigos. Members of the Abakuá secret society.

Negrismo. Poetic movement of the 1920s and 1930s by white Cubans that concentrates rhythm and images of what they perceived to be Afro-Cuban religion and culture.

Nganga. The spiritual charged pot or cauldron of the Palo Monte or Mayombe religion.

Nzambi Mpungu (Sambi). The supreme being of the Afro-Cuban Congo religion.

Obatalá. Our Lady of Mercy.

Olodumare. A god among the Yorubas. He is known as Olofi.

Orishas. Afro-Cuban gods.

Oshún. Our Lady of Charity.

Paladares. Independently owned restaurants in private homes.

Palo (Regla) Mayombe. Afro-Cuban religion of Bantu origin.

Panetelas. Slightly larger cigars than the *cigarritos*.

Revista. Stage revue.

Ropa vieja. A popular Afro-Cuban dish made with beef brisket.

Sainete. A one-act drama of a satirical or comic nature.

Santería. Afro-Cuban religion that combines Catholic and Yoruba traditions.

Santero. A priest of Santería.

Sese, seseribó. A drum that gains the significance of the cup that holds the host in Catholicism.

Sincretismo. The coming together of Catholicism and Afro-Cuban religions.

Sofrito. Sautéed onion, green bell pepper, and garlic.

Tasajo. Jerked beef.

Viandas. Root vegetables.

Yemayá. Our Lady of Regla.

Yoruba. A Nigerian African tribe.

Zarzuela. Dramatic musical composition in which the spoken language and songs alternate.

Selected Bibliography

Only the most crucial Spanish-language sources are noted here, for accessibility.

Ackerman, Holly. "The Balsero Phenomenon, 1991–1994." In *Cuban Studies 26.* Ed. Jorge Domínguez. Pittsburgh: University of Pittsburgh Press, 1996, 170.

Álvarez, Santiago, et al. *Cine y Revolución en Cuba.* Barcelona: Editorial Fontamara, 1975.

Álvarez Borland, Isabel. *Cuban-American Literature of Exile: From Person to Persona.* Charlottesville, Va.: University Press of Virginia, 1998.

Ardévol, José. *Introducción a Cuba: La música.* Havana: Instituto del Libro, 1969.

Atlas demográfico de Cuba. Havana: Empresa de Geodesia y Cartografía de Ciudad de La Habana, 1979.

Barnet, Miguel. *Autobiography of a Runaway Slave.* Trans. Jocasta Inness. London: Bodley Head, 1966.

———. "La novela testimonio: socio-literatura." In *La canción de Rachel.* Barcelona: Editorial Estela, 1970. 125–150.

Benítez Rojo, Antonio. " 'Viaje a la semilla,' o el texto como espectáculo." *Discurso Literario* 3, 1 (1985): 53–74.

———. *The Repeating Island: The Caribbean and the Postmodern Perspective.* Trans. James Marannis. Durham, N.C.: Duke University Press, 1992.

———. "The Role of Music in the Emergence of Afro-Cuban Culture." *Research in African Literatures* 29, 1 (Spring 1998): 179–184.

Bettelheim, Judith. *Cuban Festivals: An Illustrated Anthology.* New York: Garland Publishing, 1993.

Blocker, Jane. *Where Is Ana Mendieta?* Durham, N.C.: Duke University Press, 1999.

Blutstein, Howard I., Lynne Cox Anderson, Elinor C. Betters, et al. *Area Handbook for Cuba*. Washington, D.C.: U.S. Government Printing Office, 1971.

Boudet, Rosa Ileana. "New Playwrights, New Challenges: Current Cuban Theatre." In *Bridging Enigma: Cubans on Cuba*. Ed. Ambrosio Fornet. *The South Atlantic Quarterly* 96, 1 (1997): 31–51.

Boswell, Thomas D., and James R. Curtis. *The Cuban-American Experience*. Totowa, N.J.: Rowman and Allanheld, 1985.

Brenner, Philip, William M. LeoGrande, Donna Rich, and Daniel Siegel, eds. *The Cuba Reader: The Making of a Revolutionary Society*. New York: Grove Press, 1989.

Brower, Leo. *La música, lo cubano y la innovación*. Havana: Editorial Letras Cubanas, 1992.

Burton, Julianne. "Film and Revolution in Cuba: The First Twenty-Five Years." In *New Latin American Cinema*. Ed. Michael T. Martin. Detroit: Wayne State, 1997. Vol. 2, 123–142.

Cabalé Ruiz, Manolo. *Teófilo Stevenson: grande entre los grandes*. Havana: Editorial Orbe, 1980.

Cabrera Infante, Guillermo. *A Twentieth Century Job*. Trans. Kenneth Hall and Guillermo Cabrera Infante. London: Faber and Faber, 1991.

Casanovas, Martín, ed. *Órbita de la Revista de Avance*. Havana: UNEAC, 1965.

Chanan, Michael. *The Cuban Image*. Bloomington: Indiana University Press, 1985.

Collazo, Bobby. *La última noche que pasé contigo: 40 años de farándula cubana*. San Juan, P.R.: Editorial Cubanacán, 1987.

Constitution of the Republic of Cuba. Havana: Instituto Cubano del Libro, 1975.

Cuervo Hewitt, Julia. *Aché, presencia africana: tradiciones yourba-lucumí en la narrative cubana*. New York: Peter Lang, 1988.

de la Pezuela, Jacobo. *Historia de la isla de Cuba*. Madrid: Imprenta de Bailly-Bailliere, 1878.

Diccionario geográgico, estadístico, histórico, de la isla de Cuba. Madrid: Imprenta del Establecimiento de Mellao, 1863. Vol. 3.

Domínguez, Jorge. *Cuba: Order and Revolution*. Cambridge, Mass.: Belknap Press of Harvard University Press, 1978.

Faber, Samuel. *Revolution and Reaction in Cuba, 1933–1960*. Middletown, Conn.: Wesleyan University Press, 1976.

Fermoselle, Rafael. *Política y color en Cuba*. Madrid: Editorial Colibrí, 1998.

Frederick, Howard H. *Cuban-American Radio Wars: Ideology in International Telecommunications*. Norwood, N.J.: Ablex Publishing Corp., 1986.

Friol, Roberto. In *Suite para Juan Francisco Manzano*. Havana: Editorial Arte y Literatura, 1977.

Galán, Natalio. *Cuba y sus sones*. Valencia: Pre-Texto/Música, 1983.

Giacoman, Helmy F. "The Use of Music in Literature: 'El Ocoso' [*sic*], by A. C., and Symphony No. 3 (Eroica), by Beethoven." *Studies in Short Fiction* 8, 1 (1971): 103–111.

Gómez, Juan Gualberto. *Por Cuba libre*. Havana: Editorial Ciencias Sociales, 1974.

González Echevarría, Roberto. *Alejo Carpentier: The Pilgrim at Home*. Ithaca, N.Y.: Cornell University Press, 1977.

———. *The Pride of Havana: A History of Cuban Baseball*. New York: Oxford University Press, 1999.

González Freire, Natividad. *Teatro cubano (1927–1961)*. Havana: Ministerio de Relaciones Exteriores, 1961.

González-Whipper, Migene. *Rituals and Spells of Santería*. New York: Original Publications, 1984.

Gutiérrez Alea, Tomás. *The Viewer's Dialectic*. Havana: José Martí Publishing House, 1988.

Hidalgo, Narciso J. "The Son and AfroCuban Discourse." Ph.D. dissertation, Indiana University, 1999.

"Homenaje a Virgilio Piñera." *Encuentro de la cultura cubana* 14 (1999): 3–44.

Howe, Linda. "Afro-Cuban Intellectuals: Revolutionary Politics and Cultural Production." *Revista de Estudios Hispánicos* 33, 3 (1999): 407–439.

Jrade, Cathy L. *Modernismo, Modernity, and the Development of Spanish American Literature*. Austin: University of Texas Press, 1998.

Leonel-Antonio de la Cuesta. "The Cuban Socialist Constitution: Its Originality and Role in Institutionalization." *Cuban Studies* 6 (1976): 18–20.

Lluriá de O'Higgins, María Josefa. *A Taste of Old Cuba*. New York: HarperCollins, 1994.

López, Oscar Luis. *La radio en Cuba*. Havana: Letras Cubanas, 1981.

Luis, Carlos M. *El oficio de la mirada*. Miami: Ediciones Universal, 1998.

Luis, William. "America Revisited: An Interview with Edmundo Desnoes." *Latin American Literary Review* 11, 21 (1982): 7–20.

———. "Cinema and Culture in Cuba: Personal Interview with Néstor Almendros." Trans. Virginia Lawreck. *Review: Latin American Literature and Arts* 37 (January–June 1987): 21.

———. "Autobiografía del esclavo Juan Francisco Manzano: versión de Suárez y Romero." In *La historia en la literatura iberoamericana*. Ed. Raquel Chang-Rodríguez and Gabriella de Beer. Hanover, N.H.: Ediciones del Norte, 1989. 259–268.

———. *Literary Bondage: Slavery in Cuban Narrative*. Austin: University of Texas Press, 1990.

———. "Historia, naturaleza y memoria en 'Viaje a la semilla.' " *Revista Iberoamericana*, no. 154 (1991): 151–160.

———. "Culture as Text: The Cuban/Caribbean Connection." In *Translating Latin America: Culture as Text*. Ed. William Luis and Julio Rodríguez-Luis. Binghamton, N.Y.: Center for Research in Translation, 1991.

———. "Cultura afrocubana en la Revolución: Entrevista a Elio Ruiz." *Afro-Hispanic Review* 13 (1994): 37–45.

———. *Dance Between Two Cultures: Latino Caribbean Literature Written in the United States*. Nashville, Tenn.: Vanderbilt University Press, 1997.

————. "How to Read *Sab.*" *Revista de Estudios Hispánicos* 32 (1998): 175–186.

————. "*Lunes de Revolución*: Literature and Culture in the First Years of the Cuban Revolution." In *Guillermo Cabrera Infante: Assays, Essays, and Other Arts.* Ed. Ardis L. Nelson. New York: Twayne Publishers, 1999. 16–38.

————. "El lugar de la escritura." *Encuentro de la Cultura Cubana* 15 (1999–2000): 50–60.

Lumsden, Ian. *Machos, Maricones, and Gays: Cuba and Homosexuality.* Philadelphia: Temple University Press, 1996.

Madden, Richard. *The Life and Poems of a Cuban Slave: Juan Francisco Manzano.* Ed. Edward Mullen. Hamden, Conn.: Archon Books, 1991.

Martin, Michael T., ed. *New Latin American Cinema.* Detroit: Wayne State, 1997. Vol. 2.

Martínez, Juan A. *Cuban Art and National Identity: The Vanguardia Painters, 1927–1950.* Gainesville: University of Florida Press, 1994.

Martínez, Julio, ed. *Dictionary of Twentieth-Century Cuban Literature.* Westport, Conn.: Greenwood Press, 1990.

Martínez Furé, Rogelio. *Diálogos imaginarios.* Havana: Editorial Letras Cubanas, 1997.

Martínez Torres, Augusto, and Manuel Pérez Estremera. *Nuevo cine latinoamericano.* Barcelona: Editorial Anagrama, 1973.

Matibag, Eugenio. *Afro-Cuban Religious Experience: Cultural Reflections in Narrative.* Gainesville: University Press of Florida, 1996.

Méndez, Adriana. *Cubans in America.* Minneapolis: Lerner Publications Co., 1994.

————. *Gender and Nationalism in Colonial Cuba: The Travels of Santa Cruz y Montalvo, Condesa de Merlin.* Nashville, Tenn.: Vanderbilt University Press, 1998.

Menton, Seymour. *Prose Fiction of the Cuban Revolution.* Austin: University of Texas Press, 1975.

Montreal, Pedro. "Las remesas familiars en la economía cubana." *Encuentro de la Cultura Cubana* 14 (Fall 1999): 49–62.

Moore, Carlos. "Le Peuple noir a-t-il sa place dans la révolution cubane?" *Présence Africaine* 52 (1964): 226–230.

————. *Castro, the Blacks, and Africa.* Los Angeles: Center for Afro-American Studies, University of California, Los Angeles, 1988.

Moore, Robin. *Nationalizing Blackness: Afrocubanismo and Artistic Revolution in Havana, 1920–1940.* Pittsburgh: University of Pittsburgh Press, 1997.

Orovio, Helío. *Diccionario de la música cubana.* Havana: Editorial Letras Cubanas, 1981.

————. *El bolero cubano.* Santiago de Cuba: Editorial Oriente, 1994.

————. *La conga, la rumba: columbia, yambú y guaguancó.* Santiago de Cuba: Editorial Oriente, 1994.

————. *El danzón, el mambo y el chachachá.* Santiago de Cuba: Editorial Oriente, 1994.

———. *El son, la guaracha y la salsa*. Santiago de Cuba: Editorial Oriente, 1994.

Mosquera, Gerardo. "Cultures" and "Painting, Graphic Arts and Sculpture." *The Dictionary of Art*, vol. 8. Ed. Jane Turner. London: Macmillan Publishers, 1996. 228–231, 233–234.

Oroz, Silvia, *Tomás Gutiérrez Alea: los filmes que no filmé*. Havana: UNEAC, 1989.

Ortiz, Fernando. *Cuban Counterpoint: Tobacco and Sugar*. Trans. Harriet de Onís. Durham, N.C.: Duke University Press, 1995.

Partido Comunista de Cuba. *Plataforma programática: Tesis y resolución*. Havana: Editorial Ciencias Sociales, 1978.

Pau-Llosa, Ricardo. "Latin American Artists of the United States." *The Dictionary of Art*, vol. 18. Ed. Jane Turner. London: Macmillan Publishers, 1996, 834–835.

Père, Gérard. *Havana Cigars*. Edison, N.J.: Barnes and Noble Books, 1997.

Pérez, Louis. *Cuba: Between Reform and Revolution*. New York: Oxford University Press, 1995.

Pérez Firmat, Gustavo. *The Cuban Condition: Translation and Identity in Modern Cuban Literature*. Cambridge: Cambridge University Press, 1989.

———. *Life on the Hyphen: The Cuban-American Way*. Austin: University of Texas Press, 1994.

Pérez-Stable, Marifeli. *The Cuban Revolution: Origins, Course, and Legacy*. New York: Oxford University Press, 1993.

Perfiles culturales: Cuba 1977. Havana: Editorial Orbe, 1978.

Pettavino, Paula J., and Geralyn Pye. *Sport in Cuba: The Diamond in the Rough*. Pittsburgh: University of Pittsburgh Press, 1994.

Portes, Alejandro, and Robert L. Bach. *Latin Journey: Cuban and Mexican Immigrants in the United States*. Berkeley: University of California Press, 1985.

Portuondo del Prado, Fernando. *Historia de Cuba: 1492–1898*. Havana: Editorial Pueblo y Educación, 1965.

Ripol, Carlos. "*La Revista de Avance* (1927–1939), vocero de vanguardismo y pórtico de revolución." *Revista Iberoamericana* 30 (1964): 261–82.

Roses, Lorraine. *Voices of the Storyteller*. Westport, Conn.: Greenwood Press, 1986.

Salwen, Michael B. *Radio and Television in Cuba: The Pre-Castro Era*. Ames: Iowa State University Press, 1994.

Sarduy, Severo. *Severo Sarduy*. Madrid: Museo Nacional Centro de Arte Reina Sofía, 1998.

Thomas, Hugh. *Cuba: The Pursuit of Freedom*. New York: Harper and Row, 1971.

Ulloa, J. C., and L. A. de Ulloa. "José Lezama Lima." In *Modern Latin American Fiction Writers, First Series*. Ed. William Luis. Detroit: Gale Publishers, 1992.

Valdés, Nelson P., and Rolando E. Bonachea, "Fidel Castro y la política estudiantil de 1947 a 1952." *Aportes*, no. 22 (1971).

West, Dennis. " 'Strawberry and Chocolate,' Ice Cream and Tolerance: Interview with Tomás Gutiérrez Alea." *Cineaste* 21, 1–2 (1995): 16–19.

Index